SIXTY-FOUR YOGINIS
CULT, ICONS AND GODDESSES

SIXTY-FOUR YOGINIS
Cult, Icons and Goddesses

ANAMIKA ROY

PRIMUS
BOOKS

PRIMUS BOOKS

An imprint of Ratna Sagar P. Ltd.
Virat Bhavan
Mukherjee Nagar Commercial Complex
Delhi 110 009

Offices at CHENNAI   LUCKNOW
AGRA AHMEDABAD BANGALORE COIMBATORE DEHRADUN GUWAHATI HYDERABAD
JAIPUR JALANDHAR KANPUR KOCHI KOLKATA MADURAI MUMBAI PATNA RANCHI VARANASI

First published 2015

Reprint 2018

ISBN: 978-93-84082-12-3

Published by Primus Books

Laser typeset by Digigrafics
Gulmohar Park, New Delhi 110 049

Printed and bound in India by Replika Press Pvt. Ltd.

Contents

Illustrations

Preface

IN 2002, a chance visit to the Yogini Temple at Bheraghat in Jabalpur, led to a long academic journey into the mysterious and esoteric world of the Yoginis. Little did I realize while working on this project that this journey would turn out to be an enduring pursuit of what was a forbidden realm. As I was not initiated in the Tantras, a number of Acaryas were not forthcoming in revealing their secrets, the villagers were hesitant of the wrath of the Yoginis and the drivers were reluctant to drive into the interiors. In these moments of anxiety and frustration, what kept me going was the statement of one of my teachers that the work will be completed only by the wishes and the blessings of the Yoginis. Though it has taken long to complete this, the Yoginis appear to be finally pleased with me.

In this eventful journey, I am indebted to the different Acaryas for having shown the way, though I am forbidden by tradition to record their names, despite their reluctance, I did manage to engage in valuable dialogue with them. I would like to thank the drivers, local guides and the villagers from Banda (Uttar Pradesh) to Bolangir (Odisha), who helped me in their own ways. I am also thankful to my teachers, colleagues, and friends, who though encouraging, were apprehensive for this project and expressed it at different stages. I acknowledge my gratitude to Professors Vidya Dehejia, Kamalesh Dutt Tripathi, Devangana Desai, Hari Priya Rangarajan, and Acarya Ram Chandra Shukla for their wisdom and to Stella for her encouragement and friendship. The comments and suggestions that came from the anonymous referee were extremely helpful in sharpening some arguments and removing ambivalences in others. I am beholden to the UGC for the Research Award which I availed for three consecutive years, for facilitating this research. I thank the library staff of the following Universities and Research Institutions: the Department of Ancient History Culture and Archaeology, Allahabad University; the National Museum Library Allahabad; G.N. Jha Sanskrit Institute, Allahabad; Sampoorna Nand Sanskrit University, Varanasi; Indira Gandhi National Centre for the Arts, New Delhi; and Darbar Hall, Nepal, for all the help they extended to me.

I am indebted to Anupama, Hemang and Pakhi, who found my passion to my work bizarre, but never complained, to Jai—critic, cameraman, and field work companion. I dedicate this work to my late parents Usha and Siddheshwari who through their own example, taught me the virtues of selflessness, of giving and sharing without expectations of return.

Allahabad   ANAMIKA ROY

Introduction

WHO ARE THE Yoginis? When did their worship start and how were they depicted? How can one identify a Yogini image? One may answer with diverse conceptual tools, going to tantricism, to art history, or to religious thought.

Yogini is a generic term. Always present in groups, Yoginis are of different types. Ascetics, there is a Yogini Dasha in astrology, Yoginis as attendants of the Goddess and so on. In some tantra texts, Yoginis are the deities of the directions. In the *Kalika Purana* it is said that the eight Yoginis should be worshipped before worshipping the Goddess. They are also supposed to be playing with the Bhairava. It could be the reason that in circular Yogini temples there is a Bhairava in the centre.

Yogini temples emerged from the AD 900–1200 and this was the period when most of the tantra texts and the Purāṇas were written. The Yogini temples stand distinct from the main stream of the temples. There is no *Vimana*, *Shikhara*, platform, or *Jangha*. Most Yogini temples are circular and open to the sky. There are eighty-one, sixty-four, or forty-two niches in the inner wall to accommodate the Yogini images. The temple wall is not very high: from six to ten feet and the thickness is from twenty-five to one hundred and twenty-five feet. All these will be discussed in detail in Chapter 7.

The Yoginis and their worship did not have its origin in orthodox Hinduism. The Yoginis originated as simple local deities and village goddesses. With the spread of tantricism there was an elevation and transformation of these village deities. The texts were written for them and independent temples were built for them. As local deities they retained names such as Phanendri, Tarala, Tarini, and Badari. They were said to be sixty-four in number, figure that is said to be of convenience or auspicious. Thus village deities installed under trees or in a shrine, were assimilated as a group of sixty-four. The earliest reference to such ferocious deities may be found in the Gangadhar inscription of Mayurakshaka, AD 423–4. Mayurakshaka built a temple for the Matrikas along with Chamunda and it was surrounded by invisible Dakinis.

A second such important temple is mentioned in Skandagupta or Budhagupta's vihar inscription. It is significant as it mentions the erection of a yupa stambha and a temple for *Skanda Matrikas, Bhadrarya* or *Bhadrakali*. And *Devaniketamandala, mandala* here means either group of temples or *yantra.* Reference to temple of mothers may be found also in the *Rajatarangini* of *Kalhana. Kalhana* writes that *Ishana Devi* wife of king *Jaluka,* built *matricakras,* circle of mothers at a number of places of his empire. The *Agni Purana* mentions the method of carving of Yogini images. The Yogini images are usually huge: while body is sensuous, they may have fearful animal heads.

The tradition of the 'Yoginis' of the Yogini Kaula is preserved in some of the tantric texts of which the *Kaulajnananirnaya* is the most significant. The date of this manuscript is thought by P.C. Bagchi to be no later than the 1100 AD. H.P. Sastri says that the manuscript is of AD 859. Abhinavagupta, however paid homage to Matsyendra Nath, it means he must be earlier than Abhinavagupta. The text consists of 1,000 verses and the MS belongs to the Darbar Hall Library No. 11.262 (H). The texts published do not bear the name of the author. Matsyendra Nath seems to be propounder of a section of the Kaulas known as Yogini Kaula school. There are 24 patalas in the book. It is in the dialogue form between Bhairava and Devi. It is about creation, destruction, moksha (liberation), meditation, rituals and how different types of Shaktis should be invoked and how different types of vessels should be used in rituals. Surprisingly, same arrangement is found in the *Kularnava Tantra* also. The conversation emphasizes the merit of the Shastra, which is known to each and every woman of Kamarupa. The most significant is that Bhairava informs the Devi that the Yoginis and Rudras can be worshipped either externally with flower, incense and offering or internally.

For the study of Sixty-Four Yogini's *Matottara Tantra* is also important. It is from Darbar Hall Library of Nepal edited by Janardan Pandey. It says that the followers of the Kaula path become specially dear to Yoginis. It also describes the Yoginis as capable of creating and destroying the world. Like most tantric texts it mentions Shiva at centre of the group of the Yoginis.

The *Yogini Hridaya,* also known as *Nitya Hridaya* and *Sundari Hridaya* is said to be one part of entire work known as the *Nityashodashikarnava,* the other part being often separately treated as the *Vamakeshvara Tantra.* This work which abounds in elliptical terms and code words is divided into three chapters corresponding to three parts (*sanketa*), described as chakra (or yantra), mantra and puja or worship.

Tantraloka is masterpiece of non dualistic Kashmir Shaivism. It contains the synthesis of the sixty-four monastic agamas and all works in both ritualistic and philosophical aspects. The condensed version of *Tantraloka* is known as *Tantra Sara. Tantraloka* is translated into Italian by Raniero Gnoli. The English translation by Mark Dyczkowski is still awaited. It mentions

Macchendra Vibhu (Matsyendra Nath). Verse nos. 371 and 382 mention Yoginis, but it is not clear which Yogini they mean.

Vijnana Bhairava Tantra is a key text type of the trika school of Kashmir Shavism. It is discourse between Shiva and his consort. It briefly narrates the 112 methods of meditation. It mentions sixty-four Yoginis as *Svara* and *Mantra* on page numbers 98 and 172. It is edited by Jaideva Singh as *Vijnana Bhairava* or *Divine Consciousness*.

Tantra Raj Tantra is edited by Sir John Woodroff. Its verses 58–70 of Chapter VII narrate as to how to control *Apsaras* and *Yakshinis*. Chapters XVI and XVII deal with *Dakinis*. Verse 49 of Chapter XVII gives details of the rituals and fruits gained by them. Verses 50–58 mention the nature of 36 *Yakshinis* and verses 60–67 talk about 64 *Chetakas*. This text is supposed to be the king of all tantra texts, this is why it is called *Tantra Raj Tantra*.

The *Tantra Sara Sangraha* edited by Pt. M. Duraj Swami Aiyangar describes *Yogini Nidra*.

The *Mahanirvana Tantra* is edited by Arthur Avlon. It has 14 chapters. It also describes rituals for worshipping the Yoginis. Arthur Avlon says that some part of it is interpolation, and added by Raja Ram Mohan Roy.

Rudrayamala is used as a source by many other agamas, but the original appears to be lost.

Sri Kularnava Tantra is also a dialogue between Shiva and Parvati. *Kularnava Tantra* is supposed to be situated in the hearts of the Yoginis. Abhinavagupta in his *Tantraloka* explains it like this. The process of dispensing of God through joy, knowledge and desire is known as *Kauliki* Shastra.

WHO WAS MATSYENDRA NATH?

It is said that Matsyendra Nath who started Yogini Kaula, was of Nath cult and was the first Nath. Women have no entry in the Nath cult. Matsyendra Nath deviated from his path for some time. He was engrossed in the company of women and introduced a new cult known as 'Yogini Kaula'.

The oldest known legend about Matsyendra Nath is preserved in the *Kaulajnananirnaya*. The date of which can be fixed around AD 1100–1200 as Abhinavagupta has mentioned Matsyendra Nath, he must have been born before Abhinavagupta. In the sixteenth chapter Shiva says that he is super hero among fishermen (V.II) and in the 21st and 22nd verses tells Devi that it was Shiva himself, who has revealed the secret knowledge to her at Kamarupa. This secret knowledge, Shastra was stolen by Kartikeya (V.29) and he threw it into the sea. The Bhairava (in the incarnation as Matsyendra Nath) went to the sea caught the fish, which has swallowed the Shastra. He cut the belly of the fish and recovered the Shastra.

There is a late puranic legend in the Nagarkhanda of the Skanda Purana. It says that Matsyendra Nath was born in the *Gandantayoga*, thus was inauspicious for his family. To avoid it he was thrown into the sea and was swallowed by a fish. Once Shiva was travelling with Devi and Kartikeya in the ocean of milk, Shiva initiated Parvati in the knowledge of *Dhyanyoga* and *Jnanayoga*. Kartikeya listened to their dialogue. From the ocean arose a big fish, and Matsyendra Nath from the belly of the fish narrated the events and told that after listening the conversation he has also attained the *Jnanayoga*. Extremely pleased Shiva said that since the boy in the belly is a brahmin, thus is like his son. Matsyendra Nath then came out of the belly of the fish and Shiva gave him the name Matsyendra Nath.

HOW THE WORKS EVOLVED?

Not much has been written on sixty-four Yoginis. It rather got a lukewarm treatment from the art historians.

In 1974 Charles Fabri wrote *History and Art of Orissa* and has concentrated upon two Orissan temples, Hirapur and Ranipur-Jharial in one chapter. In comparison to subsequent works Fabri's work appears to be shallow. Fabri was of the opinion that the Yogini Kaula cult was born out of or was associated with Sahaja-Yana. His work could not go into the details of the images and architecture. Mostly, he has discussed the Yogini images like any other feminine beauty of the period.

After him in 1978, R.K. Sharma in his monograph, *Chaunsath Yogini at Bheraghat* has done the study of Bheraghat Yoginis. He discusses the prevalence of different Shaivite sects like Pashupata, Lakulisha, Matta Mayura and Yogini Kaula. There is a description of all the images and the history of the temple of Bheraghat, therefore history of the rise and fall of Shaktism in central India during medieval period. He has not tried to answer the riddle of Golaki Mutt. His book does not answer why the temple was built for eighty-one Yoginis.

H.C. Das (1981) in *Tantricism: A Study of the Yogini Cult,* like all other scholars has concentrated more upon Orissan temples. He has tried to find out a regionalism in the images. His work is commendable for studies on the tantras.

The real path-breaking work came in 1986, by Vidya Dehejia, *Yogini Cult and Temple: A Tantric Tradition.* Dehejia has gone deeply into the meaning of 'Yogini', rituals, legends, and temple architecture on the basis of original tantric and popular Sanskrit texts. She has shown how the concept of 'Yogini' of Yogini Kaula evolved through generic term Yogini. The real value of the monograph lies in explaining 'Yoginis' of Yogini Kaula through all the aspects.

She has also discussed the historical figures associated with the temples and their so-called patronage.

A very significant work, though a chapter only was done by Devangana Desai in *The Yogini Shrine and Cult* in the monograph 'Religious Imagery of Khajuraho' in 1996. She has raised some important issues, which have been overlooked by the scholars. She has pointed out the fact that the Yogini-Pithas have been found near the capitals of ruling dynasties suggests that the kings worshipped them for the protection of their kingdoms. She gives a precise date for Khajuraho temple, i.e. AD 900, whereas there has been a vast range of dates from AD 900–1100. She also gives a clue for the rectangular shape of Khajuraho temple stating that it was regional speciality as we find same shape temple at Rikhiyan 240 km. away from Khajuraho. Her other significant contribution is that she asserts Yogini Kaula and Yogini Temple were different as Yoginis of Kaula were female ascetics and not the deities. Over the places she also agrees with Dehejia.

In 2001 Francesco Brighenti published *Sakti Cult in Orissa*, where she has discussed the sixty-four Yoginis. Brighenti like N.N. Bhattacharyya is of the view that the Yoginis were earlier probably human beings, women of flesh and blood, priestesses who were supposed to be possessed by the goddess, and later they were raised to the status of divinity. She says that the deified Yoginis of the medieval epoch may have been, thus, regarded by their tantric devotees as the mythical ancestresses of the mundane Yoginis. She seeks their origin from Yakshis. She like Fabri rejects the theory that the number sixty-four is actually multiplication of eight matrikas. Unlike Vidya Dehejia she says that matrika and Yogini cult developed side by side with several reciprocal trends.

In 2002 Thomas Donaldson has picked up the thread from Dehejia in *Tantra and Sakta Art of Orissa* and categorized four traditions of the Yoginis. In the first, there is a circle of the Yoginis, in the second they are the ganas or group of the Yoginis. In the third tradition Yoginis and matrikas are used as synonyms and in the fourth tradition there are Yoginis of Yogini Kaula. Donaldson was doubtful for its sectarian origin and according to him it has its alliance with Shaivite sect also especially with Kapalika and Matta Mayura.

Donaldson's work is commendable as it has discussed iconography on the basis of the texts. He starts with *Caturvarga Cintamani* of Hemadri, *Pratisthalakshana Sara Samuccaya*, and *Takkayagapparani*. It should, however be noted that most of these texts were written after AD 1200, when most Yogini temples were already constructed. Donaldson like Dehejia talks about magic number eight and as the number is auspicious so number sixty-four is more auspicious. It is in his monograph that the iconography, weapons, features, functions, colours and the attributes of the Yoginis have been discussed on the basis of the texts.

Other than these works V.W. Karambelkar has done a wonderful article on 'Matsyendra Nath and his Yogini Cult' in *Indian Historical Quarterly*, vol. xxxi in 1969. Besides discussing Matsyendra Nath and the beginning of Yogini Cult, he points out that the circular shape and an absence of roof of Yogini temples find a justification in some ancient legends about the Yogini themselves, according to which these deities used to roam about in a group in the air and when they descend down they always displace themselves in a circle. *The Kiss of Yogini* by David Gordon White, published in 2003 concentrated basically on the tantricism. The unpublished thesis by Margrit Thomsen, *Kult and ikonographie der, un 64 Yoginis* also deserves mention. Most scholars who worked after Dehejia had either accelerated her theory or supported their views with her arguments.

All these studies have predominantly been occupied with the tantric aspect, and are therefore limited in their treatment of the subject. None of these works have gone beyond tantricism. The amalgamation of the tribal deities and their elevation to the status of the Great Goddess in the form of sixty-four Yoginis needs to be placed in a broader framework which can identify the processes of cultural change, and the historical contexts within which this change took place. The Yoginis are mentioned in contemporary literature, in Sanskrit texts and in the Purāṇas. It may be argued that a study based solely on tantric texts may not do full justice to the subject. The problem which then emerges is whether one can address the question of the elevation of tribal deities as the sixty-four Yoginis within the framework of cultural anthropology. Such a treatment may require a paradigm shift and a change in methodology.

The perspectives of art historians have also been changing, one vanishing where another emerges. Art historians have been perplexed by the peculiar structure of Yogini temples, which do not conform to the norms of *silpa sastra* or to the architecture of traditional temples. However, while expressing their bewilderment, they do not seek a rational explanation for the unique temple forms, as something more than mere deviation from the norm. By and large, in what is often stated as an attempt to maintaining objectivity, scholars have remained cautious and steered clear of this path. Charles Fabri (1974), for example, has alluded to the inaccessibility and inscrutability of the temple forms, pointing to the difficulty of knowing what happened within the closed world of four walls. H.C. Das (1981) on the other hand, has ascribed regional specificity to the difference in temple forms.

I have used literary texts, inscriptions, and the Purāṇas as sources, and have tried to remove the veil of secrecy that seems to shroud the reality of the Yoginis. Even as it proceeds to unveil the secrecy this work does not claim to be an objective document. Objectivity in religious history keeps changing. Moreover Jan Myrdal has stated, 'writers' explanations reveal as much about their traditions of telling as they do about the tradition they attempt to explain. The art historian derives his vision from circumstances different from the ambitions and intentions of the creator or builder. Significance of Yoginis in religion and history needs to be retold.

In the tantric tradition Yoginis are allotted different parts of the human body and they are presented as protectors of regions. Yoginis in this tradition are the energies of the Goddess belonging to the categories of Dakini, Lakini, Shakini, Hakini and Yakini. For example, the Yoginis protect the Prayag region. In later texts and myths they are presented as the protectors of the directions, thereby equal to the Kshetrapalas. Significantly, in the folklore of Kumaon and Garhwal, the Yoginis are invoked along with the Kshetrapalas. Presumably, the thread was picked up at this stage and the Yoginis are now celebrated in folk songs and lores across the Himalayan range. Interestingly, none of these places in these hills has reported a Yogini temple. Similarly, scholars have pointed out that these temples had been found only in the tribal belt of UP, MP, and Orissa but none has been reported from Bengal and Assam,[1] the stronghold of tantricism. This aspect of the Yoginis has not been fully considered, but I intend to examine it by emphasizing that a distinction has to be drawn between the Yogini cult and the Yoginis of the temples. Dehejia (1986) refers to this distinction only in passing. I argue that it is important that this difference be studied in all its complex details, including the distinctiveness of the tribal background of the regions, and the reasons behind the construction of temples in their respective areas. I find strong political and social reasons behind the building of Yogini temples. An analysis of the inscriptions by the kings, however compels us to revise the theory of royal patronage and monuments.

In order to examine the significance of Yoginis in religion and history, and to retell the story, either ignored or told in a manner which occludes specifics, I have adopted a two-pronged approach. I have attempted to remove the inscrutability that shrouds the Yogini temples. In the process of unravelling the 'mystique' which seems to have contributed to the inaccessibility of the Yogini temples, I have attempted an approach that engages with the female body, trying to go beyond the object, so that the sculptures do not remain enigmatic. For this purpose, I have studied their gestures, expressions and limbs and tried to co-relate them with contemporary myths, combining these readings of image and form with a reading of texts (Sanskrit, tantric and purāṇic). I examine whether the depiction of the female form in the temples may in any way be read as reflecting the position of women in India.

The Yoginis themselves have in some ways borne the brunt of normativity, being pushed into categories, the female ascetic, the attendants of the Goddess, or the Goddess herself. In the popular Prakrit/Sanskrit texts *Karpoor*

Manjari, Rajatarangini, and *Malati Madhava,* the Yoginis are witches or women of special powers. The Purāṇas on the other hand, mention their religious and popular aspects. The *Agni Purana* mentions the norms for carving of their images whereas the *Skanda Purana* narrates the stories about Yoginis.

The Tantric texts like the *Kularnava,* the *Kaulajnananirnaya* and the *Yogini Hridaya* describe different rituals for, and the power of the Yoginis. *Kaulajñananirnaya* also preserves the tradition of Matsyendra Nath, the progenitor of the Yogini cult. Similarly, in the *Yogini Hridaya* these beings are not only givers of boons, but also equal to Shakti. Mark Dyczkowski (1988) has identified the body of the Yogini with tantric deliberations. They both are one. Here again, it becomes difficult to distinguish between Yoginis of the Yogini temple and flesh and blood Yoginis.[2]

A reading of 'feminine' forms into the images may be fraught with confusion. Forms are diverse and often there is an overlapping of images and their textual descriptions/categorizations. Some of the Yoginis are included in the Matrika (mothers) groups. Different tantric and pauranik texts which provide lists of Yoginis include them in the Matrika group. This tendency in categorization has been translated into imageries and has often misled art historians. They often call any sensuous image a Yogini (Kaimal, 2005). Such is not the case as Yogini images are always depicted in groups. It is true that Charles Fabri (1974) had sought that the Yogini images of Ranipur-Jharial and Hirapur temples have influenced Alasa Kanya and Sura Sundaris, but calling such individual Nayikas, 'Yoginis' will do injustice to religious history.

My research asks why the artists portrayed some Yoginis as animal-faced, others with a fierce face, but with beautiful bodies. It would be worthwhile to examine whether this was indeed a fusion of beauty and mysticism. These 'terrifying beauties' are intriguing. The *Skanda Purana* and the *Kaulajnananirnaya* narrate interesting accounts as to how these Yoginis have come to bear animal faces.[3] The *Skanda Purana* has provided a list of the names of animal-faced Yoginis.

In this work, I have tried to look for explanations by traversing a trajectory and a perspective that go beyond the usual recourse to *Sastra* and *Parampara* (tradition). I will address an issue raised by Alf Hiltebeitel (2002: 12) concerning the statement, 'We worship them as goddess, but prefer them as women.'

In first chapter I have addressed the question, 'What do the Images Convey?' Harper (1989) addresses the same problem for Matrika images, and Panikkar (1997) for the Sapta Matrika images. For my observations, I have analysed Fabri's hypothesis (1974), about the Ranipur-Jharial images. Fabri has asked if these were dancing Devadasis. He had his own reservations in pushing his theory. In 2001 Brighenti, an Italian scholar of Shakta tantra discusses Fabri's theory but he too pauses at this point. Among the latest works that attempt to go beyond tantricism is that of the Donaldson (2002) but this work also does not discuss this aspect. The Yogini images had so far been marginalized either as tribal deities or as matrikas. Research has ceased at the point of enlisting/enumerating their images and discussing them under the rubric of tantricism. In the Puranas, the Yogini images do not however betray a tantric influence, and I have tried to tread cautiously.

In Chapter 1, I have considered that the images themselves are the statements. In the sculptures of Ranipur-Jharial one finds a very strong tribal influence on dress and features. This could not be the only reason for the 'gestures' conveyed by the images. Again, instead of Bhairava in the centre, here we have dancing Shiva.

To address this problem I have worked on two hypotheses, each exploring the possibilities of a specific relationship in a particular region. The first is the relation between Devadasis and the Yogini cult in Orissan temples. The second is the relation between Devadasis and modern Jogatis or Joganis of Andhra Pradesh and Karnataka.

The texts like *Karpoor Manjari* and *Rajatarangini* celebrate the valaya (circular) and fierce dance of the Yoginis. The Yoginis are *Khe Charis* who roam in the sky, the circular temples are open to the sky so that dancing and wandering Yoginis could descend into them.

Today the Jogatis or Joganis, dedicated to the native goddesses, are covered by the Devadasi Act, but before 1988, Devadasis served in the Jagannath Temple of Orissa and the old Orissan texts narrate that the Sixty-Four Yoginis served Jagannath.

I have tried to explain this relationship through a triangle:

To my mind, the attempt to establish this relationship marks a departure from the traditional approaches, and opens up an explanatory framework that neither art historians nor social historians have as yet touched.

In the second chapter I have raised some questions: Was the artist following the narration of Kashi Khanda of the *Skanda Purana*? Was there a tantric influence as the stories are to be found in *Kaulajnananirnaya* also? Is this reminiscent of the tribal roots of the Yoginis? Last, were the fierce faces of the Yoginis intended to conceal the 'self' and reveal the 'other'?

It is not always easy to apply the anthropological approach to religious history. In Chapter 3, it is shown that the acceptance of tribal deities into orthodox Hinduism is generally seen as signalling the 'history' of the sixty-four Yoginis. In third chapter I have covered the debate in anthropology from 1952–74 and argued that such debates fail to explain the 'traditional' history of the Yoginis.

Chapter 4 tries to dispel the notion that much work has already been done in the area of tantras. I have referred to the *Mahanirvana Tantra*, the *Kularnava Tantra*, and a Newari Manuscript from Nepal namely *Pratisthanirnayasarasmuccaya*. I have also touched upon the current controversy whether the sixty-four Yoginis belong to the Shaivism or Shaktism.

Sung and celebrated in the folk songs of Himachal Pradesh, Kumaon and Garhwal, Yoginis are invoked along with the local deities in the *Jagar* songs. The cult may be obscure, but in the 'low rituals' and 'popular belief' they are very much alive and well known. I have collected folk songs from Kumaon and Garhwal and folklore from the Himalaya to see how the Yoginis have 'lived on'. This aspect has been brought out in Chapter 5.

The sixty-four Yoginis were originally native deities. Their temples are in the tribal belts. In Chapter 6, I have analysed the views of three scholars on this topic, A. Eschmann (1984), R.S. Sharma (2001) and B.D. Chattopadhyaya (2003). Eschmann shows that in the process of Hinduization a sign becomes an icon. Chattopadhyaya on the basis of epigraphic evidence asserts that grants were given for the maintenance of the temples of local deities and goddesses in the dense forest from the eighth to the tenth century. He calls this a tension between vana and janapada. Sharma looks for the agencies behind the assimilation of these deities in orthodox Hinduism. He finds the answer in contemporary social and political situations. While all three theories may provide some explanation for the emergence of the sixty-four Yoginis from the tribal goddesses, no individual theory gives the total picture. Besides I have appended to Chapter 6 a list of current living tribal deities of these regions.

Most perplexing, is the form of the Yogini temples. No one has discussed the problem beyond a conventional scrutiny; most scholars arrive at the conclusion that they were deviant forms. At the most they were considered as the concrete expression of the *mandala, yantra* and other tantric diagrams. I have tried to address this problem by examining present-day tribal ritual and Buddhist practices in Chapter 7.

The Yogini temples were built in the territories and period of the Pratiharas, Chandellas, Parmaras and Kalachuris. Scholars like Dehejia (1988) had shown that the temples of 81 Yoginis were especially built for royal people. The question of power and patronage has also been raised by Stoller Miller (1992) and Dehejia (1988) in the context of artist, royalty, and monument. The *Skanda Purana*, the *Kularnava Tantra*, and the *Brahmanda Purana* discuss the power of Yoginis to grant boons to royalty. Thus the *Kularnava Tantra* says: And Shiva says: if a king worships the Yoginis with total devotion,

O Devi, his fame will reach the shores of the four oceans of that there is no doubt.

In Chapter 8, I move to the inscriptions of the concerned rulers. I tend to differ from the views of the above scholars, as I have tried to explore the reality of the builders of the gigantic Bheraghat and the enchanting Hirapur temples.

In Chapter 9, I have examined the sculptures from all the temples. The sculptures show the local touch. The Bheraghat and Naresar Yogini images create an awesome atmosphere. The Hirapur Yogini images delineate local traits whereas the Ranipur-Jharial images demonstrate dancing posture, and Yoginis from Hingalajgadha betray divinity. Thus each site of Yogini images addresses different questions.

The prominence of the sixty-four Yoginis marks in some ways the 'elevation' of goddesses hitherto marginalized. The *Kularnava Tantra* says that Rajaki Ganika, and Shilpi should be worshipped as a substitute of the Goddess. Thus Chapter 10 addresses the following questions: Was the Goddess a metaphor for the empowerment of the women? Can the sculptures be translated into or read as, gender roles, such as mother, spouse, warrior and savior?

NOTES

1. In Assam they are still worshipped on paper by making a Yogini Chakra.
2. Mark Dyczkowski's monograph is being published by Indira Gandhi Center for Arts.
3. *Varahi,* the Matrika is also included in the group of Yoginis.

PART I

CHAPTER ONE

Why do the Yoginis Dance?

Song symbolizes Mantra and Dance means meditation, so the singing and dancing Yogini always acts.
                                                            —HEVAJRA TANTRA

YOGINI IMAGES HAVE been marginalized either as tribal deities or as matrikas (mother goddesses). No art historian had engaged with them as female bodies; they were always seen as divinities. While the female gender of the Yoginis have been noted by some art historians, few scholars have actually seen gender as having reiterative significance, so that we miss out on a crucial analytical theme. Scholarship in art history and theology is to that extent limited. The images themselves are statements of their time. Sometimes they correspond to the pauranic descriptions, at other times they can be translated into literary inscriptions. The dance of the Yoginis should not be set aside as the imagination of the artists. The Yoginis dance because of a deep-rooted tribal connection and a native trend can easily be detected in all Yogini images.

In this chapter I deal with Yogini images from the Ranipur-Jharial (Illus. 1)[1] temple in Orissa. Here we find a very strong tribal influence on dress and features (Illus. 2 and 3) and the Yoginis dance around Shiva Bhairava. The question that comes is whether these dancing Yoginis hold the clue to what happened within the circular walls of the temple. Fabri (1974: 84) wondered whether these images were those of dancing devadasis. He compared their graceful gait (Illus. 4, 5 and 6) with Sura Kanya and Alasa Kanya of the Orissan temples, and was of the view that it was these Yogini images that had inspired them.[2] Both traditions were contemporary. The devadasis were married to the temple god and the Yoginis danced around Shiva and Bhairava. Scholars were, however, hesitant to develop Fabri's theory. Indeed, an uncomfortable pause seems to have followed Fabri's observation. F. Brighenti (2001: 305) comments that Fabri's question, though full of possibilities, remained unanswered and unexplored in the context of the then dominant Indology. It is perhaps important to revisit the question.

The devadasi tradition was not unknown to Orissa, the land of Jagannath. Until 1988 the devadasis danced in the temple of Jagannath for the evening rituals. Among the five makaras of tantric worship the maithun has been replaced by the dance of the devadasis.[3] According to the *Bata Abakash*,[4] an Orissan text, Jagannath was served by sixty-four Yoginis who were earlier human beings, gradually deified. Traditions preserve the narratives of the powers and magical charms of the Yogini. Thus the *Uttama Carita Kathanaka*[5] narrates that princess Ananga Sena was in fact a Yogini who could turn a prince into a parrot.

From the classical texts to the Puranas and from the Puranas to the tantra literature different aspects of the Yoginis emerge. Despite Dehejia's skilful classification (1986: 11)[6] there had always been an academic dilemma regarding the true interpretation of Yoginis. It became a generic term, referring to some characteristics in common.

In this context one can draw attention towards the tradition concerning Jogatis or Jogani, still prevalent in Maharashtra, Andhra Pradesh and Karnataka. Who are these Joganis or Jogatis? How can we associate them with the Yoginis of the Yogini cult? The Joganis known as Basavi in Karnataka and Maharashtra, are real women, but they are not ascetics. They are considered to be lower goddesses. They are also taken to be a lower form of devadasi. The point to be noted is that because of their rituals and lifestyles, they are known as religious prostitutes, but are not considered quite as fascinating and enchanting as devadasis.

The worship of Jogatis or Joganis is most popular in Andhra Pradesh, especially in Telangana. Most of these Jogatis hailed from the lower castes, and were dedicated to local goddesses. Jogatis are supposed to avert calamity and disease in the family and village. They cannot marry their whole life, but can be approached by any man; they had to dance at funerals and beg for alms in the harvest season. The custom is still prevalent and Gandamani, a Jogati is dedicated to the local Goddess Yellamma; Savithri, another Jogati or Jogani of Govvur village, is in her turn dedicated to the goddess Pochamma of her area to cure her ailing father.

These Joganis or Jogatis are also covered by the Devadasi Law. The Devadasis were supposed to be the wives of the gods, married to either Shiva or to Vishnu, whereas Jogatis or Joganis were dedicated to the local goddesses and they hail from the lowest Hindu caste system. Both were linked to the Yogini cult. This relationship can be understood in terms of a triangle.

Devadasi   Jogati

Yogani

If Jogatis or Joganis were dedicated to the local goddesses, the Yoginis were basically those local goddesses who were elevated to the forms of the Great Goddess and the Goddess herself after their assimilation in orthodox Hinduism. This relationship goes a long way in revealing that both the trends of Jogatis and Yoginis must have influenced each other.

The Joganis or Jogatis carry an effigy of Yellamma on a bamboo. Scholars believe that this custom may have come to the surface when the Nath cult became dominant in Karnataka. The Yogini cult is not unknown in these regions. In Maharashtra, the Yogini vrata is performed for the safety of children. The Yogini cult was also related to the Nath cult, as Matsyendra Nath, initiated the Yogini and the Nath cults. Traditions and legends associate him with the beginning of Yogani cult. It seems that after Matsyendra Nath, his disciples parted ways, scattering all over the state. Parts of this cult, were regenerated, in the form of Joganis or Jogatis in Karnataka and Andhra Pradesh. This instance provides an understanding of how the dance was associated with the Yogini cult even after its disappearance.

If we try to translate what the images convey, Bheraghat (Illus. 7), Lokhari (Illus. 8, 9 and 11), Hirapur (Illus. 14 and 15), Ranipur-Jharial (Illus. 16, 17 and 18) all are different from each other. The images from all these places have an easily identifiable local features. Myth, history and oral traditions confirm the fact that the Yogini sculptures are not deity images only. They address some untold facts and tradition.

The question then arises, why were images of devadasis carved in stone? It should be remembered that only the Ranipur-Jharial images (Illus. 20, 22, 23, 24 and 25) are in dancing posture, whereas the Hirapur Yogini images (Illus. 26, 27, 28 and 29) are identified with the puranic deities.

Scholars have argued over whether the devadasis of Orissan temples indulged in sacred prostitution like the devadasis of Tamil temples of the Chola period. Ghonda (1981: 76–7) points out that devadasis had a quasi religious function, whose origins are to be traced back to the incorporation of Shakta ideas into medieval Shaivism. Figures of dancer prostitutes were believed to irradiate joy and bestow prosperity because of the magical power of their sexuality, which was regarded as an earthy reflection of the energy of the supreme Shakti. Their role was, thus, conceptually akin to that of the Yoginis of the Kaula tradition. Unlike the Yoginis, the devadasis were generally approached by all common people. Ghonda's discussion points to the amalgamation of Shaivism and Shaktism at some stage; devadasis may have danced in Shakta rituals, which later found expression in image carvings. The dancing Yoginis tempt us to dig further into this question.

As stated earlier, until 1988 Jagannath had been served by the devadasis. The devadasis performed twice daily in the temple (Apffel 1985: 217–40). The morning ritual consists of a dance accompanied by songs. The dance takes place simultaneously with the first major offering in the inner sanctum behind closed doors, and also in the dance hall and in the public. The Shaktas call the dance at the time of morning meal *Kali Uchchista* or *Shakti Uchchista*. This has neither an oral tradition nor a puranic myth to support it, but it did have a legendary background.

The dancing Yoginis were supposed to generate energy. At Konark the dancing devadasis who dragged the chariot of the sun god were considered to be Yogini Shakti. Even the dancing Ida and Pingala at the temple wall of Konark were construed as dancing Yogini Shaktis.

The *Bata Abakash* of Balram Dasa describes Jagannath attended by Sixty-Four Yoginis.[7] It is not far-fetched to link the devadasi ritual dance before the god with the sixty-four Yoginis, attending the god.

Besides, it may be that the cult of devadasis and the Yogini temples in Orissa are contemporary. All this points to the fact that temple of sixty-four Yoginis at Ranipur-Jharial did not evolve in total isolation but incorporated several trends of the period.

Dancing and singing were associated with the Yogini cult. The prominence of the cult, as stated earlier, began with Matsyendra Nath, a Shaivite. The *Kaulajnananirnaya*[8] indicates that Matsyendra Nath was fond of the company of women. Matsyendra Nath or Mina Nath as he is often also called, used to roam in the Kadali forest (banana forest) with 1,600 women. Even yogis were not permitted there, only female dancers had access. These dancers were actually Yoginis, who created illusions to mesmerize Matsyendra Nath. In the *Kaulajnananirnaya*, Matsyendra Nath is addressed as *Macchaghnapada* and *Macchendrapada*[9] also. Here the term *Macchaghna* is significant. Abhinavagupta in his *Tantraloka* uses the term 'Macchanda' for Matsyendra Nath as metaphor. According to him one who ruins the corrupt activity of mind is *Macchanda*. Commentator on *Tantraloka,* says that the people of fickle-mind are known as *maccha* (fish), whoever comes out of these is 'Macchanda'.[10] Among the Kabir Panthis *Maccha* is still used for a fickle-minded person. The term is not accidental. Matsyendra Nath[11] is described in the popular texts as discarding the Yogic path and surrounding himself with the company of women. The story of Mina Nath and his association with women is narrated in the *Goraksh Vijaya* of Faizullah. It is compiled in Sukumar Sen's *Bangala Saihityer Itihas*, which says that Mina Nath was enchanted by Bhuvan Mohini, who was the Goddess herself. Bhuvan Mohini cursed him that he would lose all his knowledge and roam in the Kadali Desh with 1,600 girls. The rest of the story may be summed up like this. Matsyendra Nath's disciple Goraksh Nath came to know about his master's captivity. He disguised himself as a Yogi and came to know from a woman of Kadali Desh that his master was roaming with queens Mangala and Kamala, surrounded by 1,600 damsels. Yogis were prohibited there. Only dancers could have an audience with Matsyendra

Nath. Goraksh Nath took the form of a beautiful dancer, but the queens banned her from seeing Matsyendra Nath because of her beauty. Consequently, Goraksh Nath played a musical instrument. Hearing the sound Matsyendra Nath called out. Goraksh Nath again played the instrument, and brought Matsyendra Nath out of the forest.

In *Yogisampradayaviskriti*,[12] there is another narration which also associates Mina Nath with dancers. The story says that the queen of Triya Desh (Sinhala Desh) was not satisfied with her husband. She had received a boon, another husband, from Hanuman. Hanuman sent Matsyendra Nath to her. His disciple Goraksh Nath reached there, but the queen barred the entry of the Yogi. Hence Goraksh Nath entered there as the tabla player accompanying the dancer Kalinga. Matsyendra Nath was enjoying the performance of Kalinga, when Goraksh Nath played 'awake Matsyendra, Matsyendra Nath awake'. This sound awakened Matsyendra Nath.

This narration indicates that at some stage Matsyendra Nath was captivated and enchanted by dancing beauties. All the texts preserve this tradition and it may not be accidental. It may also be a veiled allusion to the dancing images in stone.

It is thus difficult to draw a line demarcating the Yoginis of rituals and Yoginis of flesh and blood in legends and actual thoughts.[13] Remnants of narratives about Matsyendra Nath, Goraksh Nath, Stri Desh or Kadali Forest, and beautiful Yoginis with magical charms are still preserved in popular memory from Bengal to eastern UP.

At Dinajpur in Bengal, the disciples of Goraksh Nath sing vulgar songs known as *Dhamali*. Scholars have frowned upon them, and wondered how Yogis came to sing such songs. It has also been suggested that perhaps these songs are *Sandhya Bhasa*, that is, a coded language. In some very obscene songs sung, a local tradition in eastern UP and Bihar, especially on the occasion of Holi, are known as *Jogida*.[14] After *Jogida*, *Kabira* is sung. In his study of Nath sect, Dwivedi (1981: 54) raises a question regarding the relevance of the singing of *Jogida* by Kabir Panthis. He also says that these are meant to have an inner hidden meaning. It may be taken as the most rustic form of a tradition preserved in the layers of time.[15]

This entire discussion is substantiated by archaeological evidence. At Shahdol, in dense forest a Yogini temple has been reported and sculptures are now preserved in different museums. There also exists a temple of Matsyendra Nath, which may have been associated with Yoginis also. Currently, the Kabir Panthis perform their rituals there.[16] This discussion establishes that the Yoginis were dancers. It is true that Yogini images betray local features, puranic features, tribal features, folk features and ritualistic attributes, but they also present Yoginis as dancing girls. These images have been marginalized so far.

The Yoginis stand at the juxtaposition of the cult and popular believes. The *Kathasaritsagara*[17] narrates an incident where Chandrasvamin saw a circle of mothers headed by Narayani and Yoginis danced with Bhairava.

The *Karpoor Manjari* describes women dancing on the occasion of *vata savitri* as the reminiscent of the *valaya* (circle) dance of Yoginis. It seems that the dance of Yoginis had become a prevalent ritual by this time. It was a mystic dance but there was no secrecy in the circle dance of the Yoginis. Their temples were open to the sky so that the *khecharis*—the sky wanderer Yoginis may descend and join in. The fourth canto of the *Karpoor Manjari* describes the *vata savitri vrata* in the royal household. Under the influence of tantricism, Chamunda was worshipped. The king was invited to watch the rituals, including a dance of thirty-two dancers, in a strange circle.[18]

Another couplet describes the dance of women in a circle like that of Yoginis. The fourth canto that describes the festival of *vata savitri* makes two obvious departures from the original. In this verse Chamunda is being worshipped, and in the rituals a Yogini-like dance is performed by women of the palace.[19] In the texts, the dance of the Yoginis is ferocious, with no suggestion of a vulnerable or feminine feature. Even the *Rajatarangini*, in which the magical powers of Yoginis are described, speaks of the ferocious nature of the dance in the cremation ground.[20]

Obviously, such dance was not purposeless or for merry-making. They were to be performed for a ritual or to gain an objective. Not only the classical or popular texts but religious texts too describe the dance of the Yoginis. It is a dance of victory, a fierce form of the dance. The *Padma Purana* (Ch.VI v.18 and 110–25) narrates such a dance of the sixty-four Yoginis with Shiva after killing the demon *Jalandhar*. The Yoginis had sharp nails and huge bodies. Even today (at this time), they seize the flesh so that demon Jalandhar, killed in battle, may not get up. In the *Linga Purana* (Ch. 106, v.1–28) after the defeat of the demon Daruka, the Yoginis danced with Kali in the midst of ghosts.

The Yoginis are not always awesome ogresses: sometimes they are in their appearance enchanting. Thus the *Lalita Sahsranama*[21] says eight beautiful Yoginis are to be worshipped and refers to them as *nayika*. This may be vague, but it refers to their physical charm. The *Tantra Sara*[22] describes them as Yakshini, Yogini or Nayika and their physical charm is implied.

Thus the dance had always been associated with the myths and rituals of the Yoginis. Their temples were open to sky (Illus. 30) so that the dancing circle of Yoginis may descend from the sky. In stone as well as in the texts they are depicted as the beautiful nayikas. This attribute leaves aside the Yoginis as mother or divine being. The sculptor would have been aware of the myths and he translated them into stone. Popular stories of Yoginis found place and occupied the imagination of poets. Here we have a category that was esoteric, but not secretive. The dancing Yoginis were part of that ritual and class. The dancing Yoginis do correspond to the puranic mythology. But that cannot alone explain the distinctive dilemma concerning Yoginis. Dance has been associated with esoteric practices in Buddhism also. In Vajrayan Buddhism, the dance is still practised. The Dakinis, the Buddhist counterparts of the Yoginis, also dance. These are the five wisdom Dakinis, who guide human beings through their magic dance.

You are our Wisdom Dakinis
Effortlessly guiding us with your magic dance.
From ordinary beings to sublime beings.
Into desireless qualities
                        —NORBU 2003: 6

In Nepal, the masked dance is performed by priests in Buddhist monasteries of Vajracarya. Secrecy is maintained as they are performed within the tantric sanctuary. After worshipping all the deities of the mandalas for three hours, various priests dance. The main guru, dressed in white, dances as Vajrasattva, his wife is in red, as Vajradan, the assistant in yellow as Manjuvajra, and so on. In Leh, dance is performed in honour of the eight aspects of Guru Padma Sambhava at the Hemis monastery in Ladakh. It is popular belief that the Chama dance began around AD 811, for the protection of the Dharma (Khanna 2004: 304–15). It is intriguing that while in Nepal the dance is performed by the Hinayana sect, in Bhutan it is supposed to be a transformation from Hinayana to Mahayana.

Another Newari dance (Vergati 2004: 199–209), performed in Nepal, is the ritual dance of Nava Durga. Though Newari literature is quite rich, the narrative about this dance are preserved only in oral tradition. Here the dancers wear the masks of the goddesses and dance around the streets of Bhaktapur during Navratri (October). These dancing Nava Durga are supposed to be the link between this material world and the mystic world.

In tribal Bengal (Sarkar 2004: 221–31) in the months from Chaitra to Ashadh (April to July) a masked dance is performed around Shiva, by men wearing masks of Kali. This dance, the Gamira, and another such dance known as Chandi are performed by men alone. Women are totally prohibited and the dance is carried out under tantric influence.

The question remains why Yoginis in sculpture dance. What does the image convey? There is not one single answer. It is webbed in the mystery and mysticism of the cult. The dancing Yogini images are the manifestation of the rituals where the Joganis or devadasis or women in the roles of the different goddesses danced in the temple. Even before the development of the cult the dance may have attached to some magico-religious practices, they may have been performed in the forest or in a secret place to gain a desire. Subsequently, they were expressed in stone and they also became associated with esoteric practices of the temples, and the dancing Yoginis ultimately may have become dancing devadasis. Usually eroticism and esoterism are taken as two sides of one coin. Questions have often been raised regarding the aesthetic value of tantric art. Were these Yogini images carved to perform rituals only? Did they have a utilitarian value?

Popular texts and the Puranas mention the dance of the Yoginis. Obviously, it was not for the rituals only. Their movements must have produced power: the *mudra* (gesture), *hast sanchar* (hand gesture), *pad prakshep* (leg movement) were not carved at the fancy of the sculptor. Thus the Yogini imageries were not merely the sculptures in stone delineating tantric and folk influence, but these are the images that correspond to the visual performance of the age. There are *tandava, bhava, vibhava, vatsalya* gestures and expressions. The hand gesture, expressions in eyes, and the leg postures are significant. They signify rituals, and also the zenith of the aesthetic sense. When Yoginis dance around Shiva Bhairava (Illus. 31), the Lord of the Dance, it is the dance that generates energy that gives life to sprouting seeds. Even today, women paint the earth with different geometrical designs and vibrant folk dance delineates the legends and mystics of these ancient cults. It indicates a long history of energetic and powerful female memories. The dance of the Yogini is a cosmic dance, it is to fertilize the earth. Here the Yoginis may have been portrayed as demons, dancing to celebrate their victory and magical power. They may have been fashioned into historical feminine figures, dancing as bloodthirsty deities. But this was also a dance of divine ecstasy, representing a hermeneutical world of complex interpretations.

NOTES

1. Yogini Badari (Illus. 45) from Shahadol is also in Tandava posture.
2. Charles Fabri (1974: 84) says that Devadasis, were women of easy virtue, whose contributions to the prostitutions of many religious practices are widely known and universally accepted. While the women in Hirapur shrine are shown in great variety of poses, those at Ranipur-Jharia are without exception all in one and the same dancing pose, an adavu (The Odissi a in posture with widely spread knees).
3. It is based on the oral tradition of Puri.
4. Balarama Dasa, *Bata Abakash* (Oriya), 1930, pp. 17–2.
5. Penzer, *Uttama Ramcarita Kathanak,* 1924–28, p. 60.
6. Her division runs likes this: Yogini as an adept in Yoga, Yogini as partner in cakra puja, Yogini as sorceress, Yogini of astrology, Yoginis of internal cakra, Yogini of Sri cakra, Yogini as the Great Goddess, Yogini as aspect of Devi, Yoginis as attendants of the Great Goddess, Yogini as acolyte of the Great Goddess. The question, however, is whether any of these titles, can be applied exclusively to the figures in the Yogini temples, or whether these Yogini are a category apart.

7. K.C. Behera (1967) provides a very interesting clue. He says that in the *Bata Abakash* of the poet philosopher Balarama Das (sixteenth century), Jagannatha is served by sixty-four Yoginis. The mode of worship of Jagannath incorporates the *panca tattva* of tantricism through substitutes. Fish is substituted by vegetables, meat by ginger, wine by coconut water, and maithuna by dance of devadasi offering Aparajita flowers.

8. P.C. Bagchi, *Kaulajnananirnaya*, 1934.

9. *Macchaghnapada: Kaulajnananirnaya*—Illus. 1, 2, 3, 4, 5, 6, 7, 8, 9, 10, 11 and 14. *Machendrapad*: ibid., Illus. 13, 15 and 17.

10. *macchaha pashah samakhyatahcapalahcittavrtyah,*
    cheditastu yada tena macchandasten Kkrtitah. I.17
    (The fickle-minded people are known as fish. Whoever penetrates it known as Macchanda, the killer of fish.)

11. H.P. Dwivedi, 1981: 53.

12. Dwivedi, 1981: 54.

13. Dwivedi has shown how this cult was popular among Muslims also. He has given a vivid explanation of *Sandhya Bhasha*, the language of the dusk. The Nath cult was prevalent from the Punjab to Garhwal. Its followers are still found in eastern UP and Bengal. Those Hindus who were not followers of Vedic religion, or were not accepted in orthodox Hinduism, accepted Islam and joined the Nath cult.

14. A boy dressed as a girl dances and the rest of the people sing *Jogi Ji Dhire*.

15. Kabir Panthi, Nath Cult and Joganis are associated in oral traditions, and in the texts of Nath Sects.

16. At Ujjain, there is a shrine of Macchinder Nath (Matsyendra Nath), which is worshipped by both Hindu and Muslim. Earlier it was in the possession of Muslims. There is a site of 64 Yoginis at Ujjain, though now there is a modern construction.

17. Sarasvathi, 1961 Ch.8 Vs. 172–178.

18. These thirty-two dancers are dancing in a strange circle, their foot steps are in a rhythm. Therefore there appears to be a 'danda rasa' in your courtyard. Rajashekhara, *Karpuramanjari*, ed. Sten Konow, tr. Charles Rockwell Lanman, 1963 Act IV.II.

19. Some women are making kinkling sound from the small bells. Some are singing in a rhythm and some are dancing in a circle like Yoginis with the tinkling sound of the anklets (Act IV.III). The *Karpuramanjari* mentions Bhairavanand, a tantric Yogi. The noteworthy aspect is that he calls himself involved in Kulamarga, and through this way he hopes to attain Moksha. It is not co-incidental that the text mentions the Valaya dance like the dance of Yoginis. The tantric Acarya, a convert in Kaula Marga, the dance like Yoginis and the image of Camunda, which has no place in the rituals of the fast, point to a prevalence of Yogini cult in a secret way.

20. The narrations of *Rajatarangini* runs like this. Minister Sandhimat was assassinated by king Jayendra, his bones were consigned in a cemetery by Guru Ishan. He wanted to bring him back to life. The story further runs that at midnight Ishan who has lost sleep owing to anxiety, suddenly smelt perfume of the divine incense. He heard an uncanny sound of the clang of many anklets and bells struck violently and a loud din of tambourines. On opening the window he saw

Yoginis on Yogini cakra standing inside a halo of light. Noticing their excitement and also that the skeleton had been removed Ishan ran towards the crematorium with a sword in his hand. He saw the skeleton hidden behind a tree and the Yoginis trying to bring him back to life after joining the limbs.

21. *Lalita Sahasranama*, Bhaskararaya's commentary, R. Anant Krishnan Sastry, 1951, Ch. 62, V. 50–52.

22. *Tantra Sara Sangraha*, Ch.VI, V. 2–3, ed. Durga Swami Aiyangar, 1992.

ILLUS. 1: Yogini in Dancing Pose
(Ranipur–Jharial)

ILLUS. 2: Yogini with Six Hands two Holding Weapons Rest in Dancing Position
(Ranipur–Jharial)

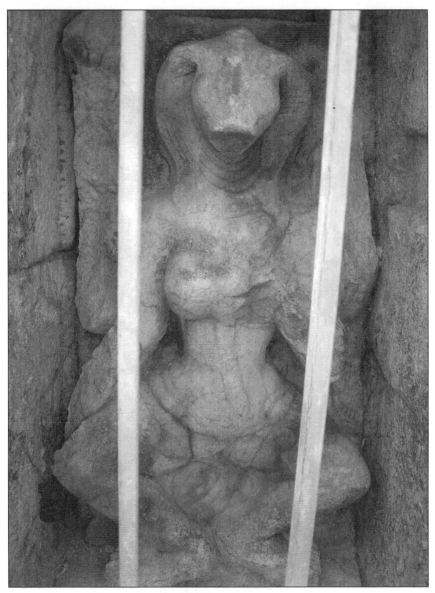

ILLUS. 3: Yogini in Dancing Position
(Ranipur–Jharial)

ILLUS. 4: Perplexed Position
(Ranipur–Jharial)

ILLUS. 5: Hand on Mouth
(Ranipur–Jharial)

ILLUS. 6: Decorating in the Mirror
(Ranipur–Jharial)

Illus. 7: Sri Varahi
(Bheraghat)

ILLUS. 8: Shashanana
(Lokhari)

Illus. 9: Sarpa Mukhi
(Lokhari)

ILLUS. 10: Hayanana
(Lokhari)

ILLUS. 11: Mrigashira
(Lokhari)

ILLUS. 12: Temple
(Hirapur)

Illus. 13: Temple Entrance
(Hirapur)

ILLUS. 14: Chandika
(Hirapur)

ILLUS. 15: Tara
(Hirapur)

ILLUS. 16: Dancing Yogini
(Ranipur–Jharial)

ILLUS. 17: Warrior position
(Ranipur–Jharial)

ILLUS. 18: Yogini with folded hands
(Ranipur–Jharial)

ILLUS. 19: Maheswari
(Hingalajgarh)

ILLUS. 20: Yogini in Dancing Posture
(Ranipur–Jharial)

ILLUS. 21: Yogini
(Mandasor)

ILLUS. 22: Hands on Knees
(Ranipur–Jharial)

ILLUS. 23: Hands on Knees
(Ranipur–Jharial)

ILLUS. 24: Adjusting the Dress
(Ranipur–Jharial)

ILLUS. 25: Hands Holding a Cup
(Ranipur–Jharial)

ILLUS. 26: Narmada
(Hirapur)

ILLUS. 27: Yamuna
(Hirapur)

ILLUS. 28: Mahananda
(Hirapur)

ILLUS. 29: Varuni
(Hirapur)

ILLUS. 30: Temple Outskirts (Ranipur–Jharial)

ILLUS. 31: Shiva in the Centre
(Ranipur–Jharial)

The Mask of
the Yogini

W ITH THEIR BEAUTIFUL limbs but weird faces the Yoginis challenge the reader-viewer to look beyond the obvious. Aesthetically they have been marginalized as bizarre. The commonly accepted understanding of their apparent fierceness is that they were carved under tantric influence. This notion of tantric influence, however, reflects an entrenched orthodoxy; it displays incomprehension and a lack of knowledge of such images. Part of this incomprehension stems from the web of mystery spunned around their appearance, with intricately wound threads of cultural lore, scenes, legends, and mysticism. Together these cast a ferocious mask, that needs to be unravelled. What are these images trying to convey, and where does the hand of the artist come into play? What is it that the artist conveys and addresses, and to what purpose, by carving the image of the Yogini, with deliberate and conscious inconsistency, which goes against the norms of aesthetics, i.e. by bringing together the irreconcilable, a fierce face on a beautiful body?

Are these animal-faced Yogini images (Illus. 32, 34, 35, 36, 37 and 38) reminiscent of certain set of tribal rituals or were these goddesses the human forms of certain animals? The Kashi Khanda of the *Skanda Purana* gives a list of the animal faced Yoginis, which tempts one to speculate whether the artist carving such images was following this list of animal faces: *shashanana* (rabit-faced), *hayagriva* (horse-necked) and *vaidali* (cat). The tribal element in the carving of the images cannot be denied, leading to the question, whether, such images are still part of the tribal religion. If such is the case, then this proposition would necessitate a revision of the theory that tribal and local deities were in the course of time elevated to, and accepted in orthodox Hinduism.[1] They remained as tutelary deities of a place. It would appear that despite elevation, in their artistic expression, the artists preferred to depict the folk origins of the Yoginis, which lingered on in the culture and memory of the artist. The faces of the Yoginis conveyed that they were malevolent. These images, however, did not have the sanction of the Agamas, so most of them are the product of the creative liberty of the artist. It seems, therefore, that it was not a particular text, but popular beliefs that captured the artist's mind.

The Kashi Khanda of the *Skanda Purana* narrates an interesting story regarding the tendency among Yoginis to assume different forms (VII.11–31). Shiva sent the Yoginis to the earth to lure king Divodasa, of Kashi. The Yoginis fancied Kashi so much that they refuted Shiva and started roaming here in the form of ganika, astrologer, owl, monkey and fox.

The world has always been mesmerized by their forms, at the threshold of divinity and folk tradition. The *Kaulajnananirnaya* narrates (XXIII.2–7) that on earth the sixty-four Yoginis exist in the form of turtle, dove, vulture, swan, hen, bitch, wolf, owl, hawk, bee, jackal, goat, cow, buffalo, and tigress. One should respect these creatures as Yoginis may reside in them. One may seek protection from the sixty-four Yoginis who wander about in various forms, disguised as animals.[2] And one should always pay respect to women as they are Shakti (XXIII.12).

Other than the animal face, however, the Yoginis also have fierce faces. The question asked earlier was whether this face was the 'real' Yogini, or a mask. The face does not take you to the interior, rather it is a barrier, that conceals the true Yogini. This fierce mask signifies a malevolent character. Indeed, the Yoginis have never been considered benevolent. It was their awful character that was celebrated in the texts.[3]

The Yoginis had magical charm also, through which they assumed different forms and could transform human beings into animals. The fierce face is thus also a metaphor conveying the ease with which the Yogini could transform herself. The tales of the Yogini preserved in the *Rajatarangini* narrate, for example, the episode (Chapter 1) in which minister Sandhimat who was murdered by King Jayendra was brought back to life by some Yoginis. Thus narrative points that the Yoginis were not ordinary female ascetics and possessed supernatural power. They were shamans and they knew witchcraft. There was, however, an amalgamation of fearfulness and sensuousness in their deeds.

The *Kathasaritasagara* also preserves similar fascinating narrative about the powers of the Yoginis.[4] Could this be the message the artist wanted to convey? Or is it a mask that becomes ordinarily acceptable through the passage of time? While the exterior signifies that the Yoginis have the power to destroy evil and anti-life forces, the attribution of extraordinary powers also serves the purpose of taking the Yoginis out of the realm of human existence. With such powers they transcend the human sphere to become the deities. Thus the mask of the Yogini serves the dual purpose of suggesting that she was in fact not what she appeared: she could be one or another, apparently human in form but with powers that went beyond human capacities. On the other hand, the mask was also metaphorical: it concealed the (human) identities and cultural contexts of the Yoginis, to give them a transcendental deification.

The latter is evident in a series of narratives which may be extracted from a variety of sources. These stories may not indicate that the Yoginis were shamans but point to rituals where they manifested extraordinary magical powers. For example, in medieval period the simple rituals were transformed and loaded with tantras.[5] The reference in *Karpoor Manjari* (ch.IV: v.IX) to women dancing is important, for it points also to the extraordinary form that dance took. They were making terrible sounds, groaning, shrieking, and crying. Significantly, they were also wearing masks of night-wandering ogresses.

It appears to be a popular narration of the time that the 'mask' conceals the true self. It was the mask that was the bridge of their journey from women of magical powers, witches, and shamans to divinities. It also shows that despite being maidens with beautiful limbs carrying babies they possesed powers of extraordinary nature. The *Kaulajnananirnaya* (ch. VI) too describes the magical powers possessed by Yoginis. Their appearance has to be contextualized. Here is the face of ritual par excellence. In Bheraghat all the sculptures are stamped with local names. Lokhari and Naresar delineate a tradition of their own. Whether it is group of Yoginis or the Yoginis including the group of matrikas, or the Yoginis as the ganas on the paintings, they all have different faces.

As stated earlier, Yoginis in disguise is a common lore in the *Skanda Purana*. There is, however, another side to it, which open up an interesting debate regarding their identification. Anand Krishna (paper presented at International Conference on South Asian Religious Art Studies at Lucknow, 1984, on 'Sasti') identifies the Yoginis of the Deccani miniatures with the Jogatis of the Bijapur region. M.L. Verma[6] logically argues in his paper that *Rauzutul Auliya Bijapur* written by Mohammad Ibrahim in about the eighteenth century mentions that in Bijapur women of the Muslim noble families had adopted sufism and were revered by Hindus and Muslims.

Nigam[7] describes the portraits, now in the Salarjung Museum and observes that Islam does not allow the female ascetic to move in the forests. He says that Shaivism appears to have gained an upper hand in south India during the early medieval period. A number of Shaivite sects such as the Pashupata, Kaula or Kalamukha, Vira Shaiva and Aradhya are known to have existed in the Deccan with Srisailam as the main centre. The Shaiva ascetics lived in solitary places and indulged in various occult practices. Nigam argues in this connection that the *Mathanavi, Saharul Bayan* written by Mir Hasan Dehalavi during the late eighteenth century presents an account of the Yoginis of that period: Princess Badr-e-Munir had a dream that her beloved was taken captive to an unknown place. She was so filled with sorrow that she thought of committing suicide. However, her friend Najmunnisa consoled her saying that she could go in the garb of a Yogini to seek her beloved. How she dresses her up as a Yogini is instructive: she wears a brocaded pyjama, *khesa* (upper garment) of saffron and a zari dupatta. She applies qashqa (sandal paste) on her forehead and goes out on her mission chanting Hara Hara. She is successful in her mission with the help of an angel (Lalit Kala, vol. 23, p. 36).

This narrative resonates in one of the stories of the *Kathasaritsagara*. The Puranas too narrate that Yoginis disguise themselves as ganikas, astrologer, etc. It seems that popular narrative of the Yoginis did not cease with the construction of temples and Sanskrit texts. It kept coming up in other narratives as well. The manifestation of the Yoginis in the sculpture does not, however, have corresponding verbal material. Descriptions in the *Agni Purana* do not match the sculptures, since they do not describe face, gesture, or posture. The Yoginis have diverse manifestations. They are not just awful, they are depicted variously, as *Sarvatomukhi* (Illus. 40), *Mahismardini* (Illus. 41), animal-faced (Illus. 42, 43 and 44) or beautiful girls (Illus. 45). Moreover, the exterior depiction of the Yoginis is diverse and varies from one place to another, so much so that they can be numbered in a group, but cannot all be grouped together.

Though the temples are of a similar form, the sculptures bear local features. Sculptures, like the lists, are found in different texts, but vary. The images from Hirapur, Ranipur-Jharial, Bheraghat, Naresar or Lokhari do not show homogeneity.

As part of the Shakta tradition Yoginis are expressions of the Goddess. As far as Shaivism is concerned, the Matta Mayura sect was prevalent in Bheraghat and Kaula Kapalika in Khajuraho. Despite the fact that different sects were prevalent in different regions, one cannot trace the shades of any sectarian influence on the sculptures.[8] Yet the other question is whether the Yogini imageries conceal a local tradition. The fact may not be denied that Yogini groups in all places have their own stamp and the mark of their native place. It appears that while carving, local popular beliefs and traditions were assiduously followed. There are two contradictory descriptions, however, which make the task of arriving conclusively at this assumption, more challenging. First the *Devi Bhagavat Purana*[9] describes the enclosure walls of the Mahavidya, where sixty-four chakra reside. All have 'luminous faces with long tongues, fire and their eyes red with anger'. They utter 'we will drink all the water and thus dry up oceans, we will annihilate the fire, we will flow the air, today we will devour the whole universe' and so on. On the other hand, in the *Talkayagapparani*,[10] a twelfth-century south Indian work by Ottakkattar, the Yoginis in the temple of Paramesvari are said to resemble the goddess Mohini, by constantly meditating upon the latter.

The mask can be explained through other events also. Aloka Parasher Sen (2001: 28) argues this point through an example of the Narasimha *avatara* of Vishnu and its enigmatic relationship with Chenchu Lakshmi in the context of the proliferation of his temples in Andhra Pradesh. This had a direct implication for the way rituals and performances evolved so that the 'other' found place in some important religious and artistic expressions. In my view, therefore, the mask was not only an artifact of concealing but one of revealing as well.

Thus, the face actually concealed the true identity of the Yogini as a goddess or as a beautiful girl, and equally successfully revealed the other side of the myth. This ignited the true self of the Yogini. It peeled away layers of the Puranas, tantra, folklore, diverse traditions, and also brought to the forefront the question of regional identity. Had there been no mask, the Yoginis would not have been inscrutable; there would have been no challenge to unmask them. They would have remained sixty-four aspects of the Great Goddess. Their forms and the question regarding their images would have remained unasked and unanswered.

NOTES

1. From Dehejia (1986) to Singh (1992), art historians have worked upon this theory. While I have also said so, it seems to me that the deities were not totally severed from their local roots.
2. The *Kaulajnananirnaya* (X.138–44) also describes other deities like snake-faced Dakini, owl-faced Rakini, horse-faced Kakini, cat-faced Shakini and bear-faced Hakini. The only exception was Lakini, who is not described as animal-faced, but holding a skull.
3. The *Padma Purana* and the *Linga Purana* narrate the tales of Blood Sucking Yoginis.
4. The stories of the *Kathasaritsagara* tell us that there was a Yogini Sukhasaya, who taught her friend Banhudatta, to transform her lover into a monkey. There was yet another Yogini Somada who put a magical thread around her lover's neck and metamorphosed him into an ox (Saraswath 1961, 1973: Book VII, ch.3 vs. 109–37 and 150–71).
5. B.D. Chattopadhyaya (1994: 223–32) shows the influence of tantra on Shaivism and Vaishnavism. Act IV of the play *Karpoormanjari* refers to the installation of an image of Chamunda, a Kaul Kapalika deity par excellence in a sanctuary by Bhairavananda, during Vata Savitri rituals. The sanctuary is constructed at the foot of a Vata tree. The king is invited by the queen to witness from her palace terrace, certain spectacles in connection with the ritual. What he sees is a series of dances, performed only by women, which are distinctly connected with the vrata ritual.
6. Lalit Kala, vol. 23.
7. Lalit Kala, vol. 23, p. 36.
8. The Yogini images of Bheraghat very strongly suggest some rituals. The images from Lokhari, Shahadol also correspond to it. The Hirapur Yoginis are identified with puranic deities. Despite, they establish the direct connection with any sect, one can only point that these premises were platforms for such rituals.
9. Barua, *Visva Kosa*, XII.11.1–30.
10. Donaldson Thomas, *Tantra and Sakta Art of Orissa,* 2002, p. 651.

ILLUS. 32: Sri Aingini
(Bheraghat)

ILLUS. 33: Periphery of the Temple
(Ranipur–Jharial)

ILLUS. 34: Ganesh
(Bheraghat)

ILLUS. 35: Sri Pimgala
(Bheraghat)

ILLUS. 36: Sri Tokari
(Bheraghat)

ILLUS. 37: Sri Ranjira
(Bheraghat)

ILLUS. 38: Indrani
(Hirapur)

ILLUS. 39: Vrishanana
(Lokhari)

ILLUS. 40: Sri Sarvatomukhi
(Bheraghat)

ILLUS. 41: Sri Teramva
(Bheraghat)

ILLUS. 42: Dancing Ganeshini
(Bheraghat)

ILLUS. 43: Ajanana
(Lokhari)

ILLUS. 44: Gomukhi
(Lokhari)

ILLUS. 45: Sri Badari
(Shahdol)

ILLUS. 46: Padmavati
(Hirapur)

CHAPTER THREE

Small Goddesses and the Great Goddess

There is no Great Goddess, When elevated all Goddesses are the Great Goddess.

THE HISTORY OF sixty-four Yoginis begins with the acceptance of minor goddesses within the fold of orthodox Hinduism. How and why were the local deity or the deities of the aborigines recognized by brahmins and identified with the great goddess? There are different factors, suggested by the scholars, regarding the assimilation and elevation of these deities. Vidya Dehejia (1986) identifies tantricism, while R.S. Sharma (2001) looks for economic factors.

The theory which argues that in order to gain their livelihood brahmins offered their services to various folk deities, is not acceptable to R.S. Sharma (2001: 236). The brahmins had indeed moved to the periphery or tribal belt of the Madhya Desh (central India) to places where the cult of the mother goddess was widely prevalent. Deities of the region were accepted in the Hindu society. During this period (c.900–1200) a number of tantra texts were written, which mention the local deities. Most of the Purāṇas written during the period give the list of the sixty-four Yoginis. Nepal, Assam, Bengal, Orissa, and Bihar became the strongholds of the Shaktas. The *Kularnava Tantra* which describes the sixty-four Yoginis may have been followed by a particular sect. The Kolas are 'outcastes' in eastern Uttar Pradesh and still follow the *Kularnava Tantra*.[1] The *Agni Purana* mentions the iconography of the sixty-four Yoginis and the construction of their temples. On the other hand, the *Narada Purana* mentions tantra in the worship of goddesses like Lakshmi, Saraswati, and Radha as Jagadamba, whereas the Agni Purana which follows the *Harivamsa Purana* is silent on Radha. One may tentatively suggest that since the *Narada Purana* refers to the higher tradition, it avoids the mention of Yoginis and refers to the higher goddesses. Indirectly, therefore, it supports that Yoginis had their origin in folk deities and they have a regional flavour. The different lists containing the names of the Yoginis are not unanimous. Even the label inscriptions of Bheraghat Yoginis differ. Some of the names are non-Sanskritic in origin. Despite Hinduization, they could not cast off their original attributes. The recognition and identification of these deities with the main goddess was an attempt to bring the religion of tribal people and lower-caste Hindus into the mainstream. Besides, there is a political context. The Yoginis were associated with the royal people. As kings constructed temples in their conquered territories, the Yoginis retained their local names. Presumably when kings wanted to please conquered people, they incorporated their deities in the main current.

This phenomenon of fusion is indeed intriguing. It reminds us of the debate in cultural anthropology about the Great and Little traditions. In India the dialogue was initiated by advocating the model of Sanskritization of the deities, developed by M.N. Srinivas in 1952. His 'Sanskritization' framework was narrowly defined. It was not cultural mobility that he traced, but emulation of the upper castes. For Srinivas, 'Sanskritization' is a process by which a low-ranking group changes its customs, ritual, ideology, and everyday life in the direction of a higher caste. Not only there was an upward mobility in the caste system, but also in the field of religion. When tribal deities were assimilated in the orthodox Hindu pantheon tribal men started functioning as priests.

A much talked of theory of the Chicago school of anthropologists, namely Robert Redfield and Milton Singer, suggests a two-tier formula, Great Tradition and Little Tradition, for the study of religious processes and influence. When Robert Redfield (1956) talks of the two traditions he says both are independent of each other, but it cannot be denied that they have long influenced each other. Thus Great and Little Traditions can be taken as two currents of thought and action, distinguishable, yet flowing in and out of each other.

Redfield emphasized the case of India and its ancient and complex processes of interaction. In 1972 Milton Singer revised Redfield's model. For him human culture was a composite human growth, gaining nourishment from borrowed cultural elements. Most cultures remodel these alien elements according to their own needs. When they become rudimentary and lose their original attributes, they give the borrowed culture a distinct form. Yet, Milton could not take Redfield's concept much further. His idea of civilization and culture as a dialogue between Great Tradition and Little Tradition was not markedly different from Redfield's.

Srinivas' model of Sanskritization falters because of an overemphasis on the Brahmanical model. Pocock (1955), for example, took recourse to the kshatriya or royal model. Singer went one step ahead and said that in the model of Sanskritization even merchants and peasants could be emulated. The historical process shows that in the trend towards Sanskritization, not only did the commoners modify their rituals and religious elements, their religious elements were incorporated in the orthodox tradition as well. Actually these models cannot answer the question of the historical process or the historical, social reasons behind it. In the ninth and tenth centuries the tantric religious elements were accepted in the main framework. According to Sharma (2001: 243) the brahmins migrated to the periphery from Madhya Desh, and came into close contact with the Sabaras. The inscriptions make a mention of Sabarasvami, indicating that the Sabaras were in authority in that region. An inscription mentions one Pulindabhadra as a donor of land.[2] The Purāṇas celebrate the great goddess residing in the wilderness and roaming over the mountains. One of the goddesses was known as Parnasabari.[3] This implies not only the problem of livelihood but also brahmin domination over tribal people in these regions. This was a phenomenon unique to Brahmanical religion. Here all models become conspicuously silent.

What Redfield and Singer term as Great Tradition and Little Tradition, Indian anthropologists (Dube 1991: 42) call 'classical' and 'local' traditions. The 'classical' tradition is constituted of not one element, value or religion, but many. In fact diverse philosophical values and ideals were incorporated in the Great Tradition, and some of their elements were then assimilated in the local or regional tradition. The latter, however, maintained their distinct forms. The Great Tradition reflects the normative forms, or ideal, and the Little Tradition, the way it is practiced in daily life.

Local traditions were regional traditions and the regional traditions were also associated with Shastriya traditions. Local traditions have always been stronger than classical traditions. The latter never tried to absorb local traditions. It was co-existence which saved Indian society from disintegration. McKim Marriott (1955) also talks about interchanging universal and regional concepts, native features becoming the part of the Great Tradition; regional traditions molded a number of elements of the Great Tradition.

Brahmanical religion is understood through symbols and not gestures. How can we explain these phenomena? Are the symbols lower or greater? Apart from symbols, the non-Sanskrit deities like female folk deities were accepted in the Sanskrit framework by denoting them a Sanskrit image. Even in the Sanskrit fold, they retained their original name and their rituals were not substituted.[4]

There is religion of the subjects (janapad) and of the kings (sastriya).[5] One cannot, however, categorize religion into two watertight compartments. There is religion of sreni and religion of the people, Shastric (classical) religion and Prakrit (common) religions. The religious way is different from the ritual and custom. Culture is not a matter of custom, it is a matter of knowledge.

In Brahmanical religion there has always been a debate on Sanskrit gods and native gods. The Sanskrit goddesses have spouses, whereas the tutelary goddesses are mothers. This was initiated by Kosambi (1962: 90), who stated that they are mothers, no father is required for them. Modern historians call such goddesses subaltern deities (Spivak 1999).[6] There is other side of the debate also. In the *Atharva Veda* the sage says, 'the earth is my mother and I am her son'. Male gods, were not worshipped as the Father but as saviours.

Indeed, it is the fusion of both trends, that is known as the popular religion. R.C. Hazra (1975: 243) has called such trends composite dharma. This, he suggests, can be found in the Purāṇas and their rites and customs. The ancient seers had before them the question of accommodation of diverse ideas, as also of resisting culturally the onslaught of dissenting sects. Orthodox Hinduism was essentially a spirited process in which attempts were made to accommodate the myths and symbols of commoners. Some native deities were accommodated by imprinting upon them the stamp of the Upanishads. They were so much moulded and modified that it is difficult to say that they did not have their origins in the Upanishads or the Vedas. It is to be noted that the Purāṇas were basically intended for the popular mind and were supposed to conserve as tradition compendia of all ancient beliefs.

This point may be emphasized by taking the case of sixty-four Yoginis. Originally these were folk deities, residing on the trees, and equated with witches. They are given to girlish giggling. In some villages they are more important than the main deities. They are the saviours of the children and protectors of the fields. After elevation, these Yoginis were recognized as the sixty-four forms of the Great Goddess, sixty-four embraces of Shiva to the Devi, or the Goddess herself. There has always been a synthesis between Brahmanical and folk deities. Most deities bear local names, though iconographically they correspond to the Great Goddess. In popular culture one comes across regional influences. At Kamrupa, Kamakhya is known by the name Nona or Naina Yogini.[7] This Nona Jogan in another part has become Nona Chamarin in magico rituals.[8] Here one is reminded of the analysis by Mandelbaum (1964: 10–11), in which he argues that Sanskrit gods are supposed to bestow the long term boons, while the local deities are worshipped for day-to-day gains, for removing disease and for individual benefit. He also admits that despite their pragmatic and transcendental natures, there is no antagonism between the two usages and little or no frictions between their respective practitioners.

The Yoginis in Maharashtra are worshipped for removing the evil eye from children, and the same Yoginis were worshipped by kings for their political benefits.[9] At Khajuraho the icon of Mahismardini bears the local name 'Hinglaju' and at Bheraghat, it bears the epithet 'Teramva' (Illus. 40—Chapter 2). In fact these Yoginis form such a tradition where the ideas and images have arisen, it is the autochthonous people, who have kept the ancient stories alive and passed them from one generation to the other. Yoginis in Himalayan folklore are equated with minor deities. In Jain texts they are listed along with the fifty-two Bhairavas. The highest tantric or philosophical aspect can be observed in the Yoginis of the Sri Cakra. The Sadhaka desirous of achieving self-realization has to pass by each set of Yoginis and to push forward the centre. Thus the difference between the local and classical tradition or Brahmanical and tribal deities is more publicized than real. Actually early village beliefs and practices had a great hold over the society. These are the under currents of the main flow of the period (Roy 2004).

Can we point towards a two-tier formula for this religious tradition, where one belongs to Sanskrit texts and other to the folklore. Aghenananda Bharti (1978: X–XI) criticizes this formula, stating that it does not explain in the behaviour, at best it gives a name to something which does not need a name for any serious student of the situation; and there is such an enormous overlap between elements in the one or the other tradition, that it ceases to be operational at any important step. More recently K. Chakrabarti (2001: 92) has argued that the concept of Sanskritization and Great and Little Traditions, qualified and refined, have come to be recognized over the years as analytical tools of considerable value. These concepts are however, not the same. Great and Little Traditions provide us a tool to understand the evolution of a culture, where two diverse and differing units work. The answer to the question how this tradition developed through historical processes, can be sought. But the theory of Sanskritization concentrates upon elevation in the caste hierarchy, not on two differing traditions.

Another question is whether symbols of Little Traditions are absorbed in the Great Tradition and whether they subsequently merge into one another. The other issue, so far ignored, is that these traditions neither complement nor supplement each other. The examples from Islam and Christianity quoted by Chakrabarti, show that the Great Tradition supplied substitutes for symbols of the Little Tradition. Did then, the Great Tradition develop at the cost of the Little Tradition? Did Sanskritization totally wash away (diminish) elements of the Little Tradition? Radha was elevated from Gopi to Goddess in the Purāṇic literature of the ninth-tenth centuries. But medieval Hindi literature celebrates the romantic attributes of Radha as a heroine. And so far as the sixty-four Yoginis are concerned, they were taken from the folk and tribal deities, the tantra elevated them; surprisingly the *Narada Purana* describes tantra, but not the sixty-four Yoginis. It refers to Radha as the highest deity. The *Agni Purana* on the other hand nowhere mentions Radha in the description of Krishna and the Gopis, but it refers to sixty-four Yoginis a number of times. Thus when a specific situation occurs this theory fails to answer any query. These theories are applicable, therefore, to a limited extent. They provide an understanding through the models of other cultures, but in a multicultural society like India suffer limitations.

In any society, there exists a religion of the ordinary/common people, and a religion of the elite. The models mentioned above can provide an understanding of how the religion of commoners, gradually became the religion of elites. But it does not explain the symbols and signs of religion. In the Brahmanical traditions, religion begins with symbols and ends in icons.

First there is an idea then there is a form. The image does not lead to the idea. There is a tension between the form and the formless. Where can we place the tantric phase of religion and tantric deities? Tantricism is a distinct way of worshipping the deity. It has a different rituals and symbols. Tantra is not different from the purāṇic religion, it only crosses the boundaries of purāṇic religion.

It is not that two traditions or currents have not been recognized in Indian tradition. In music and language a distinction is made between the classical and the folk, Margi and Desi. Classical art is higher in aesthetics and follows Shastric norms, whereas Desi is the common person's art. Folk art rarely provides aesthetic pleasure. Similarly the Sanskrit language belonged to the elites while Prakrit is the language of the people. Thus Robert Redfield and Milton Singer were not hitting any new chord. Their 'model' is heuristic, it does not actually divide culture into watertight modular forms. There has always been a bridge, which overcomes the hiatuses. In Indian tradition the classical and lower trends have different bases. Philosophers and thinkers look to the Upanishads for values in tradition. The common people preferred the Purāṇas and such other texts. There is a difference in the approach of a thinker and the anthropologist or historian. Where a thinker ignores local or regional trends, the historian is aware of their significance. The popular belief that the regional tradition developed under the umbrella of classical tradition may not be true. Actually there has always been an interaction and rivalry between the two, leading to the generation of several new values and models, which emerged from this interaction. This interaction and interrelation needs to be studied.

NOTES

1. This is R.S. Sharma's hypothesis proposed in *Early Medieval Indian Society*, 2001, p. 250 n. 49. Sharma himself had some reservations about it. *Kularnava Tantra* was written in *Sandhya Bhasha*. The names of low caste women as goddesses occurs in the *Kularnava Tantra*. It may have been the basis of Sharma's theory, but these names occur as Buddhist kulas in the *Kaulajnananirnaya* (P.C. Bagchi, 1934: 66).

2. He prevailed over a Bhauma Kara king in Orissa (ninth century) in donation for a Shaivite temple. Pandit Binayaka Misra (Hindol plate of Subhkora Reva), *JBORS*, vol II, 1930, pp. 81–2, text lines 18–24.

3. This is a form of the Buddhist Goddess Tara, who saves her devotees from epidemic. She is supposed to be incorporated in Buddhism from tribal deities. From Hirapur temple one of the Yogini image has been identified as Parnashabari.

4. In art, music, and language the two traditions have been recognized. An art is classical or folk, Margi or Desi. The Raga is classical or folk. The language is Sanskrit or Prakrit.

5. The tantra loaded religion of the royal household has been discussed by Chattopadhyaya (2005: 223–32). He very aptly shows that the rituals of the royalty deviated from the traditional ways.

6. Gayatri Spivak (1999: 181), 'Moving Devi', in *Devi: the Great Goddess*, ed. V. Dehejia. Spivak says that the Great Goddess, or Maha Devi as she is known in India, burst into the Hindu religious stage in the middle of the First Millennium of the Christian era. That is yesterday's talk. I am in the history of the (globalizing) period, I must let foolish commonsense interrupt power of the knowledge and declare: There is No Great Goddess, When Elevated each Goddess is Great Goddess.

7. In Mithila, Nona Jogin is depicted in the Kohbar (the honeymoon room) to band the evil eye on the newly weds.

8. In the pain of the eyes and in stomach aches, they are invoked as follows: Hail to Naina Chamarina (*Naina Chamarina ki Aan*), they are similarly invoked in wedding mantras.

9. Discussed in detail in Chapter 8.

PART II

CHAPTER FOUR

Yoginis in Tantric Tradition

THE SIXTY-FOUR YOGINIS in tantric tradition have been a favoured subject of previous research. The Yogini Kaula, which was started by Matsyendra Nath, is found in dialogue form and was transmitted to Parvati from Shiva. The scattered portions of it are believed to have been compiled by Matsyendra Nath.[1]

In this obscure cult, there are different levels of development—simple Yakshinis, mystic Yoginis. According to tantric texts, these are the Yoginis residing in different parts of the human body;[2] the Yoginis of Mula Cakra, the Yoginis of the subtle body, and Yoginis of different ksetras.[3] Initially the Yoginis were associated with the Yakshinis.[4] In the Kaula literature also at the initial stage the Yoginis are associated with kula trees. It is said that one should not walk under the kula trees as Yoginis live on them.[5]

The Kaula texts show the similarity between Yakshinis and Yoginis as they both symbolize productivity and they have an association with the trees. The *Kularnava Tantra* (ch. XI: V.66) describes the kula trees and says that Yoginis reside in them. The *Bhairava Padmavati Kalpa* (Shukla 1971: 334–5) narrates that a Padmavati Yakshini possesses magical power and her worship will bestow eight boons. It will not be out of the way to point out that in Hirapur (Illus. 46) (Orissa) and in Shahdol (MP) two Padmavati Yoginis have been recognized. This is the manifestation of the first level of development. The *Tantra Raj Tantra* (V. 49) mentions with specific names, sixty-three Yakshinis who grant all wishes. These Yakshinis are mentioned in the context of the worship of the Goddess. The Yoginis are Khecharis or Wanderers in the sky. This tradition is not different from tantric and early trends. The *Tantra Raj Tantra* (V. 58) describes that on the hilltop, where at night the palash flowers blossom, the Khecharis (Apsaras, Yoginis) happen to meet.[6]

In the second level of development Yoginis are regarded as deities of the directions. It is said that they come from all four directions. They are equated with Kshetrapalas and Vatukas here. In the course of their development in the *Kalika Purana* and *Kaulajnananirnaya* the Yoginis became attendants of the goddesses or the Goddess herself. Yoginis are assigned ksetras also. Sri *Matottara Tantra* (ch. 19) assigns eight sacred regions (ksetras) and subtle parts of human body with dakini presiding at the head. In the *Kularnava Tantra* they are equated with the Khetrapalas and Vatukas.[7]

YOGINIS AS DAKINI

These Yoginis form a set of eight deities: Dakini, Rakini, Lakini, Kathim, Sakini, Hakini, Yakini, and Kusuma. The Yoginis are described as belonging to the family of Lakini,[8] merging from Sakini's limbs, or from the womb of Yakini.[9] The *Tantra Raj Tantra* (V.59–71) mentions the Shaktis, Dakinis and others, but they are not placed in the same order as in Shatakarani Puja and Dhyani deities. They are described as beings, like Nitya. The *Mahanirvana Tantra* refers to Yoginis several times, but most of the time, it highlights their negative and furious aspects. They are depicted as inauspicious and equated with Dakinis.[10] The *Kularnava Tantra* mentions the worship of Yogini along with Dakini and Sakini. There is a *mantra*[11] of 50 letters that is recited during the worship.

YOGINI AND BHAIRAVA

The Shiva Kaula associated with Bhairavas had also been very popular in different parts of India. The narration of their birth follows the story of the birth of Yoginis. The *Vamana Purana*[12] thus narrates that there was a great war between Mahadeo and Andhakasura. Andhaka hit the head of Mahadeo and there was a flow of blood, and this blood produced the Bhairavas. Each group of Yoginis is associated with a Bhairava. The Yoginis are always a group and the Bhairava associated with each group is supposed to be playing with Yoginis.

THE YOGINI CAKRA

In *Sri Matottara Tantra* (ch. 20) the circular formation of the Yoginis is depicted as the unfolding of a lotus flower with a Yogini seated on each petal. Shiva and Shakti are seated at the outer edge of the petals. The Devi desires to create twelve Yoginis, who are intoxicated with their own youth and sway with the effect of wine. A later section of *Sri Matottara Tantra* (ch.20) provides explicit instructions on how to draw the yantra of the Yoginis.

YOGINIS AS PRESIDING DEITIES
OF SVARAS

In tantric tradition, there are other attributes and aspects of the Yoginis who are the presiding deities of Svara, Mantra and Akshara. In the *Vijnana*

Bhairava, they are mentioned as Svara mantra (Jaideva Singh 2003: 98, 172).

A, A, I, I, U, U, R, RI
Lri, Lri, Ai, O, Au, Am, Adam

These are the svaras, one utters in one breath. They are uttered at the meeting place of Mahayogi and Mahayogini along with Yoginis. The *Yogini Hridaya* (100: V.17) also states that by Shiva and Shakti's combination, Vira Virendra and Yoginis produce Mantra. The *Yogini Hridaya* (173: V.66) narrates that Yoginis and Dakinis preside over the letters.[13]

YOGINIS AND MATRIKAS

The association of Yoginis with Matrikas has been written by other scholars also, but this was usually perceived from the sculptural point of view. The tantra draws a clear-cut dividing line. Thus the *Kularnava Tantra* (8.32) clearly describes that Bhairava is depicted surrounded by Yoginis and is surrounded by the mandala of matrikas.

WORSHIP OF YOGINIS

It is usually agreed that the rituals and mode of worship of the Yoginis is not known. While rituals for individual or independent worship may not be known, however, Yoginis are worshipped as attendants, along with, the Kshetrapalas and Vatukas. This indicates the close association of Yoginis with them. Thus the *Phetakarni Tantra* (Dehejia 1986: 6) states that the Devi as Shamshan Kali is to be worshipped together with the circle of Yogini along with Mahakali. The *Kularnava Tantra* (ch. 7: V.30–6) delineates that Yoginis were being worshipped before the worship of Devi. Even in the Durga Puja Paddhati of Raghunandana three lines run like this:

On the sandhi on Astami and Navami (the juxtaposition of the eighth and ninth day),
Devi should be worshipped along with the Yoginis,
with the offer of different articles and the sacrifice of animals.[14]

Govindananda also informs that it was a local custom (desacara) among the Gaudiya (people of Bengal) to worship Devi along with Yoginis on Astami and Navami.[15]

The *Kularnava Tantra* also describes rituals for Yoginis. In these there is a provision for sacrifice. The vessel with which the ritual is performed is known as vira patra (vessel for the semi divine) and bali patra (vessel for sacrifice). In fact the verse 46 of chapter 6 is totally dedicated to the types of vessels for rituals.[16] Verse 53[17] describes a sequence for sacrifice: first it was Kalika, after her Vatuka, and then Yoginis to be given Bali (sacrifice). The *Kalika Purana*, mentions the worship of Kalika and Yoginis, but in the *Kularnava Tantra*, the occurrence of Vatukas, points to a later tantric or local development.

Yogini patrasanathena sayudham saparikasam
santapyar kalikamadyam vatukebhyo balim haret
(ch.6: V.57)

It is in the later tantric texts the Yoginis are associated with the Vatukas and Kshetrapalas.[18] Like the *Kularnava Tantra*, the *Mahanirvana Tantra* (ch. 6: V.46) also establishes that the Bali should be placed in Yogini vira patra. One can identify a sequence here: after Parameswari, Kali, Kalika, Vatuka, and Yoginis should be given *bali* (sacrifice). The *Mahanirvana Tantra* also says that Yoginis should be given *bali* on the right side of the mandala[19] and Kshetrapalas on the western part.[20]

It is interesting to note that the verse recited to please the kshetrapalas during the sacrifice is of sixty-four letters. In the seventh chapter of the *Kularnava Tantra*, where rituals for the Yoginis are prescribed, the Yoginis are clubbed with Vatukas, Kshetrapalas, and sometimes spirits. It says that the index finger, ring finger and middle finger should be used for offering sacrifice. After this the Goddess should be worshipped by Kulabapalas. The instances of *Kularnava Tantra* show that, Yoginis attendants of the Goddess in the early *Kalika Purana* and whose ritual, were very simple are now equal to deities like Vatukas and Kshetrapalas.

Not all the texts prescribe complex rituals. The *Yogini Hridaya* (V.98–9: 250) prescribes Pushpanjali (offering of flowers) for the Yoginis: these Yoginis are Prakata Yoginis, after this the flowers should be placed on Sri Cakra.

BLESSINGS OF THE YOGINIS

The Yoginis, if pleased, give a boon; annoyed, they ruin a person. The *Kularnava Tantra* (ch. 8: V.76) says that followers of the Kaula sects are favourites of Yoginis, and those who oppose them will be the target of the wrath of the Yoginis. It further says that only fools criticize the Kaulikas. The Yoginis worshipped by the Kaulas destroy such people.[21]

Sri Matottara Tantra declares that followers of Kaula path become dear to Yoginis. The *Kaulajnananirnaya* states that the blessings of the Yoginis fall on the followers, and their curse on the enemies of the Kaula Cakra. Thus most tantric texts highlight the malevolent nature of the Yoginis, prescribing that the Yoginis should be worshipped to ward off their wrath.

RITUALS

Despite these discussions it may not be clear what really happened within the circular walls of the temple. One thing appears to be clear is that Yogini Kaula propounded by Matsyendra Nath, may have been followed as a mystic cult in isolation and the temples of sixty-four Yoginis were built, for a purpose other than these rituals. Some Yogini images (Illus. 47, 48, 49 and 50) however, appear to manifest the rituals of this sect. The practice of Yogini Kaula may have granted a desired object. The *Kaulajnananirnaya* (ch. VIII: V.11–15) mentions fifty-five and sixty-four Yoginis. It further says (ch. VIII: V.32–44) that one should meditate on the circle of the Yoginis. The text describes that the Yoginis should be worshipped on eight cakras. Eight multiplied by eight cakras (sixty-four) belong to the Yoginis. The first cakra gives power. Worship and meditation of the second cakra gives the power of all attractions. Meditation and worship of the third cakra enables the worshipper to enter into others' bodies. With the worship of the fourth cakra, one crosses the boundaries of time and becomes another Kamadeva. The fifth great circle bestows speech like a rishi and movement like wind. The sixth great circle is the giver of Dharma, Artha, Kama and Moksha, whereas in the seventh great circle the meditater attains the power to enslave. When the worshipper enters the eighth great circle, he motivates *iccha* (desire) and *siddhi* (boon) and wins over the causes of death. It is also said that the Yoginis give *siddhis* (boons) only when the worshipper grasps these sixty-four rules. The *Yogini Tantra* (p. 127) mentions the steps of the practice as Mahayaga. Earlier I describe, rituals of Yoginis in tantric mode with, mansa and madira. Thus the *Goraksha Samhita* (ch. 20) describes that inebriated and in jovial mood, a Yogini had swollen eyes. The *Kularnava Tantra* (ch. 5: V.21–22) also mentions drink. The Yoginis were fond of blood and wine. The *Brihaddharma Purana* describes dancing Yoginis, drinking blood and wine. It appears that sacrifice being so important in the worship of the Yoginis, in the practice of Yogini rituals blood and flesh had become very important. Thus the *Tantra Maha Sadhna* (Gautam 1973: 369) says that in its practice blood and flesh are important.[22]

It appears that Yoginis are connected with the corpse ritual.[23] The *Varahi Tantra* (Sharma 1971: pt. III, 139) describes that Yoginis were associated with headless human body. *Sri Matottara Tantra* (Pande 1976: ch. 4) also mentions the Shava Sadhana (Illus. 48) which it states is performed in front of Bhairava, and Bhairava is surrounded by Matrikas. The corpse should be young, beautiful, and undamaged.

MAITHUNA

In Yogini Cakra worship, Maithuna is most important. The *Kularnava Tantra* (ch. 10: V. 84–89) describes Bhairava embracing the Yoginis. In Yogini Cakra worship, the eight women practice it on male Yogis or worshippers, and the ninth Yogini assists them to obtain the highest bliss or happiness. It is not certain where this exercise or ritual was performed, whether in the temple or some secret place.[24] This ritual was performed perhaps on Yogini Cakra or Mula Cakra.[25] As the worship of Yoginis is not for ultimate bliss but for more mundane achievements,[26] *Sri Matottara Tantra* (Pandey 1976: ch. 20) describes that by practising the Yogini Cakra, the worshipper can achieve eight types of *siddhis*—Anima, Mahima, Laghima, Garima, Prakamya, Isitva, Vasitva, and Kamavsayita.

YOGINI KAULA

Shaiva or Shakta?

This Kaula has been surrounded by myths of secrecy and mystery. It is generally taken that Matsyendra Nath initiated this Yogini Kaula. As discussed earlier, it is said in myths and legends that Matsyendra Nath was mesmerized in the company of women at Kadali Desh. He wrote the *Kaulajnananirnaya* and started Yogini Kaula, most probably in Kamrupa (present-day Assam), where he came into the company of women and where each woman was a Yogini. The *Kaulajnananirnaya* (ch. 20: V.10) says that the text was available in every household of the Yoginis in Kamrupa, and Mastyendra Nath most likely only compiled it.[27]

The *Kaulajnananirnaya* narrates simultaneously the old and the new cults of Matsyendra Nath. The texts of the *Akuraviratantra* given therein agree on the main points with the texts of Nathas as contained in the *Goraksha Samhita*[28] and may, therefore be said to represent the new secret knowledge attained by him amongst the Yoginis of Kamrupa. Karambelkar (1955: 362–74) says that the new Yogini Kaula marg of Matsyendra Nath was different from his old Akula Marg. The new cult was a Shakta cult as opposed to the old yogic Shaivism. It aimed at propitiating the Shaktis through the medium of Yoga as well as by external worship. *Sri Matottara Tantra* (ch. 27) says that eighty-one Yogini temples were built for the kings. V.V. Mirashi (1950: 10–11) associates the Bheraghat Yogini temple with Matta Mayura sect.[29]

Whatever Mirashi said indeed goes out against Karambelkar's theory. There are other scholars who think that the Golaki Mutt and Matta Mayur sect, both had alliance with Yogini temples (Brighenti 2003: 654). In this line there flourished the great Shaiva teacher Prabhashiva, who established the tradition of Golaki Matha, a branch of which was situated at Bheraghat and Ranipur-Jharial. Since both Bheraghat and Ranipur-Jharial have Yogini temples, it has been suggested that this form of Matta Mayura Shaivism incorporated some ideologies of the Kaula School and was responsible for the construction of the temples. The Yogini cult has been taken as an integral part of the Bhairava cult, which is a form of Shaivism, the circle of the Yoginis evolves from the Shaiva Siddhant School (Panda 1974). There is an opinion that they are the counter forms of the sixty-four Bhairavas. Just like the Bhairavas, the terrifying aspect of Shiva multiplied into sixty-four Chamundas, the ferocious aspect of Shakti also multiplied into sixty-four Yoginis (Pradhan 1983). It is also said that the Yogini cult is part and parcel of the Bhairava cult, which is a form of tantric Shaivism, and the circle of sixty-four Yoginis is evolved from the Shaiva Siddhant school (Panda 1974: 90–1).

Thus, though the Yogini cult may have eventually become associated with, or integrated into, the Kaulacara tantric and Shaiva sects, it is also affiliated with other mystic tantric sects. It is curious, however, that royal patronage appeared to have ceased along with the influence and acceptance of Kaulacaras throughout northern India. In Orissa, Yogini temples appeared in the middle of the tenth century and coincided with the advent of the Kaulacaras and the widespread acceptance of erotic rituals associated with Kapalikas. By the eleventh century the Kaulacaras appear to have supplanted the Kapalikas in popularity.

In fact the entire *Kaulajnananirnaya* was transmitted to Devi through Shiva. Various Kaula works single out Bhairava as the leader of the Yoginis and he is frequently visualized at the centre of circle of Yoginis while other texts such as the *Sri Vidyapithamat Sara* the *Guhyasiddhikarma* and the *Varahi Tantra* mention Shiva's presence in the midst of the Yoginis.

Though usually the scholars[30] have taken Yogini Kaula as a Shakta cult, this view is not universally accepted. A school of scholars has raised a different view.[31] In a tradition preserved in the *Brahma Yamala*, Shiva communicated the knowledge of Tantric Sadhana to one Sri Tatra who then composed 12, 500 verses in the *anustubh chanda*, which he explained among his disciples. The first person who put right tantric lore was called Bhairava who dispersed his knowledge to other Bhairavas. The last Bhairava gave it to a brahmin named Devadatta, who belonged to the Odra country (Rajaguru 1971: XXIX).

Whether in the tantric texts, popular texts, or Puranas, the Yoginis are always associated with Shiva. Even in the Yogini temples it is either Bhairava or Shiva who is in the centre of the temple. The *Kularnava Tantra* signifies the relation between Shiva and Yoginis. It (V.8: 31) delineates the fact that sixty-four Yoginis are always involved in Shiva.

Yajanti devyo harapadapankjama
Prasanndhamamrtamoksadayakam
Arantasiddhantabhayaprabodhakam namami
Castastakayoginiganam.

The *Yogini Hridaya* (100: V.17) states that by Shiva and Shakti coupling, Vira Virendra and Yoginis produce mantra. The oft-repeated narration of Kashi Khand of the *Skanda Purana* is well known, where Shiva sends Yoginis to Varanasi. Now I come to the problem of Yogini Kaula. Though the time of its emergence is still debatable but it is well established that by ninth century, Matsyendra Nath had set the Yogini Kaula perhaps at Kamrupa.[32]

It seems it has become a legend to associate the tantric texts with the women of Kamrupa or Assam. Thus how far is it correct to presume that when *Kaulajnananirnaya* was compiled it was added or it was an interpolation. The *Kularnava Tantra* also preserves a similar couplet. It says that this knowledge was concealed in the heart of the Yoginis and was revealed to the world by Shiva.[33]

Now the question is what is Kula?

In the introduction to *Kaulajnananirnaya* (Bagchi 1934), kula is defined as a state in which the mind and the sight are united the sense organs lose their individuality. One's own Shakti becomes identical with jiva and the sight merges into the object to be seen. These facts nowhere point out that Yogini Kaula propounded by Matsyendra Nath was a Shakta cult. The *Rudrayamala* mentions 64 Bhairava (Gupta 1972: 76). The *Tantraloka* (VIII:17) the tenth century text written by Abhinavagupta also mentions sixty-four Bhairavas.[34]

In fact *Kaulajnananirnaya* is a dialogue between Devi and Bhairava and P.C. Bagchi (1934: 69) admits that when this account was written Matsyendra Nath was already believed to be the incarnation of Shiva. Abhinavagupta in his *Tantraloka* describes him as Macchand Vibhu and thus gives him a place equal to that of Shiva. So it is only through legends and folklores that it is established that for some time he deviated from his original path and propounded a new Shakta cult.

I have already shown that famous couplet of the *Kaulajnananirnaya* is also found in the *Kularnava Tantra*. Hence it was a common belief that women of Kamrupa were Yoginis and had expertise in Tantra. Bagchi (1934: 69) admits that Yogini Kaula is quite similar to Buddhist tantricism. The Yogini, Dakini, and Vajrayogini point to a stage of amalgamation.

There is a very interesting point perhaps overlooked by Bagchi. Bagchi says that in Buddhist Tantra generally the five Kulas are mentioned and they are Nati, Rajaki, Dombi, Candali, and Brahmani (Bagchi 1934: 66). These are the five women that the *Kularnava Tantra* mentions who should be worshipped as the substitutes of the Goddess. Bagchi (1934: 68) says that 'last of all, in the use of mystic phraseology, the *Kaulajnana* seems to have in certain cases greater affinity with the Buddhist texts than with the Brahmanical Tantras.

Of the mystic power enumerated before, at least two, santika and paustika, which have been interpreted as 'the power to bring peace to the mind and the power to increase the capacity of mind are not met within the Brahmanical texts'. He (1934: 69), however becomes defensive and says that

these points of similarity between Yogini Kaula of Matsyendra Nath and later Buddhist mysticism, raise the deeper problem of common basis on which both later Brahmanical and Buddhist mysticism are founded. But that is a subject that cannot be treated in the present state of our knowledge.

The *Kularnava Tantra* mentions, Nati, Rajaki, Dombi, Candali as the substitutes of Shakti, or to be worshipped before Shakti. In the Buddhist tantra they are called the five kulas. It seems that at some stage these tantric texts and rituals got mixed up and it became difficult to draw a demarcating line among the different sects. It is true that in tantra, a dividing line cannot be drawn between later Buddhist and Hindu tantricism, making it difficult to talk about Shaiva and Shakta cult.

Thus there are Yoginis, on a very primitive level, they are Yakshini. Yoginis are 'Ksetra Rakshikas' also. There are Yoginis presiding over different organs of the body. Yoginis are associated with different regions too. There is Yogini Cakra and Mula Cakra. The most important aspect of Yoginis, is perhaps the different rituals associated with them. Charles Fabri once said that what happened within those walls is difficult to know. Although this chapter appears to focus on the esoteric, a historical approach makes the study challenging and interesting. The chapter has thrown light on the relation between Yogini and Dakini. In Buddhist tantric practices Dakinis are the counterform of the Yoginis. The worship of the Yoginis was thought to be for the mundane gains on the basis of *Sri Mattotara Tantra* and *Kularnava Tantra*. But the *Kaulajnananirnaya* shows that Yoginis were also worshipped for Moksha.[35]

NOTES

1. The emergence of Kula (Devi) with Akula (Shiva) is Kaula. Akula is activated by joining Kula. The highest stage of a Shakta worshipper is known as Kaula. Matsyendra Nath was founder of this school. According to legends and *Kaulajnananirnaya* (XVI) Matsyendra Nath was the first to reveal the kulagama. It seems that by the time *Kaulajnananirnaya* was compiled it had a long history. The *Kaulajnananirnaya* mentions other Kaula schools: Vrasanotta, Vanni, Kaulasadbhav, Padorrishta, Mahakaula, Siddha, Jnananirniti, Siddhamrita, Sristi, Chandra, Shaktibheda, Urmi and Jnana Kaula.

   Interestingly, *Kularnava Tantra* is also a dialogue between Shiva and the Devi In *Saundarya Lahiri* (V.31) Shiva says that he has created this tantra independent of all sixty-four tantras, especially for Bhagavati (Goddess). The other tantras bestow the boon as per their names, but this tantra is the giver of all the Purusarthas.

2. *Sri Matottara Tantra*, Janardana Pandey, ed. *Goraksasamhita*, 1977: ch. 20 identifies the different parts of human body and the corresponding Yoginis; Dakini—head, Eyebrow—Rakini, Nose—Lakini, Secret part—Hakini, Vagina— Yakini, leg—Kusuma.

3. Though Dehejia (1986) includes Yogini of 'Sri Cakra' in her list, usually 'Sri Cakra' Yogini is not included among the sixty-four Yoginis.

4. A.K. Coomarswamy (1928–29: 9) was first to propose the theory.

5. V. Taranatha and Arthur Avalon, *Kularnava Tantra*, Ch. XI, Verse 66, 1915.

6. In Almora there is a temple of Jakhini Devi, which is obviously the temple of Yakshini Devi. The temple manifests the level where the Goddesses were worshipped as Yakshini.

7. In the folk songs, when they are not associated with the tantra they stand with Ksetrapals.

8. *Lakini kula sambhuta*
Shakinyanga samudbhuta
Yakini garbha sambhuta.

9. The *Kathasaritsagara* equates Yoginis with Dakinis. It (XII.IXXV.1639) narrates that queen Kuvalayavati was disguised as a Dakini (III.XX24a). It further describes that a band of Yoginis collected from different parts at the cemetery and they offered the corpse of the son of king Karnotpala to the Bhairava. The *Tantra Sara* narrates that any woman who takes this mantra not only becomes Dakini with other Dakinis, but loosing her husband and son, she becomes a perfect Yogini.

10. *Alakshmih, Kalakarni Ca Dakinyo Yogini Ganah*
Vinashyantvabhishiken Kalibijatadita
Mahanirvana Tantra 10th Ch. V. 177, p. 313
(Kalakarni, Dakini and the group of Yoginis are inauspicious, they will destroy if invoked by Kalabija)

11. The Mantra runs like this:
Om! Om! Om! Sarvayoginibhyah, dakinibhyah, shakinibhyah, trailokya vasinibhyah, imam pujam, balim grihya grihya svaha!
Kularnava Tantra Chs.10–12
(Hail! Hail! Hail! By all Yoginis, Dakinis and Shakinis accept this worship.)

12. N.N. Basu, ed., *Visva Kosa*, no. 13, p. 548.

13. *Vidyantarbutashaktyadyaih Shaktaih Sadabhistathaksaraih*
Yoginitvam ca Vudyaya rashitvam cantyavarjite
(Yoginis reside on the six letters)

14. In Hazra's 'Sakta Upapuranas' there has been a discussion regarding the date of the Kalika Purana, Hazra says that these lines belong to earlier Kalika Purana, which is not available.

15. *Gaudiya tu Astami-Navami Samdhau-Camundarupam dvyatva upacair abhyarcya bali-danam Kurvantiti desacarah*, Varsa Kaumudi, pp. 241–3; Hazra on the basis of non-tantric elements (*Dusprapya Kalika Puranantare*) fixes its date around seventh century AD.

16. *Yogini Virapatra Ca Bali Patra tah Param, Padyacamanayoh Patam Srt Navakramat.*
    Parena Samanyaghyrasya Vidhina Patranga Sthapanncareta. Chap. 6: V. 46.
17. Ibid.
18. In the folklores and Shabarmantras also, they are associated with Ksetrapalas. It is discussed in detail in Chapter 5.
19. Ibid.
    Yogini Virapatre ca Balipatre tataha param
    Padyacamanyeh Patram Sri Patrena Navakramat
    Samanyadharyasya Vidhina Patrana Sthapanancaret
    Chap. 6: Verse 46.
    (A Yogini should be presented with Veerapatra and Bali Patra)
    Yogini Patrasansthen Sayudham Saparikam
    Santarpya Kalikamadyam Vatukebhyo Balimharet
    (*Mahaniravana Tantra*, Chap. 6: Verse 53)
    (First Kalika, then Vatuka, then Yoginis should be offered bali in Yogini Patra)
20. Though some parts of *Mahanirvana Tantra* have been considered to be interpolation, they are thought to have been added later by Raja Rammohun Roy.
21. *Kaulikan Bhairavaseshan Yo Va Nindati Moodhdhibi Tam Nashyantayasandeham Yoginyan Kala Nayike.* Chap. 8: V.76.
22. Some of the Yogini images appear to be the manifestation of such practices.
23. The *Raja Tarangini* mentions it and the folk songs of Kumayun also mentions it. This has been discussed in Chapter 5.
24. It is said that as these temples are found only from the tribal belts of UP, MP and Orissa, where they must have been built to please the local people and to assimilate the local deities and not exclusively for esoteric practices. See the chapter on Tribal Deities.
25. In Assam, at some places Yogini Cakra is still worshipped.
26. Spiritual liberation (moksa) is often spoken of in the *Kaulajnana*, but it is exclusively treated in chaps. XIII and XVII.
27. The identification of Kadali Desh has been discussed in detail in Chapter 5.
28. Hazari Prasad Dwivedi has discussed it in detail, see Nath Sampradaya, *Hazari Prasad Dwivedi Granthavali*, vol. V, 2007.
29. A branch of the Mattamayura clan was founded at Bheraghat about 10 miles from Tripuri, the capital of the Kalacuris. A hypethral temple was erected on a hillock on the bank of the Narmada, where sixty-four Yoginis with Ganapati were installed. Most of the Yoginis are of the time of Yuvarajadeva I, but some are of a much earlier, perhaps Kushana Age. The place seems to have been considered holy from very early times. The hypethral temple became known as Golaki or the Round Temple from its shape. The matha or monastery established by its side became the well known Golaki matha. The Malkapuram pillar inscription says that the Golaki matha was situated in the Dahala mandala between the Bhagirathi and the Narmada. Dahala was the name of the home province of the Kalacuris with Tripuri, modern Tewar 6 miles from Jubbulpur, as its capital. Golaki matha was thus plainly identical with the matha at Bhera Ghat. This matha sent its acaryas to distant places for the propagation of its faith.

Visvesvarasambhu who had risen to the position of the chief teacher of this matha made an agrahara called Visvesvara Golaki in the Andhra country as stated in the Malkapuram pillar inscription. The inscription gives the following spiritual genealogy of Visvesvarasambhu.

Durvasas
|
Sadbhavasambhu
(contem. of Yuvarajadeva I)
|
Somasambhu
|
Vamasambhu
|
Saktisambhu
|
Kirtisambhu
|
Vimalasiva
|
Dharmasambhu
|
Visvesvarasambhu
(Contemporary of the Kakatiya King Ganapati, 1213–49)

It will be noticed that the three acaryas from Saktisambhu to Vimalasiva are identical with those mentioned in the Jubbulpur inscription as Rajagurus of the Kalacuri kings Gayakarna, Narasimha and Jayasimha. Vimalasiva hailed from the Kerala country, while his disciple's disciple Visvesvarasambhu was a resident of Purvagrama in Daksina Radha in Gauda. This shows plainly that the Golaki matha attracted learned and pious men from distant places. Visvesvarasambhu who had attained the position of the head of the Golaki matha later moved to the Andhra country where he received great honours at the Kakatiya court. He initiated the Kakatiya king Ganapati in the Shaiva faith and received magnificent gifts of lands and villages from him as well as from his daughter Rudramba. Branches of the Golaki maths were established in several other places in Cudappa, Kurnool, Guntur and north Arcot Districts of the Madras Presidency.

30. Karambelkar, V.W., 1955, 362–374; Dehejia, Vidya, 1986.

31. Other scholars on the other hand (Donaldson 2001: 624) associate the Yogini cult with various Shaiva Sects such as Mattamayura sect (Mirashi 1950: 12) and the Amardaka sect of Shaiva Siddhanta with emphasis on the worship of Uma along with Shiva and in the case of the Amardaka sect, the worship of Bhairava, one of the names of Kala Bhairava being Amardaka.

32. It is said on page 8 of *Kaulajnananirnaya, Kamarupa Idam Shastram Yogininam Grihe Grihe*

33. *Kularnavamidam satram Yogininam hridi sthitam*
   Prakashitam Maya Cadya Gopaniyam Prayatnatah. 17.102

34. *Dashashtadashdha Srotah*
    Pancakam Yattatoapyalabdham
    Utkristam Bhairavamikhyam
    Catuhsasti Vibhedikam
                Tantrasara VIII.17

35. The introduction (Bagchi 1934: 73) discusses that the worship of the Yoginis is for the liberation also. The state of Mukti, i.e. spiritual liberation is defined here. It is exclusively treated in chapters XIII (v.1–5) and XVII. In the introductory chapter, Bagchi (1934: 55) says that it is said that by uttering '*hamsa hamsa*' one attains liberation. It is generally believed that the uppermost station (sahasradalapadma) is the seat of the Hamsa. Unless the Shakti reaches that station and gets united with the Hamsa, complete Samadhi cannot be attained.

ILLUS. 47: Kauveri
(Naresar)

ILLUS. 48: Nivan
(Naresar)

ILLUS. 49: Sri Kamada
(Bheraghat)

ILLUS. 50: Sri Nandini
(Bheraghat)

ILLUS. 51: Samudri
(Hirapur)

CHAPTER FIVE

Yoginis in Folklores

A FASCINATING AND intriguing aspect of the Yogini cult is that it is still alive in rural folklores. Yoginis are invoked in the shabar mantras[1] and marana mantras, both are construed as lowly rituals. While in the *Kaulajnananirnaya*, Matsyendra Nath started the Yogini Kaula cult,[2] the Puranas, which contain the list of the Yogini names and instructions about the carving of the Yogini images, are conspicuously silent about Matsyendra Nath.[3] We have seen in the earlier chapters that like the Yogini cult, Matsyendra Nath is also surrounded by quite a few legends. Matsyendra Nath and his disciple Goraksha Nath figure in different folklores and shabar mantras, along with the Yoginis. Matsyendra Nath probably lived around AD 900. It is notable that the Yogini cult first appeared with the advent of Matsyendra Nath, and gradually diffused in the folk traditions of different regions. A most puzzling question has emerged from the earlier discussions, are the Yoginis women of magical powers, semi divine deities, or malevolent nymphs? The study becomes more interesting and perhaps more challenging too, when one finds that Yoginis are a part of living and diverse traditions. Different classes of Yoginis emerge in these traditions. Often they are the Sanskritized Goddesses, but much of the legend around them, has churned out a mythical chain of Yoginis, some with magical powers, some mundane, others malevolent. Legend and folklore testify that the Yoginis are not part of a cloistered ritual, but influence people and their lives. We see that the secrets surrounding them were actually revealed in people's expressions.

Despite all the brilliant classifications[4] usually it becomes very difficult to draw a dividing line between Yoginis of Yogini Kaula and Yoginis of flesh and blood. The legends of Matsyendra or Goraksha Nath are associated with the Yoginis most of the time.

At Kamakhya, in Assam, the sixty-four Yoginis are invoked before worshipping the main deity. According to popular belief, all the women at Kamrupa were supposed to be Yoginis possessing magical powers.[5] The Yoginis were supposed to possess charms with the help of which they allured Matsyendra Nath. The legends narrate that the Yoginis of Kadali Desh (The land of Banana Trees) had tried to seduce his disciple Goraksha Nath. Sheikh

Faizullah (Dwivedi 1967, vol VI: 38) a Bengali poet, has written a book *Goraksha Vijaya*.[6] The editor of the book Abdul Karim claims that the book must be about five or six hundred years old. In it a Yogini says to Goraksha Nath, 'You are an ascetic; I am a young female ascetic so let us get close.'

The physical beauty and sensuous charm of the Yoginis for Matsyendra Nath is celebrated in other texts also. The *Yogini Sampradayaniskriti*[7] also narrates an interesting tale where, in Triya Desh, Matsyendra Nath entered the dead body of the king of the Simhala Desh. Goraksha Nath wanted to bring his guru back from there. So he went there in the disguise of a drummer and he played the tune:

Wake up, Goraksha Nath is here. . . .

Now the question is, where was Kadali Pradesh situated. Some scholars identified it with Assam, where every woman was a Yogini. Others say it is Kumaon and Garhwal, known as 'Stri Desh'. It has also been identified with Kuloot Pradesh. In all these three regions, the tales about Yoginis were prevalent. The mantras can be found from eastern UP to Garhwal. The Nath cult must have been prevalent in Garhwal. Ajai Pal[8] is supposed to belong to Garhwal. The Shabar Mantras, incidentally, are written in corrupt Sanskrit. They are the texts of lower-caste Hindus. They may have originated in Prayag, as one of the mantras says:

Ganga, Jamuna, Sarawati—Gai charane Jai
(On the bank of the rivers Ganga, Jamuna and Saraswati the cows are grazing.)

In Uttar Pradesh, in some Shabar Mantras, it is Gorakh Nath, who was attracted to the women and his disciple recited the Shabar Mantra for him to release him:

Nari dekh Guru Gorakh aage chalyo peeche chela bachavan jaye. Guru mantar chela padhyo. . . . Guru mantar aiso bali, sab maya mit jaya
(Teacher Gorakh Nath was walking ahead after seeing a woman, the disciple was following to save him. The teacher recited a hymn, all illusions vanished.)

In one of the Shabar Mantras, they are hailed as Nava Nath:

Maya rupi Macchendra Nath, chand rupa Chaurangi Nath . . . vayu rupa Guru Gorakh Nath[9]
(Macchendra Nath was like illusion, Chaurangi was like moon and Goraksha Nath was like wind.)

Gai Gorakh Nath ki bhains Macchendra ki charne Ajai Pal ki gadar Mahadeo ki
(The cow is of Goraksha Nath, Buffalo is of Matsyendra Nath and goat is of Ajai Pal.[10] This mantra is recited in some of weddings in eastern Uttar Pradesh, and for the removal of diseases in Garhwal.)

Why was it recited for totally different rituals in two distant places? This may be explained as follows:

While earlier, the cult was part of tantric practices, it never found a place in the Puranas or in puranic rites and customs. With the disintegration of tantra it became part of occult practices, whenever there are followers of the cult, these mantras are practised in different rituals.

In the very secret Kaithi script of Bihar, the sixty-four Yoginis are remembered in a ritual known as *katora chalana*, i.e. to catch the thief.

jambh chale, jameshwar chale, swargaho raja iner chale, patal hi raja hi suko chale. chaunsath sau Jogin chale . . . katora kamsha ka katora.[11]

The Yama moves, Yamesvara moves, the king of heaven Indra moves, Shukra moves and sixty-four hundred Yoginis moves along with the katora (bowl).

They are even popular in Gujarat. Here the sixty-four Yoginis are yelling along with fifty-two Viras:

om namo humkali! chaunsath yogani hunkali.
bavan vira dasha ganthi loha ki Jharai.[12]

In Garhwal, Matsyendra Nath, Goraksha Nath, Yoginis and Devis are remembered as protectors of the directions. In the Kaula texts too Yoginis are the protectors of the directions. The *Kaula Kalpa Taru* (Shukla 1967) mentions sixteen Yoginis in the four directions, each cluster of sixteen Yoginis known as the protectors of a direction. Yoginis have been associated with Shakini and Kalaratri. The Yoginis belong to the tradition of Dakini, Shakini and Lakini. Here one is reminded of the Prabodh Chandrodaya (4.1) where Kalaratri is hailed. Most intriguing is that these Nath Gurus are described as the protectors of different directions, Goraksha Nath of the east, Chaurangi Nath of the south, and Matsyendra Nath of the west. The Nath Gurus bear a similarity with this aspect of the Yoginis described, in the tantric texts.

Devi Sakini Kali Ratri ji yame ghate ghate hana ghate pe avaha purve Gorakha Nath siddha dakshini Chaurangi Nath siddha panchi mein Mahendra Nath sidh-utar kaulo ksetrapal. . . .[13]

(Devi Shakini Kalaratri, Goraksha Nath in the east Chaurangi Nath in the south, Mahendra Nath in the west and kshetrapal in the north.)

It is believed that these Shabar Mantras were composed by Goraksha Nath himself. As the Nath cult spread upto Garhwal, the sixty-four Yoginis are mentioned there. In Garhwal folklore, the sixty-four Yoginis are mentioned in 'Marana Mantra' (hymns for death) and are invoked to remove disease.

Om namo adesham guru ko Juhar vidya ko namaskar svaguru ko okha
Gorakhnath ki tum cheli Vhayan, Sri Krisna ki tum Radhika chayan . . . chaunsatha sai
Jogan Chayan. . . .

(Hail! Wake up Master, Hail Vidya (learning); You are a female disciple of Gorakha
Nath; You are Radhika of Sri Krishna and you are sixty-four hundred Yoginis.)

Jaga vainidavadi, kanadi angadi tum jaga nau nath caurasi siddha ka dhyan jaga,
chaunsath joganiyo ka, dhyan jaga, jaga Mahadeva Parvati ka dhyan.[14]

(Wake Up. Vainivadi, Kanadi, Angadi. Invoke Nava Nathas! Eighty four siddhas!
Invoke sixty-four Yoginis. Invoke Mahadeva and Parvati.)

These hymns of occult practices indicate that the Yoginis have their alliance
with shamans. Sometimes it becomes difficult to draw a dividing line between
history and oral tradition. The historian indeed feels uneasy to bring out
history from these rituals, which have gone beyond tantric texts and the
Puranas.

One wonders whether these are the deities of the Puranas and the temples.
They are very easily accommodated with the rituals of witchcrafts. It appears
that the term sixty-four Yogini was for the sake of convenience. The Yoginis
of the Puranas and of the tribal belt and these sixty-four Yoginis of witchcraft
had a common name. They belong to the stream of the *Kularnava Tantra*,
where the goddesses had the stigma of low-caste women.

In the Hindu caste system the Nath Yogis have been considered as of the
low strata. The Nath Yogins seem to have had a close relation with Muslims.
Their centre of activity being Punjab, Rajasthan, and Afghanistan, which were
Muslim dominated. Very few Muslims had accepted the Nath cult, however,
and the social status of the Nath Yogis remained ambiguous.[15]

In Kumaon valley the sixty-four Yoginis are invoked along with local
deities. All these folk deities are the spirits or part of the witchcraft. They
sometimes possess the body. Then the local priests invoke through songs the
said deity along with the sixty-four Yoginis. These songs are known as *Jagar.*[16]
There is such *jagar* for the local god Ganga Nath, who became a spirit. The
story of Ganga Nath runs as follows: Ganga Nath was the son of King
Vaibhav Chand of Doti. He became an ascetic owing to a disagreement with
his father. But he had a relationship with the wife of a Joshi brahmin, who
got the two of them killed. As a result they became spirits. The story of Ganga
Nath is popular in all of Kumaon region and his temples are also erected all
over the region. The Jagar runs:

Bakari ki mana Chaunsath Jogana chodi guru dhyan gyana Oh! jogi Ganga Nath jogi
tumne jog le liya.

(O Ganga Nath Jogi! You left sixty-four Yoginis and on the basis of knowledge and
meditation you have accepted ascetism.)

Another *jagar* where sixty-four Yoginis got a place along with local gods is, Gangoo Ramola.[17]

Kacata mitana ko bheluva rakata ke kaluva tumhron dhyan jage Chausanth Jogina Bavan Pir tumase dhyan jage!
. . . nau sau nagini tumaro dhyan jage Chausanth Jogini tumaro dhyan jage[18]

(Kacata ke Bheluva! Bloodthirsty Kaluva you should be invoked! Sixty-four Yoginis and fifty-two Pira should be invoked! Nine hundred snakes should be invoked! Sixty-four Yoginis should be invoked!)

Kaluva appeared in Kumaon region about three hundred years ago. He used to play the flute and serve milk. He was killed by deceit, and his unsatisfied spirit is still wandering around. His first temple was erected at Kaphada Khan.

Other than the *jagar* songs the Joginis are called upon along with the Goddess at cremation pyre, where the Yoginis are recognized as the power of the Goddess.

gaila samasan aab Devi tumari ayal bayal ye samajhane hai teri aab, cali sola sai Jogan, nau sai narsing bara sai goriya aab te Devi, tumaro cha sathi yojana.

(In the terrible crematorium, Goddess, your powers are gathering. The troops are proceeding from the crematorium. They are sixteen hundred Yoginis, nine hundred Narsingh and twelve hundred Goriya.)

The folk deities of Kumaon were initially human beings, became spirits after death and were gradually deified. Some are Kul Devata (family deity) also, and often they are invoked to remove diseases.

The second such category is that of the spirits who possess human beings. In the Kumaon region folk deities are as popular or more popular than the gods and goddess of orthodox Hinduism. The belief in folk deities is so strong that in rural Kumayun, during sickness rather than a medical practitioner it is a particular folk deity whose help is sought (Lohani 1994: 159).

In some traditions, Kumaon and Garhwal regions are recognized as Triya desh where Matsyendra Nath lived in the company of the women. Kuloot Desh (present-day Kullu in Himachal Pradesh) however preserves a totally different tradition. Here, the Yoginis are the grandmothers of the gods. In the folk narratives and the stories their fearsome and malevolent aspect has been highlighted. In some of the lores they are the giggling nymphs and fairies too. In Champa, they are supposed to reside on rocks and dry mountains but in Kullu they dwell in the high mountains,[19] and are supposed to be the goddesses of rain and water. Here, lies stark contrast: despite the local colour they have not lost Puranic touch. In Kulloot, it appears, the Pauranic mythology got the form of local and folk tradition. In these Himalayan kingdom different streams were flowing all were of folk tradition. In Kullu, whenever there is famine, people go to the mountains with their drums and invoke native gods and Yoginis for rain. It is a common belief that the Yoginis will bring rain. The Himalayan people believe that the rainbows are the dancing and bathing Yoginis, so one should not see them. Another interesting taboo is that one should not go to the mountains wearing red clothes or carrying red flowers. The Yoginis of these mountains are carried away by red colour and such persons become the victims of Yoginis' wrath.

The Himalayan people relate this belief to those narrations of the Puranas, where Mahamaya sought the help of Yoginis to assassinate Raktabija. After the killing of the demon the Yoginis became uncontrollable and started drinking everyone's blood. Mahamaya had to sever her head to calm the Yoginis down.

The Yoginis of modern Himalayan lore are reminiscent of the Puranic Yoginis. In Himalayan folklore they are always feared, as their aggressive form is known in society. The fear of the aggression of the Yoginis is such that during children's hair cutting ceremony, the honour of the Yoginis is more important than the village deities.[20]

There is another interesting story of Jhina's queen, who after becoming a Jogini stepped towards divinity. She is now recognized as the goddess of rain and water.[21]

Although Yoginis are often considered the grandmothers of the devatas of Kullu, sometimes they are their rivals also. There are legends about battles between them. The Himalayan people believe if the Yoginis win, it is a bad omen.

The narratives about Yoginis or Joginis are still popular in the places like Assam, Garhwal, Kumaon and Kullu. Interestingly, Triya Desh where Matsyendra Nath was captivated by the women, has been identified with all these three regions.

It is indeed fascinating to observe that the tribal or local deities who became part of classical Hindu religion as the sixty-four Yoginis, are still alive in popular religions.

In the elite religion they cease to hold significance, but in oral tradition, in ritual and in popular beliefs, they are still very much alive.

The question is whether one can place them in watertight compartments as remnants of a dead past, or part of a living tradition which is recreated every day. It compels one to ask whether all these traditions were one or different. They may have different elements, which merged in one. Different regions picked up the thread according to their own needs and constructed tales around them.

These Jogini are not Yoginis of the Puranas and the tantra texts, but both trends complement each other. In order to understand Yogini cult, one should study it in its entirety without exercising any dimension as trivial, extraneous, or irrelevant. We cannot forget that the *Rg Veda* and the *Atharva*

Veda complement each other, the *Atharva Veda* delineates superstition, magical charm, and the beliefs of the common people, the *Rg Veda* the culture of the elites. But there is no contradiction between the two.

The Upanishadas also embody the distinct cultures. The *Kathoponishad* describes the soul, the Brahman and the Universe whereas the *Grihya Sutras* narrate the beliefs of the masses.

The Puranas very aptly sketch the amalagamation of Brahmanical religion, popular belief, regional cults, and folk tradition. The study, however, shows that local traditions delineate how a classical tradition becomes a local tradition. Even when the classical tradition become a thing of past the local tradition gives a clue to the merging of classical tradition with folk tradition.

NOTES

1. Shabar and Marana Mantras are written in a cryptic language, they are recited to invoke sixty-four Yoginis, fifty-two Bhairavas, Ismail, Macchinder Nath and Gorakh Nath.
2. Matsyendra Nath was the progenitor of the Yogini cult. He was a Shaivite, but for some time he was captivated by women and roamed around in their company in Kamrupa. Women are excluded from the Nath cult, because they are Nirguna (virtueless), formless, tigress, demoness, and illusion (*Gorakha Bani*, 7.153): The sun and the moon identified respectively with Shakti and Shiva (Shiva represents moon nectar, Shakti the female principle, sun) and fire want to cosume. This is why the Nath Yogis keep away from women.
3. Only in the Nagarkhanda of the Skand Purana it is mentioned that Matsyendra Nath was thrown in sea by his family as he was born in the 'Gandantayoga'.
4. Dehejia (1986) has classified them into four categories.
5. '*Idam Shastram Yogininam Grihe Grihe*' Kaulajnananirnaya. It shows the popularity of the fact that at Kamrupa the women are Yoginis. It also shows that the dividing line between the Yoginis of Yogini Kaula and deified Yoginis was not very clear.
6. Goraksha Vijaya is available in Maithili also, written by Vidyapati.
7. In the *Aitihasika Sandarbha Me Shakta Tantra*, described by M.C. Joshi.
8. One of the Nava (nine) Nathas.
9. Collaborated by Sri R.K. Misra, Koraba, MP.
10. In the *Lok Varta* Sri Ram Swarup Yogi mentions this mantra as described in *Nath Sampradaya* by H.P. Dwivedi.
11. Kaithi script's shabar mantra, Sri Dinesh Chadra Shastri, Sri Avadh Jyotish Karyalaya, Vaishali, Bihar.
12. Chandoolal Shah, Nemeshwardesh Street, Jamanagar, Gujarat.
13. Collected by Shivanand Nautiyal, 1994.
14. Ibid.
15. The Nath Yogis rejected the Hindu caste system and found shelter in the upper

terrains of Simla, Himalaya, Almora, Punjab, Ambala, Garhwal, eastern Uttar Pradesh, Bengal, Maharashtra, Konkan. In Bengal and eastern UP, their livelihood depends upon tailoring. Usually they are tailors, painters and cattle rearers. In the Mantras, along with Macchinder Nath, Gorakh Nath and sixty-four Yoginis, there also occurs an Ismail Jogi. In Ujjain the shrine of Macchinder Nath was under the possession of the Muslims. In Dhar along with an unreported Yogini Temple, there is a shrine of Peer Kotwal, who had his alliance with sixty-four Yoginis.

16. Jagar is a local Kumayuns dialect term it means to invoke. In Kumayun region it is used to invoke the spirit. It is believed in these regions that some people are possessed by deities or spirits. Through Jagar, one can awaken that spirit.

17. The singer of Gangoo Ramola is Kalooram Bhasaradi (Develayala) Patti, Baragisi. The Ramaula Gathas are known for their distinct tune. They are known as Ramaulani songs. They are sung in a particular tune that is known as Ramaula.

18. All these *Jagar* are based on oral tradition.

19. One is reminded here of the Devi Stotra of Arya Satva, where the Devi also resides on high mountains.

20. Together with the minor deities of excitable character—birs, jogins, rakhvalas and others, they share their blood offering during festivals. Joginis are pretty nymphs and the guardian deities of the trees.

21. The story runs like this: After the death of Rana Jhina, his wife acquired Satihood (burnt herself along with her husband at funeral pyre). Later she became a Jogan and is considered to be the goddess of rain. At the time of famine if a moustache bearing man burns leather near her temples it becomes intolerable to her and she pours rains.

CHAPTER SIX

Yoginis as Tribal Deities

WHEN THE CULT of the Goddess re-emerged in Brahmanical Hinduism in the post-Gupta period, there was an upsurge of tribal and local deities and their identification with the Great Goddess. This trend appears to have been so strong that it compels art historians and academics to recognize and identify them. The trend also manifests how a symbol gets form as an image, and a rudimentary thought becomes entrenched through complex historical and social processes. The process of entrenchment has been approached by scholars in three distinct ways.[1] Before highlighting how the process has unfolded especially around the group of sixty-four Yoginis, it would be apt to analyse the views of these scholars. The tribal deities were not accepted only as sixty-four Yoginis. There was a broader phenomenon and the Yogini cult was one of its many segments. The diverse images and names of the Yoginis was an outcome of this challenging phase of entrenchment.

R.S. Sharma (2001: 41) explains the process as an outcome of the migration of the Brahmins from Madhya Desha in search of livelihood. He highlights the socio-economic factor behind the acceptance of tribal deities.[2] On the basis of the *Kularnava Tantra,* he conjures that the new deities were mainly deities of 'sudras' and 'untouchables', several of whom were named after their native tribes.[3]

Sharma's framework may be taken as an influential explanation for the acceptance of tribal deities in the main frame of Hinduism. Socio-economic reasons may have indeed been a strong reason, but the cult of sixty-four Yoginis or tribal deities who were earlier marginalized also gradually became dominant. The question then is, how did this entrenchment and simultaneous domination of tribal deities take place. Was it an evolutionary process of reciprocity, or a constant tussle?

While the process manifests the accommodation of native divinities in orthodox Hinduism, the fact however remains that in the rapid process of Hinduization, the local identity of these deities did not totally vanish. One may cite here the example of the Bheraghat Yogini temple, where image of Mahismardini is stamped with the local name Teramva (Illus. 41—Chapter 2). At Bheraghat, Sri Phanendri (Illus. 52), Sri Amtakari (Illus. 53), Sri Tokari

(Illus. 36—Chapter 2), are all names indicating a local origin. They may have been identified with the Great Goddess at this stage but carried their original name.

Even when tribal goddesses were adopted in Brahmanical society, they continued to carry the stigma of their origin. Thus the *Jayadratha Yamala*, a work located in the twelfth to thirteenth centuries, states that in order to worship Parameshvari (Kali), it was necessary to go to the houses of oilmen and potters and then worship the goddesses in their company (Bagchi 1929: 763).[4] Actually in the countryside, it is believed that the Goddess prefers to be worshipped by the lower class than by the brahmins. This could be reminiscent of the tantric mode of worship, as the *Kularnava Tantra* very specifically states it. In the *Kularnava Tantra*[5] the Shakti has been identified with the 'untouchables' and tribal women. There are eight kulas (clans) which were considered to be pious. There could be two possibilities for such an attempt. The first is that most of the attributes of the Goddesses were taken from this class of society. Or else, there was an attempt to bring 'untouchables' and tribes into the fold of Brahmanical Hinduism through Goddess worship.[6]

Eight Goddesses have been mentioned according to profession. All these were low-profile professions. It seems that the deities of these professions were also assimilated in orthodox Hinduism.[7] It was this class that provided a background for the emergence of group of Yoginis. In many localities of Bengal, the Goddess is first worshipped by the 'untouchables' rather than by Brahmin priest. Kada Devi, a local Goddess, in eastern Uttar Pradesh is worshipped by a Mali (gardener) priest. Certain cults which include tantric elements as well, worship Sitala Devi and the priests are called Dom Pandits. Obviously it is an indication that the priests were outcasts.[8]

Goddess worship among the Scheduled Tribes whether they follow Hinduism or a combined religion, is still prevalent. Along with Kali and Lakshmi they worship their aboriginal goddesses also.[9] The accommodation of tribal deities as sixty-four Yoginis and their diffusion again as village and native deities is indeed a fascinating journey. Despite their elevation, the tribal deities were worshipped in the lowest of rituals. The study shows that despite Brahmanization, these deities remained rooted in their local contexts and origins.

It was for the territories newly incorporated into Brahmanism, that the attributes of the tribal deities were imposed upon the Great Goddess, so that the masses could recognize them and identify with them. The kings built temples to please the aborigines to accommodate their deities in the Hindu pantheon. It is for this apparent reason that the temples of the Yoginis are found in the tribal belt of UP, MP, and Orissa. Yogini temples are not found in Assam and Bengal.[10] Both Bengal and Assam are not only strong hold of tantra, but are associated with Yogini tantra and with the legends of Matsyendra Nath, the progenitor of Yogini Kaula sect.

Let us now proceed to the views of Eschmann (1978) who has considered the problem in an anthropological way. She has suggested a three-tier formulae for the acceptance of tribal deities in orthodox Hinduism. In the process of Brahmanization, she says, first a tribal deity is recognized; it becomes a village deity. The next decisive stage comes through the construction of a temple. A temple cult is subject to further development, for instance through royal patronage, and might rise to regional importance and thus become an integral part of the highest level of Hinduism valid for all India. Usually village deities are mistaken for tribal deities. Eschmann (1978: 83–4) draws a demarcating line between village god and tribal god. She also emphasizes the importance of regional tradition in this process. After the temple level, among rituals first comes *locacara*, then *desacara*. *Locacara* may be prescribed by folklorist, but *desacara* may vary from region to region. In our case study when the tribal deities become the deities of tantra, a sort of secrecy was maintained. In the *locacara*, it seems, the simple rituals of tribal deities was replaced by mystic tantric rituals.[11]

Whatever rituals were performed, they were not simple. They must have been fearsome, as is apparent from the description of the contemporary texts like *Karpoor Manjari* and *Prabodh Chandrodaya*.[12] In the *Karpoor Manjari* a fierce dance of Yoginis is described during the ritual of Bata Savitri Vrata.[13] Whatever model Eschmann[14] (1978) has suggested, the fact, however, remains that very simple formless tribal deities become an image, and get installed in a temple loaded with the rituals.

It was indeed, a journey from sign to icon, from formless to form or image. The question, however, is how a *locacara* becomes *desacara*. While answering this question one should not forget the fact that *desacara* may diminish or may give way to another ritual but *locacara* remains in the legends, lore and folk tradition. When simple tribal deities became a group of Yoginis, independent tantra texts were written for them. The Puranas provided the lists and the local texts were written for them. The Puranas prescribed the methods for the carving of the images. In this entire transition from sign to icon no tussle can be seen.

That the Brahmanization of tribal deities took place, is evident in the Puranas. The symbols and names were given to the most familiar icon. Thus at Bheraghat the icon of Mahismardini was stamped with name Teramva (Illus. 41—Chapter 2). The goddesses of the Yogini group are still worshipped in eastern Uttar Pradesh, Madhya Pradesh, and Orissa in a scattered way and individually.

The Goddesses, incorporated in the group of Yogini were the goddesses of the tribes and low-caste Hindus, with the disintegration of the cult they also went back to their roots. They neither disappeared nor remained on a pedestal.

It should, however, be remembered that this process did not begin with the cult of sixty-four Yoginis. Recognition of tribal deities, and their elevation as temple devatas started from about AD 300. On the basis of epigraphy Chattopadhyaya (2003: 176) provides a documented record of such tribal deities where villages were donated for the maintenance of their temples. Chattopadhyaya (2003: 179) mentions that this trend continued in western India also. This time it influenced the mercantile class also. Temples for Aranyavasini was constructed in a place called Arnyakgiri. Another contemporary record of the period of Guhilas comes from Dabok, where a *devadroni* was built for Sri Durgadevi, whose original name was Ghattavasini (female deity of pots). The Varahi of Orissan temple (independent, not of mother's group) is also known and depicted as pot bellied.

Among all the examples cited by Chattopadhyaya the most striking one is that of 'Sri Vata Yakshini Devi'. It is engraved on a set of copperplate inscriptions of the tenth century from Pratapgarh in south Rajasthan. It is reminiscent of Yoginis who had their origins as Yakshinis residing on kula trees. People were prohibited to go near these trees.[15] Chattopadhyaya (2003: 172) calls this phenomenon the reappearance of the Goddess. But this was reappearance with a difference.

The cult of sixty-four Yoginis organized these tribal and lower deities. It assembled them under an umbrella, named sixty-four Yoginis. The construction of the temples and the introduction of the 'upacaras' signify a process of religious change in history. The rulers wanted to please the subjects of their newly acquired territories. Their deities found mention in the Puranas. The *Kularnava Tantra* was composed during this period, where the low caste women were identified with the Goddess. It is prescribed in the *Kularnava Tantra* that the Devi should be worshipped by these women.[16] The Goddess has been identified with this class. The *Mahanirvana Tantra* (ch.10: 177) says that in order to carve the deity clay should be dug out with a boar's tooth from the door of a prostitute's dwelling. This shows that despite 'elevation' and 'assimilation' in orthodox Hinduism, there was also an attempt to maintain their roots. It points to the possibility that this assimilation was a pretext to please those people.

The queries raised by scholars have largely remained unanswered. These are regarding the shift from invisibility to visibility and from sign to icon. The shift was obvious in tantricism, and in the political upheaval of the period, when the people needed a god, who could fulfil requirements quickly. It may be a period of degeneration, where an Upanisdic philosophy was not required. The magical practices and miracles made their headway. Those deities with magic powers attracted attention. Their attributes were imposed upon the Goddess as the sixty-four forms of the Goddess. The symbols were obscure and ambiguous. These symbols are mentioned in the Sanskrit records, in the popular beliefs, in the regional cults, and in folk traditions. Here one finds how local beliefs make a classical cult and that classical cult gradually submerged into native religious beliefs.

In these three approaches regarding the cult of the Goddess, from where the cult of Yogini had picked up the thread, there is no contradictory or challenging opinion. The question raised by Chattopadhyaya regarding the shift from invisible to visible or from vana to ksetra, is answered by Sharma's theory of migration of Brahmins from Madhyadesh to its periphery in search of livelihood. So far as Eschmann's theory is concerned, there is no clash between sign and icon. In process of Brahmanization, the tribal deities were not totally uprooted.[17] Even the Puranas highlighted this fact. Thus the *Skanda Purana* provides a list of animal-faced Yoginis (Illus. 7, 8 and 10—Chapter 1; Illus. 43 and 44—Chapter 2) to imply that at some stage they must have been associated with forest people and the names of sixty-four Yoginis in the Puranas show the movement from vana to ksetra.[18] Their attributes were imposed upon the Great Goddess and eventually they came to be regarded as one Great Goddess. This phenomenon led to the development of different images, but the Yoginis retained their old names with new forms. Before emergence of the cult of sixty-four Yoginis, the worship went through many stages—the mountain dwelling Goddesses worshipped by tribal people, identification with tribal deities and rituals performed by low-caste Hindu women. It is a journey whose facts can be verified from the *Arya Stava* to the Puranas and from the Puranas to the *Kularnava Tantra*. These deities became sixty-four Yoginis with original attributes attached to them and did not discard their background. For this apparent reason the lists of their names show non-Sanskrit names and many names justify their aggressive as well as native forms. Many Yoginis of the sixty-four Yoginis group are still worshipped in villages of eastern Uttar Pradesh, Madhya Pradesh and Orissa.[19] Their temples were constructed only to accommodate the tribal deities, hence they are found only in the tribal belt of UP, MP, and Orissa. It raises a genuine query whether these temples were different from those of the cult of sixty-four Yoginis. Was the sixty-four Yogini tradition of Bengal different from the temple tradition of Banda? Was the tradition of tribal deities of Yogini temple different from the tradition of the Yogini cult of Matsyendra Nath?[20] These are the questions which are as fascinating and interesting as the cult itself.

NOTES

1. A. Eschmann 1978: 79–98 in *The Cult of Jagannath*, ed. A. Eschmann, Hermann Kulke and G.C. Tripathi, R.S. Sharma 2001, B.D. Chattopadhyaya 2003.

2. A geographical survey of land grants would show that, except in the deep south where brahmana settlements appear in large numbers from the eighth century onwards. It was from the fifth to the seventh centuries that large scale land grants were made to the brahmanas in the peripheral areas, such as Assam, Bengal, Orissa and Central India (R.S. Sharma, 2001: 241).

3. Ibid.

4. P.C. Bagchi has written about the tantric texts of ancient Kambuj. Its Nepal MS is dated AD 1642, HP Shastri catalogue of Palm leaf and Paper MSS Preface PLXI, HP Sastri, Catalogue of Palm leaf and Paper MSS 1, p. 1767.

5. *Candali Carmakari Ca Magadhi Pukkasi Tatha*
   Svapaci Khattaki Caiva Kaivarti Visvayositah
   (Whether the Shakti hails from Candali (untouchable) leatherworker, huntress, boatwoman, they are very auspicious). *Kularnava Tantra*, ch.7, verse 42, V. Taranath and Arthur Avlon, 1915.

6. *Candali Carmakari Ca Magadhi Pukkasi Tatha.*
   Svapaci Khattaki Caiva Kaivarti Visva Yoshitah.
   —*Kularnava Tantra* 7.42
   (Whether Shakti is from Candal, Carmakar Matanga and Pukkasi's house, whether she is from Svapaci, Khattaki or Kaivarta family, these eight clans are considered to be auspicious.)

7. *Kulastakamidam Proktamkulastakmucyate*
   Kanduki Saundiki caiva Sastrajivi Ca Ranjiki.
   Gayaki Rajaki Silpi Kauliki Ca Tathastami
   Tantra Mantra Samayukta Samayacarapalika.
   —*Kularnava Tantra*, 7.43–44
   (The above eight Shaktis are of kula category. Now the Akulastaka category's eight Shaktis will be described. These are Kanduki (merchant of the balls), Shaundiki (wine seller), Sastra jivi (merchant of arms), Ranjiki (Dyer), Gayaki (Singer), Rajaki (washer woman), Shilpi (sculptor) and Kuliki (weaver) these are eight akulas, they are always involved in the tantra and mantra.
   V. Taranath and Arthur Avlon, *The Kularnava Tantra*, 1915.

8. C.P.W.C. Sen HBLL p. 31, Crooke, '*Doms*' ERE IV in Payne's *The Shaktas*', 1933.

9. Refer to appendices I and II.

10. Why the Yogini Temples are not from Bengal and Assam, there is no certain answer for it. Presumably, both these places had the strong cult of Mahishmardini Durga and Kamakhya therefore the temples of sixty-four Yoginis were not built here.

11. At Assam they are invoked before worshipping Kamakhya, who was originally goddess of Kiratas. The *Kalika Purana* describes a ritual of Bengal, where eight Yoginis should be worshipped before worshipping the Goddess. The *Kaula Kalpa Taru*—23.2, 815 61 676 describes the worship of sixteen Yoginis descending from the four directions.

12. In the *Prabodh Chandrodaya* Kalaratri as Yogini has been described like this.
    Ghoram Narkapalkundavatim Vidyucchatam Dristibhiha
    Muncantim Vikaralmurtirmanalajwalpishnngaih Kacah

Drastracandrakalangkurantaralalajijhvam MahaBhairavim
Pasyantya iva Me Manah Kadalikevadyapyavepato. 4.1

Kalaratri Karalsyadantantargataya Maya
Dristasi Sakhi saiva tvam Punartreva janmani. 4.2

13. *Kinkinikidaranajjhnasada kanthagidalajantidatala*
    Jognabalaanccanakelim talneuraam viranti. 4.17

14. Eschmann (1978: 84) explains the situation with a graphic model. The canonised all India Hindu tradition is a circle composed of segments comprises regional tradition, which are represented by ellipses. The regional traditions again are composed of the segments of several ellipses representing subregional traditions, which are again interlocked with several popular and tribal traditions.

15. At Almora there is a Yakhini Devi temple.

16. The Shakti has been identified with chandali, cobbler, hunter and prostitute (7.42).

17. The appendix shows that they are still worshipped in tribal belt. Not all the folk deities could find a respectable place or were taken into Brahmanical framework. The Silpa Ratnakosa, a fifteenth century text of Orissa clearly prescribes that for the icons of village deities no auspicious day is recommended and no knowledge is required. The Shabar and other tribes worship the shapeless images.
    Gramyamurtyarthe Na Kalah Na Jnanasya Prayojanam.
    Apamurti Pujayanti are Shabarrajecathare Janah. 480.

18. Appendices II A, B and C list of sixty-four Yoginis with Animal names.

19. Appendices I and II.

20. In tantric tradition, usually a secrecy in worship is maintained. Hence the desired deity is not worshipped openly. Supposing Bagalamukhi is the desired deity, an icon of Pitambara will be carved there.

Goddesses Worshipped by Some Tribes of Central India

Goddess	Tribes
Dharti Mata (Earth Goddess)	Bijan, Baiga, Londh, Nagesia
Dharvi (Earth Goddess)	Gadla
Rat Mai (Goddess of Darkness and Night)	Baiga
Kher Mai (Goddess of Village)	Baiga, Gond, Majhi, Khaira
Sitala Mai (Goddess of Smallpox)	Habba, Biar, Kandh, Korwa, Bhaina
Banjarani Mai (Goddess of Forests and Namats)	Baiga and Gond
Thakurain Mai* (Almighty Goddess)	Baiga
Bhurj Mai (Supreme Mother Goddess)	Bhata, Bhurjia, Binjhwar, Bhaina, Bhanwari, Khairwar, Manjhwar, Birhor, Baiga
Kankalini Mata (Mother Goddess with form of a skeleton)	Binjhwar, Haebar
Sat Bahinia (Group of Seven Sisters)	Binjhwar
Danteswari	All the tribes of Chhattisgarh

*One of the Yogini names.

APPENDIX IIA

Yogini with Native Names

	Agni Purana	Hemadri	P.L.S.S.	Matottara Tantra
1.	Lola			Lolā
2.	Raksasi	Raksasi	Raksasi	Raksasi
3.		Lankeśvarī	Lankeśvarī	Lampatā
4.	Huṅkārī	Hunkārā	Hunkārā	Hunkārī
5.	Vadavāmukhī	Vadavāmukhī	Vadavāmukhī	Vadavāmukhī
6.	Mahākrūrā			
7.	Krodhanā		Hāhārāvā	
8.	Mahānanā	Mahākrūrā	Mahākrūrā	
9.		Krodhanā	Krodhanā	Krodhanā
10.	Sarvajñā	Bhayānanā		Bhayānanā
11.	Taralā			
12.	Sarakhya		Hayānanā	
13.		Rasasangrahī		
14.	Śambarā			
15.		Sabarā		
16.		Tālujihvikā	Tālājanghā	Tālajanghā
17.		Raktākṣī	Raktākṣī	
18.	Karankinī	Karankinī	Karankinī	Bhayaṃkarī
19.	Meghanādā	Meghanādā	Meghanādā	Meghanādā
20.		Kālakarṇī	Kālakarṇī	Kālakarṇī
21.				Campakā
22.				Pralayā
23.			Pralayantikā	Pralayantā
24.		Picuvaktrā		Picuvaktrā
25.	Piśaci	Piśācī		Piśācī
26.	Piśitāśā	Piśitāśā	Piśitāśā	Piśitāsava
27.	Lolupā	Lolupā	Lolupā	Lolupā
28.	Tapanī	Tapanī	Tapanī	Vakṛanāsā
29.				Vikṛtānanā
30.	Vikṛtā	Vikṛtā	Vikṛtā	
31.				Yamajihvā
32.	Yamajihvā	Yamajihvā	Yamajihvā	Pretākṣī
33.	Durjayā	Durjayā	Durjayā	Durjayā

(Contd.)

(*Contd.*)

	Agni Purana	Hemadri	P.L.S.S.	Matottara Tantra
34.		Yamangikā		Yamantikā
35.	Bidālī	Vidālī	Vidālī	Pralayī
36.	Pūtanā	Pūtanā	Pretana	Pūtanā

Source: Vidya Dehejia, *Yogini Cult and Temples*, Delhi, 1986.

Names of
Native Deities

	Jaipur MS AD 1501	S.B. 2/150 26505	Baroda 8177
1.	Pretāśī		
2.	Dākinī	Dākinī	Dākinī
3.			Kālarātri
4.	Niśācarī	Niśācarī	Niśācarī
5.	Hunkari	Kalini	Hunkarini
6.	Phetkārī	Kalaratri	Bhutadamari
7.		Vetalini	Mamsa-Sonitabhogini
8.		Ūrdhvakeśinī	Kalahapriyā
9.	Raktākṣī		Rāksasī
10.	Ghora-raktā		Ghora-raktākṣī
11.	Krodha		
12.			Caṇdī
13.	Kaumārikā		
14.	Durmukhi		Bhaya-Vidhvansinī
15.		Asurā	Krodhī
16.			Durmukhī
17.	Kantakī		
18.	Kālinī		
19.		Durmukhī	Cakrī
20.	Dirgh Lambosti	Kankālī	Kaikamuki
21.	Bhaksinī	Yamadūtī	Kakadrshti
22.		Karālinī	Mundagradharini
23.	Kāmukī		Vyagri
24.	Kinkinī		Pretabhaksini
25.	Ghorī		Ghorakapali
26.	Viśālāngulī	Kālarātri	Visabhaksini

Source: Vidya Dehejia, *Yogini Cult and Temples*, Delhi, 1986.

Skanda Purana, Kasi Khanda (Yogini with Animal Names)

1.	Gajanana	elephant-faced
2.	Simhamukhi	lion-faced
3.	Grdrasya	vulture-faced
4.	Kakatundika	crow-beaked
5.	Ustragriva	camel-necked
6.	Hayagriva	horse-necked
7.	Varahi	boar
8.	Sarabhanana	mythical creature, half horse
9.	Ulukika	owl-like
10.	Sivarava	jackal-voiced
11.	Mayuri	peacock
12.	Vikatanana	fearsome-faced
13.	Astavaktra	eight-faced
14.	Kotaraksi	hollow-eyed
15.	Kubja	hunch-backed
16.	Vikatalocana	fearsome-eyed
17.	Suskodari	dried abdomen
18.	Lalajjihva	tongue hanging out
19.	Svadamstra	canini-toothed
20.	Vanaranana	monkey-faced
21.	Rksaksi	bear-eyed
22.	Kekaraksi	squit-eyed
23.	Brhattunda	large-abdomened
24.	Surapriya	fond of wine
25.	Kapalahasta	skull-cap in hand
26.	Raktaksi	blood-eyed
27.	Suki	parrot
28.	Syeni	hawk
29.	Kapotika	dove
30.	Pasahasta	noose in hand
31.	Dandahasta	club in hand
32.	Pracanda	terribly terrible

33.	Candahasta	terrible-handed
34.	Sisughni	killer of children
35.	Papahantri	destroyer of sins
36.	Kali	black one
37.	Rudhirapayini	drinker of blood
38.	Vasadhaya	holder of earth
39.	Garbha-bhaksa	eater of foetus
40.	Sava-hasta	corpse in hand
41.	Antra-malini	garlanded with intestines
42.	Sthula-kesi	rough grip on hair
43.	Brhatkuksi	large-girdled
44.	Sarpasya	snake-faced
45.	Pretavahana	one whose vehicle is a preta
46.	Dandasukakara	Venomous one
47.	Kraunci	heron
48.	Mrgasirsa	deer-headed
49.	Vrsanana	ox-faced
50.	Vyattasya	open-mouthed
51.	Dhumanisvasa	inhale of smoke
52.	Vyomaika	the sky
53.	Charanordhvaduk	foot at the top
54.	Tapani	burning one
55.	Sosani-drsti	one with a shrivelling look
56.	Kotari	lives in a hole
57.	Sthulanasika	large-nosed
58.	Vidyutprabha	one with the glow of lightening
59.	Bakakasya	crane-faced
60.	Marjari	cat
61.	Kataputana	departed spirit
62.	Attahasa	one with a very loud laugh
63.	Kamaksi	eyes of love
64.	Mrgaksi	eyes of a deer

ILLUS. 52: Sri Phanendri
(Bheraghat)

ILLUS. 53: Sri Amtakari
(Bheraghat)

Illus. 54: Mitauli Temple Mound

PART III

CHAPTER SEVEN

Yogini Temple Architecture: Beyond Convention

T HE STRUCTURE OF the Yogini temples (Illus. 54—Chapter 6; Illus. 12 and 13—Chapter 1; Illus. 55 and 56), has indeed perplexed art historians. Charles Fabri (1974: 76), says that it is a departure from the Brahmanical trend. He is surprised to see no vimanas or sikharas, no mandapa, temple chambers, no garbha griha or sanctum, no main cult image. Fabri regarded them as totally different from contemporary Orissan temples. Not only Orissan, these temples are distinct from any other Brahmanical or Buddhist structure. L.K.Tripathi (1974–5: 33–40) on the other hand, looks for Buddhist influence on it. The particular architecture of Yogini temples, could be an outcome of an effort to accommodate eighty-one or sixty-four deities, for which they unknowingly and perhaps inadvertently followed the Vedica of the stupas.

Some scholars on the other hand, take recourse to the tantric tradition to explain the peculiarity of the architecture of the Yogini temple (Illus. 12, 13 and 30—Chapter 1; Illus. 55 and 56). They lament the paucity of any relevant documents on the subject. Thus, they bank upon terms like mandala, yantra or chakra and consider that these probably found expression in the form of circular Yogini temples. The most popular speculation is that they were built according to the tantric geometrical diagrams.

The *Nispannayogavali* (Bhattacharya 1949) mentions twenty-six mandalas, with gods and goddesses in the middle. The *Hevajra Tantra* (Sheyagrov 1959: 74) mentions that in the middle of the mandala, there are five Yoginis. The east is presided by Vajra, the west by Vajrayogini, the north by Vajradakini and the south by Gauri. In the middle there is Nairatma and in the outer mandala there are eight Yoginis.

The *Devi Purana* (Barua 1974: 371) mentions twelve mandalas. These mandalas are supposed to be the mediators of the Devi. Worship of mandala signifies the worship of all godheads. Similarly the yantra has also been considered equally important. Yantra is a graphic mode of worship. It is drawn to worship a particular god on metal, stone or paper. The *Shilpa Prakash* mentions the *Yogini Yantra*[1] of sixty matrikas, consisting of dots, with each dot presided over by a Yogini. The *Shilpa Prakash* also says that on each point of the Yantra, the Yoginis are worshipped and this worship should be conducted by the king.

The group of sixty-four Yoginis is supposed to be situated at the outer point of the triangle of the goddess. They signify the circle of day and night, divided into the muhurtas. Among the thirty muhurtas are situated two Yoginis, of the morning and the evening. The Yoginis move in circle and their temples may signify the *Kala Cakra* (circle of time). The *cakra* is drawn for a particular god. The Cakra literally means constant movement. Since the Yoginis move in circles, presumably the temples symbolize the *cakra* (Douglas 1971: 7). Nick Douglas also associates it with energy. He says that

these 'energy circles'—circular flying-saucer to the sky and astronomically located, contain the most exquisite 'passengers'. Each dancing Yogini either peaceful or wrathful perhaps with the head of a bull or lion, dancing upon full lotuses, or the crouched figure of a man and exhibiting various exact gestures and expressions, represents certain natural energies, tamed by Matsyendra Nath. These energies circle around the immovable Shiva (in fully tantric aspect), and we find them represented as Yoginis (in the early Tantras like Hevajra) and Dakinis . . . goddesses adorned with the symbolic ornaments of human bone . . . in the Tibetan tradition.

Thus Douglas' theory takes the Yoginis and their temples from mundane to super mundane. His theory is inspired by Tibetan tradition. It is supposed to be drawn in real and symbols. In real cakra the male worshipper sits with his female companion (Yogini). He is surrounded by a circle of eight Yoginis. In Yogini cakra (Illus. 109—Chapter 9), the female companion participates with one male companion. These symbols are different forms of the month. In every form, the goddess has different attributes and gestures.

In the temple architecture Shiva Bhairava (Illus. 31—Chapter 1) in the centre is Bindu and Yogini (Illus. 20—Chapter 1) around him is Mandala. When images of multiple Yoginis are thus placed within a circular enclosure, we get a Yogini Cakra, a Yogini temple (Illus. 12 and 13—Chapter 1). In advance meditating technique, the deities and Yoginis of a Cakra are sometimes visualized as existing internally within the body and are to be offered symbolic worship. The word mandala may also be understood as a square, but not rectangle, and it is hence surprising that the shrines of the mothers are always rectangular and those of the Yoginis only occasionally so.[2]

It will not be out of the way to suggest that Yogini could be the name of one of the Nakshtras. These temples are open to the sky and may have been connected to the sky. Padma Kaimal (2005: 59) sees it as the architectural realization of the Yoni. The first correlation is between Yoni and the Goddess. Sculptures from the Yogini temple at Bheraghat, in which sages worship a

Yoni that emanated from the entire figure of a goddess above it, demonstrate that this one body part could serve as an emblem of the Goddess entire being. The roofless and round Yogini temples are thought to be stone expressions of the Cakra. She says that in sexuality and building some drawing of the Goddess overlay a Cakra upon the deity's pelvic region, making explicit the diagram's physiological reference (Kaimal 2005: 21, 23 and 46). She establishes the correlation between the Yoni and the Cakra. She further says that Dehejia (1986: 39–52) and Deva (1991:567–71) have established the third correlation by demonstrating that Yogini temples are built versions of Cakras. To sum up this chain of associations, the depiction of the yoni embody the female divine, certain cakras embody the yoni, so that the hypethral goddess' temple therefore embody the yoni. These temples share with the yoni not only their outline but also their open, embracing, and containing nature. The Hirapur Yogini temple (Illus. 12—Chapter 1) articulates the shape of female reproductive organs with particular clarity. Thus in the absence of positive evidence, it may be tentatively suggested that these temples are the concrete expressions of the abstract diagrams of Yogini Kaula worship.

This is only one way of looking at these temples. There are others. These temples of initiation are circular roofless enclosures, which housed a cycle of shaktis, emanations of goddess. Based on the rays that emanated from the navel of solar plexus of the subtle body, they represent the energies of transformation. As an accurate reflection of the aspects of self, the sixty-four matrix is a point of interface between the personal and the cosmic. Its template has been constructively utilized to create a lens through which we may view the infinite as it filters into form.

In fact the problem is not so knotted as it appears. It only needs to be considered from a different angle. Before trying to give an answer for its peculiar shape, the sixty-four niches and eighty-one niches should be analysed. Other than the tantric texts, the religious texts like Puranas also provide a clue. The number sixty-four and eighty-one was not exclusively associated with the Yogini temples. These numbers invariably occur for other sacred and secular monuments of the period. Thus the *Agni Purana* (ch. 93: v.II) while describing rituals for *Vastu Purush* narrates that:

Tatah prasadamauchya vartayeyavastu mandapm
Kuryathkosthacatuhsasthi ksetre vedasakreme

Mahesvara said that on that place a sixty-four roomed Vastu Mandapa should be built.

The *Agni Purana* says:

Catuh sastipado brahma maricayadya' ca, catuspancasatpadipa apodyastau rasagnabhihi. (ch. 93: v.360)

In order to protect the country a sixty-four roomed temple should be built in the honour of Brahma and Marichi.

Incidentally the Yoginis were supposed to be Ksetrarakshika (guardians of the land). It is again narrated in the *Agni Purana* that for the development of the city, village, fort, house and palace, a structure of eighty-one rooms should be worshipped. For the rituals too eighty-one was an auspicious number. Thus for Bhoomi Pujan (worship of the land) and for installing a vase, the mandapa should be of eighty-one steps (ch.105: v.1).

Nagaragramdurgadau grhapradasvriddhaye
Ekastipadairvastu pujayetisiddhaye dhruva

For the development of city, village, fort, palace, the eighty-one steps should be worshipped.

Interestingly, the *Agni Purana* describes Pratima Laksana (attributes of the images) of the sixty-four Yoginis in chapter 52. But nowhere does it talk about the unconventional and unique structure of the Yogini temples. Perhaps it was a departure from the Shastric tradition and the writer avoided it. Art historians conveniently concluded that the temple structure responded to the tantric diagrams. Such an interesting problem should not be shrugged aside. Yoginis despite their elevation as the Great Goddess could never cast away their roots as tutetalaries. The names of the Yoginis enlisted in different texts are not unanimous, moreover they contain native names. The images also differ from crude and mundane to very sophisticated. A very simple query comes to the mind here. When all the images (Illus. 57 and 58) do not reveal the tantric influence; but a contemporary and local impact (Illus. 60, 61, 62 and 63), one must try to look beyond the tantric influence of Yogini temple architecture.

The Yoginis always move in circle. The legends preserve narrations that they descend from the sky and move around Shiva. The *Karpoor Manjari* also gives the simile of the valaya (bracelet) to the circle of the Yogini. Yoginis are always associated with the dance. Each Yogini is established on a cakra and cakra is a circle. These dancing Yoginis form a circle around Shiva. In Tibetan traditions these energies are equated with the Yoginis as dancing goddesses. Not only literature, folk tradition till today, preserve the tales of Yogini dance in the temples. A Kumaon folklore substantiates this argument, narrating that in the Neti village, the Joginis come and dance in the temple on full moon nights.[3]

There are two pieces of evidence that connect the temple with the native tradition. In the Sidhi District of Madhya Pradesh, the central triangular stones have been excavated by archaeologists from upper palaeolithic contexts. The stone is still in worship by Kol and Baiga people. The Kol tribe had made a shrine named as Kerai ki Devi, i.e. Goddess of Kerai. The shrine consists of a roughly circular platform, composed of sandstone, limestone and rubble blocks. In addition to these there is a headless figurine called Angari Devi (Goddess of Burning Coal) (Kenoyer et al. 1983: 88–9). The *Kularnava Tantra* is supposed to be practised by the Kol tribe.[4] Most of the lists of the name of the sixty-four Yogini preserve quite a few non-Sanskrit tribal names. The circular open shape of Yogini temple may have been a reminiscent of this practice prevalent in Tibet also. Near Retina (Rva sqren) is a rough circle of large stones (Phaong P'a bo'n) on the top of which flutter streamers bearing printed prayers. The site is traditionally regarded as sacred to a Dakini. Another ancient tomb, also circular in shape, was recorded by George de Reerich (Tucci 1973: 36).

The clue for this specific shape may be found in the local tribal practices. The circular shape in stone was prevalent in the ancient period. It was associated with the local female powers (Shakti). In Tibet such a shrine was associated with Dakini, a counter form of Yogini. The Yogini temples may respond to tantric practice rituals, or astronomy, but the fact cannot be denied that in their structure they followed the folk tradition. It had been a practice since upper Paleolithic period. Being non-Shastric, the Puranas did not describe it. The local and folk practices, where Yoginis as dancing goddesses descend from the sky, provide an answer for this unusual structure.

NOTES

1. An Orissan manuscript of twelfth century, Alice Boener and S.Rath Sarma, pp. 90–106.
2. It seems that temples of Khajuraho and Rikhiyan, followed the rectangle temple of mothers in architecture. The Hindu temple is based on a Mandala known as the Vastu Purusa Mandala which is combined in painted Mandala, both Buddhist and Hindu.
3. Based on oral traditions.
4. This theory is propounded by R.S. Sharma in his book *Early Medieval Indian Society*, 2001, pp. 235–65.

ILLUS. 55: Temple
(Khajuraho)

Illus. 56: Entrance
(Khajuraho)

ILLUS. 57: Yogini in Dancing Position
(Ranipur–Jharial)

ILLUS. 58: Yogini in Dancing Position
(Ranipur–Jharial)

ILLUS. 59: Indrani
(Naresar)

ILLUS. 60: Vaishnavi
(Naresar)

ILLUS. 61: Camunda
(Lokhari)

ILLUS. 62: Hayagriva
(Lokhari)

ILLUS. 63: Rksanana
(Lokhari)

CHAPTER EIGHT

Patronage:
Royalty and Reality

The king who worships the sixty-four Yoginis, he acquires victory and fame.
—KASHI KHANDA, *Skanda Purana*

THE RELATION BETWEEN royalty, temple, and deity has been understood in
many ways. While some scholars have understood it within the framework
of socio-religious relationships, others have analysed the relationship as an
expression of power. Two works focusing on these aspects of the relationship
between art and royalty are of particular significance. These are Vidya
Dehejia's edited book, *Royal Patronage and the Great Temple Art* (1988) and
Power of Art, edited by Barbara Stoller Miller (1992). Dehejia's book studies
the socio-religious constraints, which operate in the relation of patron and
the artist in different regions and periods of India. It asks how patrons and
artists perceived each other, and on the other hand, how they were perceived
by society. Miller's book also puts forward the socio-historical approach
regarding patronage. In Dehejia's work in particular, the 'power of art' has
been estimated through the relationship between kingship and artist, which
worked through particular socio-political systems, and culturally mediated
systems of authority.

A fascinating study of the relationship between king, temple and deity can
be seen in the reign of the Cholas. However, while it may be easy to decode
the network of kings as patrons of temples, the same cannot be said for
patronage of the sixty-four Yogini temples. The unravelling of the nature of
this relationship is difficult to establish precisely because of the tension that
lies in the proclamation of the authorship of these temples. The credit of
constructing Yogini temples goes to the contemporary dynasties. The
literature of the period describes vividly the powers of Yogini that mesmerized
the kings. Historians have been similarly enthusiastic in describing the
interrelation between the political powers and the builders of the Yogini
temples.[1] The present chapter tries to discover the network between Yoginis
and kings on the basis of the literature and inscriptions, which bring out some
unseen facts and the tussle between kings and deities.

The symbiotic relation between the temples and royal patronage has never been easy to identify. The period between AD 800 and 1200, to which Yogini temples have been attributed, was a period of political upheaval and chaos. In northern India, the Paramaras, Chandellas, Pratiharas, Kalachuris, and Kachchavas, were vying with each other to increase the extent of the boundaries of their respective kingdoms. From the inscriptions attributed to them, all of them claim to have built temples. The question is whether these included Yogini temples. The maximum numbers of Yogini temples have been reported from the Chandella and the Kalachuri kingdoms. The Chandellas held under their jurisdiction the area from Kalanjar in Malwa to the boundaries of the Chedis and a mountain called Gopa. Gwalior, Banda, Kalanjar, Lalitpur, Khajuraho, and Duduhi, the places where Yogini temples have been found, formed part of Chandella Kingdom. Starting their career as feudatories of the Pratiharas, the Chandellas rose to prominence on the ruins of the Pratihara dynasty. Chedi, Kosala, Malwa, Kalanjar, Mithila, and Gauda were under their direct or indirect influence. They had been at war with Mahmud Ghazanavi. The important rulers of this dynasty were Yuvaraj and Dhanga. In fact Dhanga fought with Kachchapagatas. In an undated fragmentary inscription from Mahoba of the time of Kirtivarman (AD 1060–1100) Dhanga is compared with Hamir.[2] Significantly, it was not Dhanga but perhaps Kirtivarman and Dhanga's grandson Vidyadhar, who fought with the Turks.

If one goes by the inscriptions, the rulers of the Chandella were no exception, in terms of fighting with contemporary rulers. The Pratihara period is also known for political upheavals, which finally contributed to the fall of their kingdom in the tenth century. Credit for building the gigantic Khajuraho group of temples goes to the Chandellas. Art historians, however, claim that the Yogini temple at Khajuraho was built by the Pratiharas.[3]

The Kalachuri of Tripuri or Dahal were the most significant branch of Kalachuris. The history of the Kalachuri begins with the rule of Gangeyadeva (1015–40) who rose from the position of a feudatory. Gangeyadeva was probably a ruler under Vidyadhar of Chandella dynasty. He fought with the weak Pratihara, Chalukya Jayasimha and later Bhoj of Paramara dynasty and declined the overlordship of the Chandellas after the death of Vidyadhar. Yuvaraj Deva I (915–45), was the first significant ruler of the dynasty. He fought the Chandellas and the Paramaras, though in the later part of his life he was defeated by Yashovarman of the Chandella dynasty. The credit of building Bheraghat Yogini Temple goes to him (1041–72). Karna was the most victorious ruler of the dynasty. He fought with the Chandellas, Paramaras and Chalukyas. The reign of Karna is known for building a Shiva Temple named Kamameru at Varanasi, Karnatirtha at the bank of Prayag, and a town, Karnavati.[4] The Kalachuri power declined with the reign of Yashkarna (1107–23), although it was during the course of his reign that the

Kalachuri power started waning. It is said that Yakshkarna had invaded Andhra Pradesh and worshipped Bhimesvara at the bank of Godavari.[5]

The earliest account of kings as worshippers of Shakti can be traced back to the period of the *Mahabharata*, where Arjun worshipped Durga and a host of other goddesses. The goddesses were indeed associated with warriors. The kings worshipped the goddess before their military campaigns. It is the fierce aspect of the Yoginis, however, which is highlighted in the texts of the period. The *Prabodh Chandrodaya* (4.1)[6] a text written during the reign of Chandella dynasty describes the Yogini as kalratri. Sometimes the kings are shown to be scared of the powers of the Yoginis, yet, the Yoginis were always perceived as favouring the kings. An interesting incident is depicted in the *Kashi Khanda* of the *Skanda Purana* (ch. 65) which says that Shiva sent the Yoginis to Kashi to lure king Divodas. The Yoginis liked the place so much that through their powers they disguised themselves as dancers, ascetics and witches and started living in Varanasi. The *Rajatarangini* of Kalhana (v.122) relates the story of pretty Yogeshwari, who captured King Baka as an offering to the circle of Goddess. Kalhan uses both 'Yogini' and 'Yogeshwari' synonymously.

The *Manasollasa* (ch. 67) an eleventh-century text describes the Yogini cakra. This Yogini cakra is a discussion of military strategies with the description of astrological diagrams for determining when and where to attack. The last of these diagrams, which places a goddess in each of the eight directions, is called the Yogini cakra.

Most of the contemporary sources, sacred or secular describe the tutelary role of the Yoginis. The kings consulted them at midnight for their predictions. The *Dvasraya Kavya* (ch. IV–V: v.13) an eleventh century text, describes the association of Yoginis with Chalukya monarch Siddharaja (1094–1145). It describes the Chalukya king Siddharaja confronting the Yoginis at the city wall and enquiring about the protection of the city.

(Even when the night comes) the duties of the king are by no means finished. . . . He must rise from his couch to perform the Veera Carya (Vira Practice). He goes forth, sword in hand, alone extending his rambles beyond (the city) walls to some spot frequented only by the filthy birds of night, the Yogini (Yoginis), and the Dakini (Dakinis) female spirits whom he compels to reply to the question and to inform him of future events.

The above texts very clearly indicates that the Yoginis bestow boon on royalty. This has been taken as one of the reasons for the construction of Yogini temples by the kings. In the popular and contemporary texts the military campaigns and the Yoginis have been interrelated. In this connection an interesting incident can be narrated here. The decisive battle between Chalukya Jayasimha and Parmara Yashovarma, is stated to have been fought, on a Yogini's advice to Jayasimha to go to the holy city to worship Kalika and other Yoginis, if he wanted to increase his religious merit. She also impressed upon him the necessity of establishing friendly relation with Yashovarma in order to obtain permission to enter Malwa. This enraged Siddharaj and he decided to launch an attack on the Parmara king.[7]

The *Vasant Vilasa* (canto III: v.21–3) inform us that Jayasimha brought from Ujjain the Yogini Pitha, having defeated and imprisoned the lord of Dhara, like a parrot in a cage. The Yoginis were also associated with the war. One *Yogini Tantra*[8] refers to the militant nature of the Yoginis while describing their origin.

The relation between Yoginis and royalty takes yet another significant turn when we look at temple architecture. There are two significant problems regarding Yogini temples. Although all are circular on plan, significantly the temples at Khajuraho and Rikhiyan are square. Second, the Yogini temples are conventionally of sixty-four Yoginis, in number, but the temple at Bheraghat are of eighty-one Yoginis. The worship of eighty-one Yoginis was specifically for royalty. *Sri Matottara Tantra*[9] (ch. 7: v.24) specifies that the group of eighty-one may be divided into nine subgroups, each with a presiding Yogini. Among these the seven groups are concerned only with royalty. In temple construction the mandalas of eighty-one squares is specially reserved for royalty. Thus the *Manasollasa* (Dehejia 1986: 51) a royal compendium, refers only to a plan with eighty-one squares. The concordance between these two independent sources on the importance of the number eighty-one is indeed striking.

Eighty-one is in fact the royal number for such arrangements. A passage from the *Sri Matottara Tantra* (ch.73) describes the benefits that accrue from the worship of the eighty-one Yoginis of the Mula Cakra.

On the basis of these arguments most scholars came to the conclusion that the eighty-one Yogini temples were exclusively for kings, sixty-four Yogini temples were for the common people. But such is not the case. The majestic sixty-four Yogini temples could not have been built without royal patronage. Even the sixty-four Yogini temples were supposed to grant boons to royalty.

Thus the *Yogini Sadhana* (Dhana 1974: 422) says: 'A king worships the sixty four Yoginis with the faith that his fame will reach the four oceans.'

The gigantic temple of Bheraghat was no doubt built as a royal project. The Kaula Kapalik and Yogini Kaula at Khajuraho could not have flourished without royal patronage either. The *Yogini Sadhana* (Dhana 1974: 422) itself says that Yoginis can make a commoner a king.

There is yet another fascinating side of the problem of builders. The successful rulers of Kalachuri dynasty were Yuvaraj Deva, Gangeya Deva and Karna. Yuvaraj Deva II followed the Kaula sect, which was active during his period. With the shifting of royal patronage, the scene of the sects also changed. Queen Alhanadevi had a bent towards the Pashupata sect. She had invited the Shaiva Acarya Rudraksha from Lat Pradesh. Owing to the paucity of patronage, the worshippers of the Yogini cult too migrated to Golaki Mutt, one kilometre away from Bheraghat. So we come to another problem, that of the identification of Golaki Mutt.

An inscription of AD 1261 narrates that Acarya Vishveshvara Shambhu hails from the tradition of the Acarya of Golaki Mutt. In the same inscription the Golaki Mutt has been identified as follows: In the middle (confluence) of Narmada and Bhagirathi rivers Dahala Mandala is situated. There, born in the lineage of Durvasa, a sage named Sadbhav Shambhu, Kalachuri king Yuvaraj Deva has donated three lakh villages to it.[10]

It is suggested by Dehejia (1986: 69) that Golaki Mutt was at Tripuri. Since the followers of Golaki Mutt were in Andhra Pradesh, this cannot be identified with a Yogini temple. But the Kalachuri kings had led invasions up to Andhra Pradesh. The lone victory of Yash Karna was in Andhra Pradesh. An interaction or currents and cross-currents at both the places of the cult cannot be ruled out. An inscription dated 1093 from the Bellary district of Karnataka, describes the Maha Samanta as one who has obtained the gracious boon of sixty-four Yoginis. Although this is a late inscription, it indicates that Andhra Pradesh had the influence of Yogini cults (Dash 1965: IX).

The name Golaki Mutt evidently owes its origins to its circular shape. The temple of Bheraghat must have enjoyed royal patronage at a certain stage. So far as the temples at Hirapur and Ranipur-Jharial are concerned, stylistically they are placed in the eighth and ninth centuries, the time of the Bhauma rulers, when six queens also ascended the throne. Queen Gauri Mahadevi was a devout worshipper of Shaktism. She considered herself an incarnation of Gauri or Parvati and built the temple of Gauri. Her daughter Dandi Mahadevi was also an illustrious queen and patron of Shaktism. The Hirapur temple was probably built by Hira Mahadevi, queen of Santikar II. The name Hirapur probably indicates the influence of this queen.

The dynamic rulers of the Kalachuri dynasties were Yuvaraj Deva, Gangeya Deva and Karna. Their reigns are marked with wars against their contemporary rulers. They were great builders also. To Gangeya Deva[11] the inscriptions give the credit of issuing coins stamped with Lakshmi motif. To his successor Karna goes the credit of constructing temples at Karnaghat in Varanasi and Karnavati in Prayag.

The most intriguing aspect of the problem of patronage is that despite the proclamation of the tantric texts and other texts about an association of Yoginis with the kings, none of the kings actually claimed the construction of the Yogini temples. Though the different rulers of Chandella dynasty claimed to be builders of temples of Khajuraho group, no inscription refers to them as builders of Yogini temples. For the Khajuraho temple there is a mere speculation that it was built by Yashovarman, and indeed he has admitted the ownership of different temples other than Yogini temples. Interestingly as stated earlier, the majority of Yogini temples are found from the jurisdiction of Chandellas. Even the theory that the gigantic Bheraghat temple was built by Kalachuri king Yuvaraj Deva is only a hypothesis. The controversy regarding the Golaki Mutt points to another possibility that since the inscriptions shied away from mentioning the Yogini temples, it was referred to by the name of Golaki Mutt.[12] The Bhaumakara queens of Orissa, despite their Shakta leanings, never mentioned that they built the Yogini temples of Hirapur and Ranipur-Jharial.[13]

The temples were built as a recognition of the power of the Yoginis. The Yoginis were supposed to protect kings, but kings never publicized their association in stone. Perhaps they were scared of their wrath and their fierce nature. They built the temples to gain a secret ambition, a personal favour. Thus secrecy was maintained not only in their rituals but also in their construction.

The *Brahmanda Purana* (*Lalitopakhyan* ch.3: v.8) clearly says that the person who reveals the secret of Yogini cult worship has to face the wrath of the Yoginis.

NOTES

1. The latest such work is by Dehejia 'Kalachuris and the Temple of Sixty-Four Yoginis', in *Royal Patronage and the Great Temple Art*, ed. Dehejia, 1988, pp. 77–84, where she has propounded the theory that the eighty-one Yogini temple at Bheraghat was specifically for the royalty.
2. *Nirmit Vairi Bhangah Srij Dhanga Ityavanimanga lamnvisasita
Sarena yah Bhujobhruvanatibharm Hammirmpyati Balatulyami cakara*
(Sri Dhanga defeated the group of the enemies. He was like Hammir in the art of arrows.)
CII, vol. IV, p. 293; vol.13; pp. 253–4; v.14.
3. Personal communication with Dr Krishna Deva, 1998.
4. *CII*, vol. IV, p. 293; vol. 13, p. 253; vol. 5, p. 276.
5. Khaira Inscription, Jabalpur, *CII*, vol. 4, p. 294.
6. *Ghoram Nar Kapal Kundal Vatim Vidyutcchatam Dristibhih
Muncati Vikaralmurtirmanalajvalpishankai
Dristracandrakalankurantaral lajjihvam Mahabhairavi
Pashyantaya Iva Me manah Kadalikevadyatyaho Vepate.*
7. *Dvyasraya Kavya*, Bhandarkar Oriental Research Institute, Pune, 1936, Canto XIVVV.
8. *Maharavaishcaturdiksu Yato Ghorparakramain Rasmivrindasamudbhuta Yoginyah Kotishah.* 2.55.
9. *Sri Matottara Tantra* (ch. 7, v. 24), Vidya Dehejia (1986: 125–9), and Kramarisch (1976: 46–50) have raised this theory.
10. Malka Purama Inscription 54–63.
11. *CII*, vol. IV, p. 295; vol. 13.
12. Another inscription of comparatively later period from the South Satara district

of Maharashtra of 1117 AD refers to the village Ankulye as the abode of Mahayogesvari Ugracamunda the presiding deity of the sixty-four Yoga Pithas. M.P. Dash, *A Descriptive Catalogue of Sanskrit M.S. of Orissa*, vol. V, intro, p. IX.

Dr. Hira Lal identifies it with Yogini temple at Bheraghat. A.M. Shastri (Tripuri) says that Golaki Mutt was somewhere near Bheraghat. V.V. Mirashi (Inscriptions of Kalachuri Chedi Era) revises both the theories and infers that the Yogini temple at Bheraghat was known as Golaki owing to its shape and the Mutt near it came to be known as Golaki Mutt.

13. Besides the term sixty-four yogapithas occurs frequently in the prasastis of the mercantile corporation of Ayyovall featuring in the inscription of Karnataka. Vijay Laxmi Chaudhuri (1984).

PART IV

CHAPTER NINE

The Terrifying Beauties

Most of the Yoginis have beautiful bodies and terrifying faces (Illus. 14—Chapter 1; Illus. 64, 66 and 67). These terrifying beauties, as the previous chapters have shown, are indeed intriguing. The Yogini images have been marginalized either as tantric or as 'local phenomenon', and insignificant. The Yogini images in fact pose a number of historical and cultural questions and conceal the mysteries of an esoteric yet significant cult.[1] It has often been asserted that these images do not follow the cult. But this study has shown that Yogini images, and indeed their temples are not irrelevant and ahistorical objects of an inscrutable art, but are expressions of socio-political and religious processes and contexts. There are two ways of looking at the images. How the artist had perceived them and how the art historian has visualized them. Apparently there does not seem to be any tussle between them. The tension arises owing to the difference of time and space. These Yogini images cannot be dismissed merely as a bridge between local and puranic deities. These are the potpourri of native, mythical, pauranic, classical and ritualistic deities.

The Yogini images are found in Hirapur (Illus. 68, 69, 70 and 71), Ranipur-Jharial (Illus. 67 and 73), Bheraghat (Illus. 74, 75 and 76), Khajuraho, Naresar, Mitauli, Shahdol (Illus. 65, 77, 78, 79 and 81), Rikhiyan and Hingalajgadha. But none of these images bear resemblance from the others. They can easily be identified and categorized according to the spots where they have been found. Do they then show regional features? Can we talk about the regional identity in the Yogini imageries?[2] We can easily pinpoint the indigenous features of the Yogini imageries.

These images were developed out of an interaction between the prevalent local culture, popular puranic Hinduism and Shastric mythology. The stories of the Yoginis found expression in three types of texts, the Puranas, popular Sanskrit literature and Tantric literature such as *Kaulajnananirnaya*, *Goraksha Vijaya*, *Yogini Hridaya*, *Kularnava Tantra* and *Chandi Shataka* of Sarala Das. Other than the last one, none of these texts had any bearing upon the Yogini images.

As H.C. Das (1981) had pointed out there is a regional variation in Yogini images.[3] While discussing the making of the regional tradition of Bengal, Kunal Chakrabarti (2003: 309) projects the case of the local goddess in place of the great goddess.[4] As a cult, the Yoginis may not present a regional identity but in their images we perceive the cultural identity of different regions. The temples appear similar because of their peculiar shape but in the sculpture local elements have been recognized.

There is no similarity, for example, between the sculptures of Ranipur-Jharial and Hirapur. The Ranipur-Jharial images appear like Alasa Kanya and Sura Sundari (Illus. 4 and 12—Chapter 1; Illus. 82) of the contemporary temples. They also look like the aggressive Yoginis of the *Linga Purana* and *Padma Purana* (Illus. 83 and 58—Chapter 7). For Hirapur Yogini images it is said that Sarala Das wrote his *Chandi Shatak* after visiting this temple as there is so much similarity in the descriptions. All of them are puranic, local and popular deities (Illus. 84, 85, 86 and 87). At Bheraghat all these 'awful' deities are stamped with local names. The Naresar (Illus. 65), Shahdol (Illus. 89), and Rikhiyan Yoginis are animal-faced. The Yoginis from these places, their gestures, postures, and animal expressions are different. The Naresar and Lokhari Yoginis with names like Shashanana (Illus. 8—Chapter 1) appear to be local deity. The Hirapur Yoginis (Illus. 91 and 92) with their beautiful limbs, face and specified vahanas appear to be puranic deities.

The Yoginis are part of Shakta tradition. They are supposed to be the forms of the Devi or the Devi herself. The Shakta tradition is different in Orissa and Madhya Pradesh. It is to be noted that no sectarian influence can be traced here. At Khajuraho, Kaula Kapalikas were dominant and at Bheraghat Matta Mayura sect mushroomed. The images may not have been developed under sectarian influence, but some images deserve special attention. They not only appear to be manifestation of rituals, it seems they were carved for the fulfilment of rituals. Such Yogini images have been reported from Bheraghat (Illus. 74 and 75) and Shahdol (Illus. 89). They also give a glimpse of the types of rituals performed here especially at the temples of Bheraghat (Illus. 37—Chapter 2) and Naresar. There are worshippers sacrificing the human beings, and performing the rituals. The depictions of ghouls, and skeleton all point to an esoteric atmosphere. In the present case it is neither geographical boundaries nor language that can define the regional influence. The religious and cultural identity have become regional markers.

For the Yogini sculptures the term local has also been frequently used. The question here is whether the local culture is same as regional culture. The distinct local traits or elements are absorbed and a regional culture emerges, but not all local elements take the form of regional culture as they are uprooted from their native place, scattered and assume a different shape in another places. Thus in carving the Yogini images the local trend prevailed which gave them a local identity just like the texts where lists of the Yoginis do not tally. They correspond to the description of native deities. The images in these places had distinct features but being an esoteric cult and not being very prominent deities, could not assume the prominence and prevalence of a tradition of an entire region.

In Orissa where the cult of Jagannath developed as a state cult, the sixty-four Yoginis are described as his attendants. At Bheraghat there was no such development. At Kamrupa they are invoked before the worship of Kamakhya, but they could never become the regional tradition like the cult of Great Goddess in Bengal, Kamakhya in Assam or Jagannath in Orissa, where they remain attendants of main deities.

THE TERRIFYING BEAUTIES OF
THE DIFFERENT REGIONS

Hirapur

There are several distinct features of Hirapur Yogini that mark them out as a distinct class of images. They may not be treated as regional cult, but they tend to show a different identity and cultural attribute. The artist or the patron has left the mark of his efforts to identify the regional religious cults with Yoginis.

On the outer face of temple enclosure are images (Illus. 12 and 13—Chapter 1) of nine enchanting looking female goddesses, but they all stand on severed human heads or are associated with the dog and jackal. They represent the nine Katyayanis, the awe-inspiring and ferocious manifestation of Shakti, who according to Oriya version of the *Kalika Purana* were created by Durga along with the sixty-four Yoginis for the purpose of killing the demon (Panigrahi 1961: 291).

K.V. Saundararajan (1984:139) calls the sixty-four Yogini temple at Hirapur a subtle and esoteric perfumed garden in which elements of different Brahmanical cults were strongly amalgamated. It seems, however, that Hirapur Yogini temple was constructed under puranic influence. Here one finds the leaning of Oriyan *Kalika Purana* on one hand and *Chandi Shataka* of Sarala Das on the other.

The sixty-three figures of Yoginis enshrined at Hirapur are exquisitely carved and manifest fine workmanship. Whether their vahanas had some esoteric value or they were carved only with popular mythical belief is difficult to answer. The vahanas comprise of animals like the alligator, eagle, bull, boar, buffalo, camel, crow, cow, crab, duck, deer, elephant, fish, frog, horse, jackal, lion, monkey, mongoose, mouse, peacock, ram, scorpion, serpent, and tortoise.

The artist or the patron has left his mark. He was able to create a cultural identity for Hirapur Yogini. It does not mean that there was a complete shift from the conventional idioms or orthodox theology. But when deities like Ganga, Yamuna (Illus. 27—Chapter 1), Narmada (Illus. 26—Chapter 1), Chinnamasta (Illus. 86), Kali (Illus. 70), Tara (Illus. 15—Chapter 1), and Dhoomavati (Illus. 85) all have found place in this scheme. They show a beautiful amalgamation of tribal, puranic and tantric deities. The images address prevalent beliefs and compel one to interpret beyond the subject.

Significantly, at Hirapur, the Yogini images are clearly devoid of mother images. Though by this period other than Chamunda, the Goddess images are accompanied with a baby in Orissa. Neither Hirapur nor Ranipur-Jharial has reported any such image. Hirapur has depicted some rare forms in Yogini images like Tara (Illus. 15—Chapter 1) and Chinnamasta (Illus. 86), but surprisingly the most popular Yogini image of Mahismardini is missing here. At other temples Mahismardini is carved as a local deity and not as puranic goddess.[5] Here Viraja is depicted, who is considered to be a form of Mahismardini.

The Hirapur temple houses Viraja (Illus. 97) among its Yogini icons. She was a popular deity in Orissa. Its antiquity goes back to the sixth century. Viraja is also a Shakti pitha in Jajpur, in present-day Orissa. It was only in the medieval period that Jajpur recognized Viraja as its presiding deity. Iconographically, Viraja is supposed to be a form of Mahismardini Durga.

The image of Tara (Illus. 15—Chapter 1) is also surrounded by a fascinating debate. Is the Tara image the brahmanical Dash Mahavidya, the Buddhist deity Tara, or a tribal goddess? There is a temple for tribal Tara and Tarini at Puri. The Buddhist Tara has also incorporated many earlier tribal deities like Janguli and Parnasabari. Janguli is described in the *Sadhanamala* as being old as the Buddha himself. She was known to extract poison from snake bitten people. Parnasabari, another tribal deity, destroyer of all diseases, was also assimilated in the Buddhist pantheon. Tara, Buddhist and Brahmanical had been the deity of autochthonous groups and was incorporated in both sects (Sircar 1969: 133).

Tara as Yogini may have been the Brahmanical Dash Mahavidya, as other forms of Dash Mahavidya are also carved here. But the image responds to the attributes of its aboriginal prototype. It appears that their fusion continued even after transitional phase. The hairstyle, ornaments, dress, and gestures bear the marks of local craftsmanship. The elevation and acceptance of tribal deities is very strongly expressed here. Originally, the Jain goddess Padmavati is seated on the lotus and is snake-hooded. Padmavati is the most important female deity in Jainism. The Yogini Padmavati at Hirapur also shows an association with snakes, but the iconographical similarity stops here. It seems that there was only a conceptual similarity. It is not unlikely that like Janguli and Mansa she was also a deity of aborigines. Interestingly, all these deities, identified on the basis of Sarala Das' *Chandi Shatak*, sometimes do not correspond or conform to the conventional way of expression. Chinnamasta (Illus. 86) too does not follow accepted norms. Here she has not severed her own head and is not standing on the lotus, which is a union of Rati and Kamadeva. She is not even attended by two females at her both sides, who according to the Mahabodhi Tantra are Dakini and Varini, and in Buddhist tradition are the two Yoginis.[6] She is shown standing on a corpse merely holding a head.

Why do the iconographical details differ? Is it that the understanding of the artists and the interpretation of the myth differ? Chinnamasta first severs her head and then restores it at the end of the Sadhna. Chinnamasta is alive, she is shown being nourished or sustained not by death (sacrifice) but by captivating couples beneath her (Kinsley 1986: 175). This frozen moment of temporarily decapitating her head indicates her ability to transcend the dichotomy of life and death. Another possibility, proposed by O'Flaherty is that the head which Chinnamasta appears to be holding may not be her own, but that of Shiva. O'Flaherty (1980: 85) opens up a domain of ambiguity on the question. Benard (2000: 98) agrees with O'Flaherty and says that 'the question remains ambiguous, perhaps purposely ambiguous . . . but it is possible that some tantric texts may identify the head as Shiva'. Yogini Chinnamasta at Hirapur, however, is delineated differently. Her head is restored and she is standing on a severed head. The head could be of Shiva, but it could be also construed as pointing to self-sacrifice rather than self-destruction. Presumably, by this time, the entire myth of Chinnamasta may have taken a new form and turn. Chinnamasta's legend may have been popular here, but not the conventional image.

The distinct feature of the Hirapur temple is that here the orthodox pantheon images are manifested in native forms. At Bheraghat however the carving is in the classical mode, but the images are stamped with the local name. At Naresar the images of Ambika and Aparajita are carved in original way with no impressions of native influence.

Ranipur-Jharial

The Yoginis at Ranipur–Jharial show the frozen moments of dance. They may not be identified with puranic deities, but they appear to be the outcome of puranic traditions. Other than the dancing pose they are expressed as warriors holding weapons and in attacking posture (Illus. 67). They may be the manifestations of the *Linga Purana* and *Padma Purana*. The Yoginis decorating (Illus. 5—Chapter 1) themselves appear to be the Nayikas (heroines) of the Tantra Sara or Sura Sundari or Alasa Kanyas of the contemporary temples. Many of these do not appear to be divine, but women of flesh and blood.[7] Unlike the other temples, Ranipur-Jharial does not have a religious or ritual atmosphere. The images point to popular aspects. In contrast to Hirapur, the Yoginis here, though dancing appear to be dull, lifeless, and stereotyped. In contrast the Hirapur Yoginis are seductive and sensuous.

It is interesting to note that this site of sixty-four Yogini Pitha was famous for the activity of the Matta Mayura sect of Shaivism. We do not however, find any direct evidence to connect the temple with the sect (Donaldson 2000: 674).

Bheraghat

As stated earlier, the sculptures at Bheraghat, with conventional attributes, are labelled with local names. Only a few are Sri Varahi, Sri Padmavati, Sri Vaishnavi, or Sarvatomukhi. All these images establish a dialogue between art and rituals. Although it is debatable whether or not the images were carved for the performance of rituals or to fulfil some goal as part of the tantric pursuits, it is certain that the temple premises provided a platform for esoteric practices. Sri Phanendri (Illus. 52—Chapter 6), the snake goddess, is carved seated on a ghoul. Yogini Sarvatomukhi (Illus. 40—Chapter 2) is surrounded by musicians. Yogini Vibhatsa (Illus. 75) is sitting on a phantom and is wearing a skull garland. The faces of the ghoul and the phantom are of the skulls and bodies are of skeletons. Yogini Varahi (Illus. 7—Chapter 1) is shown kicking a woman.

Significantly, all the attendants and worshippers are women. One may be tempted to raise the hypothesis that women were involved in all these practices. According to the *Goraksha Samhita*, when Matsyendra Nath was roaming in Kadali Pradesh in the company of women, the men were prohibited there. According to the *Kaulajnananirnaya* and the *Kularnava Tantra*, the text of Yogini Kaula was known to all women of Kamrupa.

D.P. Chattopadhyaya (1981: 277) has raised this issue. He says that if agriculture was the invention of women then it was only logical that agricultural magic in its origin should belong exclusively to the province of women. Tantricism too originally consisted of ritual practices in which only women participated. The reason is, that tantricism has its source in agriculture rituals. Could it be possible that this happened in Bheraghat? One of the Yoginis is given the title *Ksetra Dharmini*, i.e. bearer of the region. The Yoginis were associated with the fertility cult as well. The temple was supposed to be constructed by Queen Ahana Devi. Chattopadhyaya (1981: 277) says that the idea of ritual resting mainly or chiefly on women may appear strange to us, but the ancient world was full of priestesses. Among the Tantrikas, female shamans, Bhairavi, and Yogini still occupy an important place. Chattopadhyaya also raises the question whether men participated in tantric practices as men or dressed in the female garb. He (1981: 278) addresses the question with the evidence of the *Acarabheda Tantra*: 'Worship the five principles (panca tattva), the sky flower (*khetattva*) and Kula woman, that will be Vamacara. The ultimate female force is to be propitiated by becoming woman (*Namo Bhutva Yajet Param*).'

He enquires, 'Why should the tantrikas thus try to become women? There could be only one answer. The practices were originally associated with women and were regarded as women's functions.'

Among the various details of these representations, we find the diagram of a triangle within most of the padma figures. The triangle as we presently see is invariably representation of the female genitals. This leads to speculation that the women carved here are: Shamans, Yoginis or Bhairavis performing rituals. They are the Shamans, deified with local names. So far as the Vamacara (Vama + Acara) is concerned, even N.N. Bhattacharyya (1977) has gone to the extent of calling the Vamacara with the same meaning that it is acara, i.e. practice of vama, i.e. woman. Referring to the Buddhist concept of the female force, Dasgupta observes that in the Carya songs we find frequent references to this female force variously called as the Candali, Dombi, Savari, Yogini, Nairamati, or Sahaja Sundari, etc. We also find frequent mention of the union of the Yogin with this personified female deity. The *Kaulajnananirnaya* and the *Kularnava Tantra*[8] also mention that they should be worshipped as the substitutes of the Goddess. In Carya songs it is often mentioned that the Yogi became effeminate, when possessed by the Goddess: 'The Yogin Kanha has become Kapali (Tantrika Shamaness) and has entered into the practice of Yoga and he is sporting in the city, in a non dual form.'

Another Carya song (Dasgupta 1950: Song No. 10) says,

One is that lotus, sixty-four are the petals—the Dombi climbs upon it and dances.

The Yogini images at Bheraghat appear to be shamans performing rituals. Unlike Hirapur, they may not be puranic or local deities, but the true Yoginis. Such a view emerges owing to the productive powers of women.[9] One of the Yogini's name Ksetra Dharmini, also indicates to fertility cult. Similarly, Sri Aindrajali (Illus. 101) denotes magical powers. Sri Rangini (Illus. 99) is shown being worshipped by quite a few women. Sri Vaishnavi (Illus. 76) is sitting on a ghoul. Yogini Sri Sarvatomukhi (Illus. 40—Chapter 2) is wearing a skull necklace. Sri Jhangini (Illus. 103) is watered by a Purnakumbha. Sri Aingini (Illus. 32—Chapter 2) herself is elephant-faced and supported by an elephant. Sri Phanendri is sitting on a ghoul. Sri Simhasimha is eating the hand of a skeleton. Sri Thakani (Illus. 167) has a halo. Sri Vibhatsa (Illus. 75) is sitting on a ghoul. Sri Amtakari (Illus. 53—Chapter 6), Sri Thakini and Sri Tokari (Illus. 36—Chapter 2) all create a fearful atmosphere, surrounded by female worshippers, burning lamps human skeletons, corpses and weapons. In the same way the platform of Yogini Sarvatomukhi (Illus. 40—Chapter 2) is carved with a cobra and the word 'Hrim'. The Simhasimha Yogini image shows one of the attendants eating a skeleton. The Aindrajali (Illus. 104) shows the skeleton and a devil's bell. The phallus of Simhasimha Yogini's altar shows being worshipped by yogi. 'Sri Jhangini' (Illus. 103) Yogini shows the third eye. *Chandika* is standing on a ghoul. The male figure is lying at the foot of 'Bhisani', 'Phanendri' (Illus. 52—Chapter 6), and 'Sri Lampata' signifies the human sacrifice. It was neither a tantric ritual nor the reminiscent of tribal element. Human sacrifice had been prevalent and had its sanctity even before the *Purusamedha Yajna* (human sacrifice). The Purusamedha is loaded with rituals. According to the *Satapatha Brahmana* (6.1.1), it is held for eight days, which may be extended up to forty days. The *Srauta Sutra* (XIV.6.1) emphasizes that it should be performed either by a king or brahmin. What was the significance of this human sacrifice yajna? The *Sankhya Srauta* (XVI.10.1) depicts that Prajapati gained from *Purusamedha* what he could not get from *Asvamedha*. The *Purusamedha* was performed for political gain, it is clearly stated in the *Srauta Sutra* (XIV.6.1) and the *Gopatha Brahmana* (V.8).

This exotic yajna did not cease with the Vedic period. In puranic religion and society, although the significance of the yajna was waning because of the emergence of the tirthas, these yajnas were still in practice. The *Vayu Purana* describes the Naramedh.[10] From the Puranas it is obvious that this sacrifice was not for the ordinary people but to enable royalty to make political gain. The eighty-one Yogini temples as suggested by the *Matottara tantra* was exclusively for the kings. The Kalachuri inscriptions also mention sacrificial posts. There is no open indication that these posts were for human sacrifice.[11]

Sri Kamada (Illus. 49—Chapter 1) is surrounded by female worshippers, her triangular pubis shows the vulva coming out of it. The three dimensional, inverted triangle is the symbol of the womb and feminine power. It is also the female emblem. It is drawn at a number of Goddess worship places. The three lines, which represent rajas, sattva and tamas. Since these three gunas are found in every entity, it signals creation. In the centre of the triangle is Bindu, which signifies the abode of the Goddess. It is known as Maha Shakti Pitha (the region of the Great Goddess).[12]

A strong tantric affiliation and ritual cannot thus be ruled out. The *Kalika Purana* (ch.61: 98) associates Kamada with sexual rituals. The platform of some images show two intersecting triangles, that is Shiva and Shakti.[13]

Come what may, the worshippers may not all have been women, but were predominantly women. Kings were also worshippers of Yoginis. Did they perform rituals in the garb of women? Do men as males participate in the tantric practice? It has already been mentioned that the female power should be invoked by becoming a woman. If the stretch of imagination permits, the *Kaulajnananirnaya* was known to every Yogini in each and every household of Kamrupa. Matsyendra Nath, the progenitor of Yogini Kaul was roaming in the company of women in Kadali Desh, where men were prohibited. The Yogini images here may be Shamans possessing magical powers. After deification, they all were stamped with local names with the prefix 'Sri'. They may not have been local deities, but real women. All these images appear to be involved either in rituals or being possessed. The *Kularnava Tantra* says that in place of the Goddess, dombi should be worshipped. As already mentioned above, the carya song says that

One is that lotus, sixty four are the petals—
the Dombi climbs upon it and dances.

This indirectly supports the hypothesis.

The Bheraghat Yoginis definitely dwell in an atmosphere of mystic and secret practices. Presumably, as it was built by the royalty, the temple was reserved for such practices. The Yoginis of Ranipur-Jharial present a totally different picture. The stone used at Hirapur was fine grained-chlorite, whereas the Yogini figure of this place are carved out of coarse grained sandstone and the figures are also weather-worn. Most of these Yoginis have either two or three pairs of arms and wear a conical headdress. Their attributes and gestures are stereotyped and they are carved in a stiff dancing posture. In many cases they carry weapons, especially the two armed figures or a Kapala. The Yogini images of Naresar manifest a similar idiom as at Bheraghat and Shahdol. Here the images are so blatant that they appear to be practising rituals. (Most of these images are housed in the Gwalior museum). Yogini Vaishnavi (Illus. 111) is seated on the Garuda (Hawk). She is holding a Garuda and a flower and is surrounded by female attendants. Indrani (Illus. 59—Chapter 7) is seated on an elephant and Kauveri (Illus. 47—Chapter 4) is sitting on a ghoul. The most fascinating and intriguing is Yogini 'Nivan' (Illus. 48—Chapter 4). She is not only sitting on a ghoul, she is also holding a human head. Yogini Uma (Illus. 100) is holding a baby, such depiction is very rare in Yogini images. The gesture is to protect the child: was it a part of some ritual for child's protection? The Yogini's name 'Uma' itself signals motherhood, and Yoginis are also associated with productivity. A Yogini image at Ranipur-Jharial is also supposed to be holding a baby. Pradhan (1983: 193) however does not think that this implies motherhood. Donaldson (2002: 668) appears to be agreeing with him. He takes it to mean killing of children. The Yogini looks fierce and holds a sword in her right hand.

There could be two alternatives: either that these images are inspired by Hariti, or that they embody the local folklore. In the Himalaya, during the head-shaving ceremony the Yoginis are worshipped before Kula Devatas.[14] It is intriguing here that the motherhood of these Yoginis had never been discussed. They are depicted as awesome deities. Here a genuine question arises as to whether these deities are benevolent or malevolent, auspicious or inauspicious. Marglin (1985: 80–2) considers this auspiciousness of her character as a dangerous attribute so too Pitchman (1997: 202). This leads to another question about the Goddess with spouse. Married Goddesses are supposed to be controlled by their spouses. Wadley's (1977: 118–19) remarks are significant here, who says that Hindu goddesses who are married and have thus transferred control of their sexuality to their husbands are generally benevolent, whereas independent goddesses, who control their own sexuality are malevolent. Shulman (1980: 212, 223–6) too takes domestication and marriage as a benevolent aspect: dangerous and sinister aspects of the Goddess are changed into positive, beneficent qualities with marriage and domestication. This model has its own limitation. It is applicable only in a particular situation. In the sixth and seventh century AD the Goddess was not hailed as a spouse but as a mother. Macenzie Brown (1990: 122–25) appears to be of the same opinion. The portrayal of the Goddess in the *Devi Bhagavat* and *Devi Mahatmya* is not as a married or unmarried Goddess. Following Kurtz,[15] Pitchman (1997: 204) holds that the favourable portrayal of an individual goddess, then, may have less to do with whether or not she is a wife, than with whether or not she is a nurturing motherly female. She suggests that in this regard, an order/disorder dynamic may underline the motherly/unmotherly paradigms. When a Goddess is portrayed as threatening patterns of order, regardless of whether she is married or unmarried, she is viewed as dangerously unmotherly and malevolent. And vice versa.

The Yogini images, however, defy working within a single framework and explanatory model. In 1962 Kosambi initiated this debate, when he said that they are mothers, but no father is required. The Goddess whether benevolent or malevolent, is regarded as mothers.

Here the images under discussion also fall in the same category. Nowhere in literature, they are known as mothers. They are always regarded malevolent and to some extent inauspicious. The folklores of Himachal Pradesh and Maharashtra narrate that they should be worshipped for the safety of the children.

In Maharashtra a 'Yogini vrata' is popular for the welfare of children. In Himalayan villages during the head-shaving ceremony, Yoginis are worshipped before worshipping the local or family deities. Their lists contain the names of the mothers also. Here they are not the spouses or the uncontrolled mothers. These images are not only the religious images, they are the stamp of the rituals being performed here. They reveal the hidden superstitions and beliefs of the period.

Hingalajgarh

Hingalajgarh is situated in Bhanupur district of Mandsor. This place has reported quite a few Yogini images, housed in the Bhopal State Museum, Indore State Museum and Bhanupura State Museum today. Unlike Bheraghat

Yoginis, these Yoginis are divinities. These are indeed goddesses, and not elevated local deites.

Images of Mahismardini have been found from Bheraghat, Khajuraho and Hingalajgarh. No mysterious or tantric influence could be traced at Hingalajgarh. The image of 'Ambika' is holding an infant. This is the third Yogini image reported so far which depicts motherhood, though in the text nowhere Yoginis are associated with motherhood. Yogini Aprajita is remarkable, as it is kicking the lying Ganesha with her right foot and has three eyes. As a Buddhist tantric deity, she was popular in Tibet and Nepal and her elevation was combative and contemptuous of the dominant structures of Hindu Gods and Goddesses. Her manifestation as one of the Yogini figures shows the phase of tantricism where Buddhist deities were incorporated in the Hindu pantheon. Chamunda is in her usual fierce aspect. Vainayaki is elephant-faced and a matrika is carved at both the sides. There is Maheswari with three-faces, Indrani riding on an elephant and Nagi with a serpent's hood behind.

The Hingalajgarh images are distinct in the sense that they convey sensuousness and divinity simultaneously.

Shahdol

Although currently no trace of a temple can be seen at Shahdol, this site has reported quite a few Yogini images. It is debatable whether on the basis of style, one can raise the hypothesis of two temples. The vehicles of Yoginis are animals, ghouls and dead bodies. Most Yoginis are shown in meditating posture.

Shahdol has also reported Mahismardini (Illus. 107), and inscribed with local name Krishna Bhagavati. Some Yoginis have innovative names like Tarala (Illus. 98). Yogini Tarini also occurs in this list. Tarala and Tarini are tribal goddesses in Orissa (Eschmann 1978: 90). The name Tarala as Yogini occurs in the list of Yoginis also. Other important Yoginis are Yogini Vrishbha (Vasabha) (Illus. 81), who is holding Ganesh on the left side of her lap. This Yogini is buffalo-faced.

There is Yogini Vasuki, holding a skull and sword in her left hand. The Yogini image of Sarvamangala is quite enchanting. The most remarkable image is that of Ambika, who was a Jaina Matrika. Jaina Tirthankara Nemi Nath is also depicted here. The Jainas have their own tradition of Yoginis.[16] The depiction of Ambika shows a sort of fusion or amalgamation.[17] Most Yoginis here are holding human skulls and sword. The attendants also created a fearful atmosphere as one of the attendants is chewing a human leg. It reminds one of the Simhasimha Yogini depiction at Bheraghat. One female attendant is holding a knife.

Usually local and tribal elements are pronounced in these images. Yogini Kaula worship, a sort of shava sadhana, and human sacrifice, are also carved. These images were not just tribal deities but as soon as they found a place in the Yogini group, the tantric influence could easily be seen especially on images found at Bheraghat and Shahdol.

The other group of Yogini images of Shahdol show them in standing posture. These images show a different and comparatively inferior craftsmanship. Here two dancing Yogini images are worth mentioning. Yogini 'Badari' (Illus. 45—Chapter 2) is performing tandava while another dancing Yogini is on the back of a ghoul.

This place has also reported a Mahismardini (Illus. 107) whose local name cannot be traced. Yogini 'Tlama' is displaying her magical power. In the same tradition, Naresar has also reported the Yogini images. Most Yoginis are headless. There is an inscription at the pedestal. Yogini is significant as she is holding a kid animal. Yogini 'Nivan' is holding a head and is sitting on a human. The first image signal the motherhood, while the second appear to be indicating human sacrifice. At Lokhari also, the images are animal-faced. They are following some local tradition.

Mitauli

In Mitauli (Illus. 54), very close to Gwalior, the structural remains of a Yogini temple can be seen. Some pillars are dated in Vikram Samvat (1245–1188). They are devoid of Halo and are in *lalitasana* (a sitting posture). Another remarkable thing is that name 'Vamadeva', is also carved on the images. Whether he was the sculptor or the acarya of the temple is not certain.

Bheraghat, Rikhiyan, Shahdol, Naresar, and Lokhari, show the presence of more or less the same tradition and local names. Mahismardini is found everywhere but she was identified with the local goddesses. There was a deliberate attempt to create a frightening atmosphere. One cannot just end it by writing that all tribal deities were brought to orthodox Hinduism. Here the artist was trying to show the influence of Yogini Kaula, which is missing at Ranipur-Jharial and Hirapur. Moreover at Shahdol, a temple of Matsyendra Nath is still in use. It must have been the main centre of Yogini Kaula worship.

There is a prominence of local deities; local Puranas in Bengal and Orissa were written. As the local cultures prevailed in the Yogini cult, all the Puranas have their own lists of Yoginis and the temples have their own deities as Yoginis. When one talks about idea and image, the question is whether the image follows the idea. The 'rhetoric of images' has a dual articulation. First comes a study of 'What images say', the way in which they speak for themselves by persuading, telling stories, or describing. The second, as a study of 'what we say about the images' writing on art as such that describe and interpret symbolic meanings (Mitchell 1987: 1).

In the Puranas the Yoginis are celebrated as ferocious warriors. In the popular texts also, they are manifested as bloodthirsty warrior deities. This form found expression in the images. They also delineate occult practices, that was, the very part of Yogini Kaula cult. Their ferocious aspect is clear in the light of the texts. But they are also presented as mothers. The artist has accepted the challenge as Uma from Naresar is animal-faced and she is holding a young animal. From Hirapur the Jaina deity Padmavati is reported, but at Shahdol and Hingalajgarh Padmavati is replaced by Ambika, holding a child. These images portraying motherhood, were either sculptor's fancy, or represent the difficulty in drawing the line between mothers and Yogini.

Yogini images also show the fertility aspect. Earlier agriculture was performed by women only. Chattopadhyaya (1981) has raised the question as to what happened to those women when the agriculture was taken over by men. These images show the fertility aspect as well as women's performance in these rituals. Most attendants in these images are women, performing occult practices.

The question is whether the images follow the prevalent puranic mythology or betray tantric influence.

Alternately, can we talk of an amalgamation of tribal, tantric and puranic influences in the carving of the images?

The Yogini temples were built before the date of these texts. It could be that these images, especially, Hirapur Yoginis, influenced the writings of these texts. It is rightly presumed that Sarala Das wrote *Chandi Purana* after visiting Hirapur Yogini temple. The *Kaulajnananirnaya* merely informs that the Yoginis wander on earth after assuming the forms of various creatures like animals and birds. The Kashi Khanda of *Skanda Purana* also narrates that the Yoginis disguised themselves as animals. Both texts are of eleventh century. It seems they compiled a tradition which was originally a source for Yogini imageries and their depictions.

The Yoginis as a group, and their warrior-like attributes, got a prominent place in the sculptures. Yoginis holding different weapons had been the favourite depiction. Their feminine aspects as deity, motherhood and above all womanhood, could find a place only at Hirapur and to some extent at Ranipur-Jharial.

Yoginis are projected as power and are independent of a male consort. Yoginis are the terrifying face of the feminine power. This motion was manifested in the imageries. (Some texts describe their beauty and feminine aspects also.) The depiction raises quite a few questions. In the Yogini Kaula, the Kula trees are of much significance. It is said that the Shaktas should always pay reverence to these trees in the morning. The Kula Yoginis dwell in all the Kula trees. One should not sleep under them or harm them.

At Hirapur, Yoginis are shown with vegetation, but they are not shown residing on these trees. Likewise, no text talks about the forms and gestures of Yogini images, they talk only about Yogini Cakras. There is no Matsyendra Nath in these depictions. According to Bagchi (1934: 6) the *Kaulajnananirnaya* is of the eleventh century. The legend of Matsyendra Nath became popular in Nepal and Bengal in the fifteenth century and the temples were built in between AD 900 and 1100. There is a strong possibility that the Yoginis of Yogini temple and those of the Yogini Kaula are two streams.

Thus the terrifying beauties bring out many inferences. They project a local cultural identity, but could not become regional cults. Bheraghat, Rikhiya, Naresar, and Shahdol Yoginis show a kind of similarity. The Yoginis display local tribal elements, and also strong influence of tantric rituals and occult practices. The Yoginis are warriors as well. Other than power, they show motherhood.[18] Their beauty mesmerised the art historians enough to call them Nayika. They were also celebrated for their feminine beauty and charm. They were Surasundari and Alasa Kanya, with the proclamation of Oriya *Kalika Purana* and *Chandi Shataka*, the imageries could assume a regional identity but not develop into a regional cult. The Yogini images are carved as puranic deities with tribal name and face. Sometimes they have even created a fearful atmosphere owing to tantric influence. They were divinities but attempts were made to bring them to the human level. The sculptures of different regions and places never followed the similar trend. It was the local beliefs in popular traditions that paved the way for these sculptures.

YOGINIS OF HIRAPUR

Yogini	*Mount*
1. Chandika	standing on a dead body
2. Tara	standing on a dead body
3. Narmada	elephant
4. Yamuna	tortoise
5. Mahananda	lotus
6. Varuni	water
7. Gauri	—
8. Indrani	elephant
9. Varahi	buffalo
10. Padmavati	snake
11. Ustragriva	camel
12. Vaishnavi	owl
13. Pancavarahi	boar
14. Bhadrarupi	drum
15. Charchika	demon
16. Vaitali	fish
17. Chinnamasta	head
18. Bindhyavasini	hill
19. Jalagamini	frog
20. Ghatavarahi	lion
21. Karkari	dog
22. Saraswati	lotus, conch
23. Virupa	water
24. Kuberi	seven wealth, sapta bhandara
25. Bhalluka	flower
26. Narasimhi	flower
27. Viraja	lotus
28. Vikata Nayana	—
29. Mahalakshmi	lotus
30. Kaumari	peacock
31. Mahamaya (main deity)	lotus
32. Rati	Kama Deva
33. Karkari	crab
34. Sarpasa	—
35. Yasha	stool
36. Aghora	goat
37. Rudra Gali	crow
38. Ganeshani (Vainayaki)	donkey
39. Vindhya Vasini	mouse
40. Shivani	scorpio
41. Maheswari	bull

42.	Ambika	mongoose
43.	Kamakhya	hen
44.	Chandra Kanti	lion
45.	Parvati	sandal
46.	Kali	Shiva
47.	Narayani	flower
48.	Bhagavati	—
49.	Samudri	conch
50.	Brahmani	books
51.	Agnihotri	cot
52.	Agnihotri	goat
53.	Aditi	parrot
54.	Stuti	sandalpot
55.	Svaha	yak
56.	Chamunda	musk deer
57.	Maruta	deer
58.	Ganga	crocodile
59.	Dhoomavati	duck
60.	Gandhari	donkey
61.	Missing	
62.	Sarva Mangala	deer
63.	Surya Putri	horse
64.	Vayuvega	deer

THE BHAIRAVAS

1. Svacchanda Bhairava
2. Purva Bhairava
3. Astanga Bhairava
4. Ekpada Bhairava

LIST OF VARANASI YOGINIS

1. Simhamukhi
2. Gridhayakshi
3. Kaktundika
4. Ustragriva
5. Shuramanani
6. Ululika
7. Sivasavi
8. Astavakra
9. Kotistha
10. Kunjiri
11. Lolajihva
12. Svadrista
13. Vanaranana
14. Rishakshi

15. Rukaraksi
16. Brihatatunda
17. Surapriya
18. Kapalhasta
19. Raktaksi
20. Kapotika
21. Pashahasta
22. Dandhasta
23. Prachanda
24. Chadravikrama
25. Shishudhvasa
26. Paphridaya
27. Rudhirapayi
28. Vastradhvaji
29. Garbhabhaksya
30. Shavahastayi
31. Antrapalini
32. Sthulakantha
33. Brihatkukshi
34. Sapasiti
35. Pretavahini
36. Danta Sukaraksi
37. Krauchi
38. Mrigaksi
39. Vrishanana
40. Vyavtasthayi
41. Dhoomanishvasi
42. Vyomekacharini
43. Kotarakha
44. Sthulamasika
45. Vidyutaprabha
46. Valaki
47. Marga
48. Kathaputali
49. Mrigakshi

VARANASI YOGINIS:
IDENTIFICATION WITH TEMPLES

1.	Gajanana	Ranamahal
2.	Hayagriva	Bhadaini
3.	Varahi	Kakmandir
4.	Mayuri	Ranamahal
5.	Vikatanana	Sindhiyaghat
6.	Shushkodari	Dyodar Vira
7.	Kali	Kalika Gana
8.	Urdhvavriksha	Phoolvatika, Maduadiha
9.	Kushmanda	Vinayaki
10.	Tapinya	Kalikagali
11.	Shoshanadrishta	Raj Mandira
12.	Attahasa	Kishorimala Haveli
13.	Kamaksha	Kamakhya Mandira
14.	Mrigalochana	Lalitaghat
15.	Shakti	Jhoriya Vira
16.	Chausatthi	Chausatthi Ghat

(Both these lists were given by Dr B.S. Mehta, Varanasi)

LIST OF JAINA SIXTY-FOUR YOGINIS
(Acara Dinakara, p.270ff.)

1. Brahmani
2. Kaumari
3. Varahi
4. Sankari
5. Indrani
6. Kankali
7. Karali
8. Kali
9. Mahakali
10. Camunda
11. Jvalamukhi
12. Kamakhya
13. Kapalini
14. Bhadrakali
15. Durga
16. Ambika
17. Lalita
18. Gauri
19. Sumangala
20. Rohini
21. Kapila
22. Sulakata
23. Kundalini
24. Tripurari
25. Kurukulla
26. Bhairavi
27. Bhadra
28. Chandravati
29. Narasimhi
30. Niranjana
31. Haimakanta
32. Pretasani
33. Isvary
34. Mahesvari
35. Vaisanvi
36. Vainayaki
37. Yamaghanta
38. Harasiddhi
39. Sarasvati
40. Totala
41. Candi
42. Sankhini
43. Padmini
44. Citrini
45. Sankini
46. Narayani
47. Paladin
48. Yamabhagini
49. Suryaputri
50. Sitala
51. Krsnapasa
52. Raktaksi
53. Kala Ratri
54. Akasi
55. Sristini
56. Jaya
57. Vijaya
58. Dhurmavarni
59. Vegesvari
60. Katyayani
61. Agnihotri
62. Cakresvari
63. Mahambika
64. Isvari

SRI BHAIRAVA-PADMAVATIKALPA

1. Divyayogi
2. Mahayogi
3. Siddhayogi
4. Ganesvari
5. Pretasi
6. Dakini
7. Kali
8. Kali(la)ratri

9. Nisacari
10. Hunkari
11. Siddhavaitali
12. Hrimkari
13. Bhutadamari
14. Urdhvakesi
15. Virupaksi
16. Suklangi
17. Narabhojahi
18. Satakari
19. Virabhadra
20. Dhumaraksi
21. Virabhadra
22. Raksasi
23. Ghoraraktaksi
24. Visvarupa
25. Bhayankari
26. Vairi
27. Kumarika
28. Candi
29. Varahi
30. Mundadharini
31. Bhaskari
32. Rastratankari
33. Bhisani
34. Tripurantaka
35. Roairvi
36. Dhvansini

37. Krodha
38. Durmukhi
39. Pretavahini
40. Khatavangi
41. Dirghalambosti
42. Malini
43. Mantrayogini
44. Kalini
45. Trahini
46. Cakri
47. Kankali
48. Bhuvanesvari
49. Kati
50. Nikati
51. Maya
52. Vamadevakapardini
53. Kshemadri
54. Rakta
55. Ramajangha
56. Maharsini
57. Visali
58. Karmuki
59. Lolakakadristradhomukhi
60. Madoyadharini
61. Vyaghri
62. Bhutadipretanasini
63. Bhairavi and Mahamaya
64. Kapalini Vrthangini

NOTES

1. A. Harper (1989) has tried to address the same concept for matrika images and after her work, S. Panikkar (1997) has followed the same methodology for Sapta Matrika images.
2. N.R. Ray (1967) raised the theory of major characteristics of medievalism in Indian History. By this, he meant among other things regionalization of the schools of art.
3. Discussed in Chapter 6.
4. Kunal Chakrabarti (2003: 309) in this work has traced the evolution of Mangalacandi in preference to Durga to highlight the process by which the local goddesses were universalized within cultural space of an experienced region and to show how the newly acquired syncretic identity of these goddesses in turn helped reinforce the regional identity of Bengal.

5. At Bheraghat and Hingalajgarh the icon of Mahishmardini is stamped with local names.
6. Chinnamasta is Brahmanical Dash Mahavidya and the Buddhist deity. The severed head denotes self destruction, Shiva or human sacrifice is not evident. In the absence of substantial evidence the third hypothesis is shaky.
7. Discussed in detail in Chapter 1.
8. *Kularnava Tantra* VII.42 says Candali, Carmakari, Magadhi, Pukkasi, Svapachi, Khattaki and Kaivarti should be worshipped as Shakti.
9. The *Kularnava Tantra* says (patal, VIII) that a Vesya (prostitute) should be worshipped.
10. For a detailed study see G.R. Sharma (1957–9: 85–205).
11. The Soma and Syena sacrifices are referred to in the Rewa Stone Inscriptions (Ins. no. 67, verses 32–3). The verse runs as follows: '*This city of men is an ornament of the region here, in which the multitudes of brahmanas bring the fires of Soma and Syena sacrifices to the altars, filling the surface of the earth with golden rings of the sacrificial posts (touched) by the rays of the sun, and in which they dwell making the sides of the altar resound with mantras laid down by (rules).*' Reference to the sacrificial posts is also found in the inscription no. 98, verse 36 (*CII* IV).
12. In Buddhism there are two types of triangle associated with Vajrayogini—single or double. In Kashmir Shaivism triangle is a step towards progress as the initial vibration expand, creation occurs. The next step is visualization of the solar disc which represents the universe with form as a reflection (of consciousness) (*Vimarsa*). This is followed by the triangle which represents the three saktis (powers) known as *iccasakti* (willpower), *jnanasakti* (knowledge) and *kriyasakti* (action). These three are sources of impulses which begin the process of differentiation. See Benard (2004: 91).
13. In Buddhist tantric philosophy it is Dharmodaya, though in *Nispannayogavali* it is stated that single triangle signifies 'Dharmodaya', Benard (2004: 91).
14. Discussed in Chapter 4.
15. Hence Kurtz wants to graft a motherly and unmotherly model (1992: 24–5).
16. See Appendix at the end of the chapter.
17. Ambika is also carved at Hingalajgarh.
18. Not accepted by some historians like Pradhan and Donaldson as discussed earlier.

ILLUS. 64: Sri Naini
(Shahdol)

ILLUS. 65: Maghali
(Naresar)

ILLUS. 66: Hands Joined
(Ranipur-Jharial)

ILLUS. 67: Yogini in Dancing Pose
(Ranipur-Jharial)

ILLUS. 68: Chandra Kanti
(Hirapur)

ILLUS. 69: Svaha
(Hirapur)

Illus. 70: Kali
(Hirapur)

ILLUS. 71: Bhagavati
(Hirapur)

ILLUS. 72: Narayani
(Hirapur)

ILLUS. 73: Animal Headed Yogini in Dancing Posture
(Ranipur-Jharial)

ILLUS. 74: Sri Brhmani
(Bheraghat)

ILLUS. 75: Sri Vibhatsa
(Bheraghat)

ILLUS. 76: Sri Vaishnavi
(Bheraghat)

ILLUS. 77: Sri Krisna Bhagavati
(Shahdol)

ILLUS. 78: Sri Jyoti
(Shahdol)

ILLUS. 79: Yogini
(Shahdol)

ILLUS. 80: Chamunda
(Hirapur)

ILLUS. 81: Sri Vasabha
(Shahdol)

ILLUS. 82: Finger on the cheek
(Ranipur-Jharial)

ILLUS. 83: Gandhari
(Hirapur)

ILLUS. 84: Maruta
(Hirapur)

ILLUS. 85: Dhoomavati
(Hirapur)

Illus. 86: Chinnamasta
(Hirapur)

ILLUS. 87: Agnihotri
(Hirapur)

ILLUS. 88: Parna Shabari
(Hirapur)

ILLUS. 89: Sri Narasita
(Shahdol)

ILLUS. 90: Sri Tarala
(Shahdol)

ILLUS. 91: Jalagamini
(Hirapur)

ILLUS. 92: Ghatavarahi
(Hirapur)

ILLUS. 93: Sri Erudi
(Bheraghat)

ILLUS. 94: Sri Padmavati
(Bheraghat)

ILLUS. 95: Sri Tamaka
(Shahdol)

ILLUS. 96: Gauri
(Hirapur)

ILLUS. 97: Viraja
(Hirapur)

ILLUS. 98: Horse Headed Sri Tarala
(Shahdol)

ILLUS. 99: Sri Rangini
(Bheraghat)

ILLUS. 100: Uma
(Naresar)

ILLUS. 101: Sri Satanusamvara
(Bheraghat)

ILLUS. 102: Ustragriva
(Hirapur)

ILLUS. 103: Sri Jhangini
(Bheraghat)

ILLUS. 104: Sri Indrajali
(Bheraghat)

ILLUS. 105: Tarini
(Shahdol)

ILLUS. 106: Sri Varahi
(Shahdol)

ILLUS. 107: Mahismardini
(Shahdol)

ILLUS. 108: Vaishnavi
(Hirapur)

Illus. 109: Yogini Cakra

ILLUS. 110: Sri Kapalini
(Shahdol)

ILLUS. 111: Vaisnavi
(Naresar)

ILLUS. 112: Varahi
(Naresar)

ILLUS. 113: Purva Bhairara
(Hirapur)

ILLUS. 114: Kaumari
(Hirapur)

ILLUS. 115: Varahi
(Hirapur)

ILLUS. 116: Panca Varahi
(Hirapur)

ILLUS. 117: Bhadra Rupi
(Hirapur)

ILLUS. 118: Stuti
(Hirapur)

CHAPTER TEN

Religion, Gender, and Yogini Imageries

USUALLY IT IS asserted that there are two well established paradigms for the study of gender and history. The first is the so-called nationalist approach which is popularly known as Altekarian model, and the second is its critique by Uma Chakravarti, and Kumkum Roy. The Altekarian model has been revived in the 1990s as *The Position of Women in the Yajnavalkya Smriti* by Manjusri, which as Kumkum Roy[1] suggests, 'adopt the paradigm wholesale and re-produce it unquestioningly'.

In 1996, Jamieson tried to show that woman's role in the Vedic rituals may not have been as significant as that of the man, but she played a considerable role as a mediator not only between man and man but also between god and man. Patton (1996) has traced the history of women sages in the *Rg Veda* through subsequent traditions and thus has tried to raise the question of their views and opinions. Uma Chakravarti (1999) had tried to show that the position of women was not as glorified as it has been held.

Sutherland Godman (2000) has made a recent and innovative attempt to analyse the attitude of males towards motherhood and wifehood. She gives a detailed analysis of myths about Vac, using it as a metaphor for female. Aparna Roy (2004) followed the Altekarian paradigm. It seems that these entire advances/notions/movement revolve around certain assumptions which we shall discuss below.

There is yet another movement, in which an attempt has been made to use Devi as a Metaphor for the position of women. Two such recent publications can be mentioned here. *Devi, Great Goddesses*, by Vidya Dehejia in 1999 and *Is the Goddess a Feminist? The Politics of South Asian Goddesses* by Alf Hiltebeitel and Kathleen M. Erndl in 2002.[2]

This debate may be seen as having been initiated by Kosambi (1962: 90) as early as in 1962, when he talked about mothers at cross-roads. Kosambi tried to identify the elements of feminism in the Goddess. He tried to distinguish between the goddess without spouse and goddess with spouse, saying that they are mothers but unmarried, and no father seems to be necessary in the society in which they originated. Gatwood (1985: 133) takes it as a specific manifestation of the process of Sanskritization in the sphere of religious symbols. The spousified goddess is regarded as representative of the high-caste woman, while the more autonomous deity is viewed as typifying low-caste woman. The acceptance of such deities within the orthodox framework is an attempt to bridge the gaps.

David Kinsley (1987: 4) also takes the insurgence of the goddess as a challenge or contrary to the social roles of the female as described in the *Dharma Sashtra*. Arvind Sharma (2000: 68) on the basis of the *Devi Mahatmya* says that what the gods could not achieve singly they decided to accomplish collectively in the form of a Goddess.

Hindu society is generally considered to be patriarchal, but proclaims an ancient tradition of Goddess. It was only in the sixth century that the Goddess re-emerged and one comes across the Yoginis as her attendants. It should however not be forgotten that in Vaishnava and Shaiva traditions she has male counterparts: Narayan, and Krishna, while Parvati appears to be inseparable from Shiva. When one analyses from this perspective, Indian religion does appear to be patriarchal. Where can we place her (Devi) as mother?

It was in trantricism that one finds the highest bliss in the form of Shakti. It was the male God's Shakti that supersedes him and who is much ahead of him. How does the Goddess re-emerge? It is said, what the trinity of the Gods could not achieve collectively, the Goddess achieved singularly. The present section addresses the following dimensions:

(a) Whether the Goddess or her powers, the Yoginis, are a metaphor for the empowerment of women.
(b) How one can explain the question of feminism, the queries of western theologians and feminists, through the cult of the Goddess.
(c) The tantric view of woman and the position of women during the period as reflected in the tantric texts.
(d) The question of the Goddess/Yoginis as mother, as spouse, as warrior, and what the imagery suggests.

Recently there has been a curiosity towards a powerful existence of feminine divinity. The Western feminist activists' notion is very amusing in this context, according to which the feminist movement is not required in India, as they have the Goddess in their religion. There is no single definition of feminism, however. Western feminism differs from Indian feminism.

King (1987: 201–2) notes 'the feminist movement is for the most part still a Western urban middle class phenomenon, where women have the necessary education and leisure to articulate the deeply rooted hierarchical and patriarchal structures of oppression embedded in our male dominated culture.'

Young (1993: XI, XXI-XXII) reminds us that almost every religion in one way or the other associates women with evil, women are often equated with the body and men with the spirit. Young goes to the extent of suggesting that women are often associated with evil qualities, such as blood-thirstiness or death (Kali, Durga) because of a male fear of sexuality.

When the Goddess reappeared around AD 500 she gradually took under her umbrella all marginalized deities. This is why an observation has often been made that the myths of Goddesses mean the recovery of the voices of subaltern and marginalized women. Thus Thomas Coburn (1991) writes: '(F)rom a western perspective, it seems natural to assume that the presence of a powerful figure as the Great Goddess must result in the general empowerment of women. Indeed the pivotal text on the Great Goddess, the fifth to sixth century poem Devi Mahatmya speaks of "all women as portions of Devi".'

The question here is whether the Goddess is a symbol and can be interpreted to empower women or to dis-empower them. But it should be remembered that Goddess is not merely a symbol to be studied or interpreted but is rather a living presence who reveals herself through a cultural and religious divide.

Anthropologist Wadley (1977: 111–35) and religious historian Pintchman (1993: 144–59) point out, 'it should be possible for today's women to re-interpret goddess myths to redefine their place in society'. Dehejia (1999:24) says: 'Myths have been analysed and re-interpreted over the ages. The ancient sages would certainly have been surprised when confronted with by scholar Wendy Doniger O'Flaherty's readings, yet that does not render her interpretations invalid.'

The question arises that when all the marginal and so-called subaltern goddesses are brought into the mainstream and are not found in their native cultural matrix, they become fluid with respect to both place and time, how should one view this in a patriarchal society? Can the myths, traditions, legends, and history of the Goddess substitute for the voices of women in society? Hindu society may proclaim an ancient tradition of the Goddess, but it is generally considered patriarchal. In the Vaishnava or Shaiva tradition she has a spouse, or a male counterpart. The Goddess as spouse is perhaps an attempt to bring the gods to level of human experience. At the same time, the Goddess appears as the highest 'Shakti' even 'Radha', who is initially projected as lover-consort, becomes Jagadamba, the mother of the world.

Here a dilemma appears. The goddesses are portrayed more as mothers or saviours than as spouses. Even folk songs that invoke them before ritual, they addressed them as mothers. Goddess as wife or spouse remains fully subsumed within the power of her male counterpart, philosophically rationalized as Jivatma and Paramatma, Prakriti and Purusa. In socio-political terms the bhakti mode of relationship between god and devotee is a non-violent means of social and political control (Narayanan and Kesavan 1987).

The devotee always approaches her as mother. The Bhakta (worshipper) prefers to worship her in her role as mother but not spouse. They are mothers, but distinct, in so far as they are also divine. It is not easy to explain this paradox. It becomes even more difficult to explain the relationship as that of Shakti and women's empowerment.

The Female Body and the Goddess: 'Tantric philosophy is based on a powerful feminine principle of calm and movable material and it presents the woman as the most natural manifestation of this feminine power. The female body is regarded as the Goddess. The Goddess in tantra is not the other half of the god. There is a maternal aspect but it is aggressive and ferocious.'

The orthodox schools used terms like impure and *asaucha* for woman's body. It was a sort of negation of the existence of women's body. The purification of this body is well expressed in Tantric texts. Rita Sharma (2003: 45) suggests: 'The purification referred to in tantric texts involves a multilayered visualization process whereby the aspirant envisions the presence of the divine mother in every part of the body/mind complex (Bhuta-Suddhi) since women are Shakti incarnate their self identification with the inner Shakti is considered easier and more natural.'

According to the Abarabhuta Tantra, 'One may be a vamachara (left handed tantric) only if one can worship vama (in the Vama style) being oneself a woman'—*Karpuradi stotra* 8 (Avlon 1953). Thus the body of woman is an object of worship, the highest bliss. The female body, which according to orthodox norms is an embodiment of impurity, in tantra becomes the highest means for realizing wisdom, both for the woman herself and for her spiritual partner.

What is the difference between Samkhya and Tantra's attitudes to the female body? In Samkhya the female principle is Prakriti, literally meaning nature, the primordial material/body that envelops the spirit. This led to the development of female divinity and in ancient India the body of the woman came to be regarded as a metaphor of nature. The ancient Indian materialist philosophy the Lokayata, within its material condition may be analysed as follows (Chattopadhyaya 1981: XVIII): 'Etymologically, *lokayata* means "that which is prevalent among people" and "that which is essentially this worldly".'

The most conspicuous feature of this outlook appears to be *dehavada*, the view that the material human body (*deha*) is the microcosm of the universe, along with a cosmogony attributing the origin of the universe to the union of the male and female (Chattopadhyaya 1981: XVIII). The material basis of primitive *dehavada*, according to Chattopadhyaya, lay in the fertility magic of the early agriculturist, which rested on the assumption that the productivity of the earth and the female can be enhanced or induced by ritualistic copulation, symbolically or in actual terms (Chattopadhyay 1981: XXI).

In Purusa-Prakriti relationship, Purusa remained secondary, indifferent. According to *Charaka Samhita*, Purusa is only a part of Prakriti; meaning that the consciousness as potentially contained in the primeval matter (Dasgupta 1922: 214–15). Dyzkowski (1988: 64) says that the body of the Yogini is supposed to produce Yogi. The Yogini is the womb from which the enlightened Yogi is born and her mouth from which issues the tradition is the sacred matrix (Yoni). It is suggested in the *Karpuradi Stotra* (Avlon 1953: 8) that

a worshipper should always be like the object of his worship. Woman is Devata, and the embodiment of the Supreme Shakti, and is as such, honoured and worshipped and is . . . never (to be) the subject of enjoyment.

The next question, that arises is whether this Goddess has given empowerment to women, a new identity to womanhood. While Hindu goddess worship in general does not seem to have explicitly endowed women with greater authority or autonomy, the ubiquitous presence of the female deity has framed the notion of Hindu womanhood in subtle ways. The ways in which Hindus relate women with goddesses may not be in keeping with western feminist concepts of female power and autonomy (Sharma 2003: 25).

The Goddess/woman relationship has been made more perplexing by those writers who wish to study it out of its historical contexts. This relationship has come out beautifully in Shaktism, where it is portrayed in the framework of Shakti and real life Yoginis, Shakti and low-caste women, and Shakti as spouse and mother.

In Vaishnavism and Shaivism female ascetics had been given a certain space, but it is only in Shaktism that the alliance of Goddess and woman had become vocal. Thus Payne (1979: 72) on the basis of the Devi Mahatmya says: 'She is not merely the power of the Absolute, she is the Absolute, while the entire cosmos is the material form of the Goddess, she is specifically identified with women' (V. 114).

However, this identification was not emphasized in the Shakta tradition. While the emergence of the Shaiva bhakti movement allowed women a certain degree of spiritual self-agency, the Shakta tradition (devotionalism directed towards Shakti) developed into a male dominated sphere. It is only in Shakta tantra that Goddess/woman identification is stressed and women's right to religious self-determination is affirmed, so much so that in tantra the two form intersecting and not coinciding circles. Unlike Shakta literature the tantra literature, stresses the relation between women and the Goddess, which is evident especially in folk songs, where the devotional aspect as well as the relation and identification is quite apparent when the Goddess is invoked as human.

The Journey from Human to Divinity: In Shaktism the Yoginis are female ascetics as well as Shakti herself. Thus the term sometimes becomes quite misleading, are they human beings, or deities, or a symbol? This uncertainty has brought out interesting analyses of gender and religion.

Dyczkowski (1988: 63) stresses that a branch is sprouting through the mouth of the Yogini, i.e. *Pascimamnaya*. Similarly in the *Kaulajnananirnaya* (Bagchi 1934: 89–90), it is inscribed: O Goddess! It [Kaulajanana] is heard as residing in ear [and not found written in books] and has come down through the line of teachers. This is *kaulika* (doctrine) transmitted from ear to ear.

In the *Pascimamnaya*, as in Kaula tradition in general, women are thought to have a special role to play as the transmitters of Kaula doctrine and take it straight from her lip:

Strimukhe niksipet prajnah

The Yoginis were indeed human beings of flesh and blood initially and gradually they became attendants of the Goddesses or came to have power of the Goddess herself. Thus sometimes it becomes difficult to distinguish between human and celestial Yoginis. The same tendency can be seen in folklore where Yogini, apsaras, and nymphs are equated together.

Human Yoginis do exist and prominently in the Virshaiva and other Shaiva traditions.[3] Working on Kanaphata Yogis, Briggs (1982: 48) found that: 'Women who have been initiated into the sect are numerous. Those who are wives of yogis are of two classes, those who are themselves Yoginis (in their own right) and those who are not.'

The height of the transformation of women into Yoginis has been described as follows: 'In the case of Kanaphata sect the aim is the homologization of one's consciousness with the dormant Kundalini Shakti within deemed a much easier task as the aspirant is herself female.'

Briggs (1982:120) notes that the Yogi attempts to identify the self with Tripura Sundari (an ultimate form of Shakti) by thinking of himself as a woman. Perhaps this is the highest way of showing reverence to women. In Vaishnavism Chaitanya became Radha when he goes into extreme trance.

Rita Sharma (2003: 40–1) cites another example in which the tantric attitude towards women is quite apparent.

Female siddhas (adepts) have a long history in the Gorakhnath sects. The earliest reference to a female Nath mystic is in the legend of Queen Mayanamati, a disciple of Gorakh Nath, who came to be regarded as a highly advanced Yogini with mystical insight and magical powers. Mayanamati's son Gopi Chandra, guided to the yogic path by his mother, renounced his throne, was initiated by a Guru chosen by

Mayanamati and became a legendary Natha Yogi himself. Here again, the tantric attitude of acceptance towards women is clearly evident.

This evidence is very interesting as the legends narrate that Gorakh Nath relieved his guru Matsyentra Nath from the mystic mesmerization of Yoginis, which is also narrated in *Kaulajnananirnaya*. But even in the life of Goraksha Nath the importance of Yoginis cannot be denied.

The female body, which is in orthodox terms supposed to be infused materially, becomes in tantra the highest means of realizing wisdom, both for women and their spiritual partners. Rita Sharma asserts the identification between Yogini and Shakti very strongly. She even refers to Kashmir Shaivism to make her point. The Krama school of Kashmir Shaivism, which exhibits a distinctly tantric-Shakta-orientation (in context to systems such as the Pratyabhijna and Trika which are strongly Shiva centric), is traditionally thought to have been founded entirely by Yoginis.[4]

As pointed out (Dyczkowski 1988: 63–4) in Pascimamnaya and in all Kaula traditions in general, women are thought to have a special role to play as the transmitters of Kaula doctrines:

One should place wisdom in the mouth of a woman and take it again from her lip. The lower mouth which is the mouth of the Yogini, is generally considered by the Kaula tradition on the whole to be the source of Kaula doctrine. . . . The Pascimamnaya, like other Kaula traditions, calls this face 'Picu Vaktra' the face of Picu, incidentally the face of Yogini is also called Picu.

There is another significant feature of the Yoginis as preservers of Kaula tradition. The tradition, which emerges from Yogini's mouth, is called the Pashchimaamanaya Shaiva Shastra. The Siddhantagamas also consider the Kaula tradition to be represented by two of eight subsidiary currents (*anurotasa*), associated with five principal currents of the Shaivagama. These two are called Yogini Kaula and Siddha Kaula. The Yogini Kaula is so called because Yoginis heard it from Shiva's mouth and kept it within their own line of transmission.

It appears that when in the post-Gupta period trantricism became popular female ascetics were held in high reverence. They were identified with Shakti, to whom Shiva revealed the secret of the Kaulas, which they kept in secrecy. From human beings they became deities and thus there developed a cult. These Yoginis, who carry the secret Jnan (knowledge), crossed the threshold and became the deity themselves. The dividing line between Goddess and female ascetic became narrow, the Yogini became a symbol for women and for the Goddess.

Thus Shiva says to Parvati at the beginning of the *Yogini Hridaya Tantra* (I: 26–30) of Sri Vidya school: 'Listen! Devi, to the Great Secret, the Supreme

Heart of the Yogini. Out of love for you I will tell you today that which is to be kept well concealed that which has been taught from ear to ear, and so reached the surface of the earth.'

It seems that gradually the Goddess and female ascetic became synonyms.

The identification of Shakti with the common woman is more tricky than the journey of mundane Yogini to the super mundane. The relation of woman and the Goddess (divine mother), is not easy to explain from a western perspective. In tantra, it is not the female body that was an object of worship. Here even the priest (read priestess) is woman. There is no rigidity towards the body of the woman. The dichotomy of pure (saucha) and impure (asaucha) does not exist here. The women are not barred from participating in religious rites. Not only were enlightened or ascetic women are taken as the deity. The very low origin and outcaste women like Ganika, Shilpi, and Rajaki are to be worshipped as substitutes of the Goddess.

How do contemporary literature and the Puranas depict the position of women? Do they substantiate the description of Shakti? Or was the description of Shakti limited to their cult? Can we try to translate this reality of Shakti into Yoginis?

The Yoginis were originally the gram devatas and they owe their origin to Yakshinis also. Though with the spread of tanricism the Yoginis were also assimilated within the realm of orthodox Hinduism, the demarcating line is not very clear. They are mentioned in the later Puranas and entire tantra texts were written for them. The Puranas from the *Matsya* to the *Agni* reveal a fascinating development of these regional deities. Their assimilation into the mainstream is best referred to in the Puranas. The *Deshdharma* or *Locacara* of the Puranas strengthen this notion. These Yoginis were equated with witches and half-divine females in the folklore and tradition. It has been suggested that that they are human beings, women possessed by the goddesses. Even in the carya songs we find frequent references to the female force, variously called a Candali, Domli,[5] Sabari, and Yogini.

Women may have become spiritual preceptors in puranic society, but the age-old tradition of the Devadasi did not perish. The Lalitopakhyan section of the *Brahmanda Purana* and Kashi Khanda of the *Skanda Purana* refers to four types of the female slaves. The *Skanda Purana* says that the Devadasis hailed from Kshatriya clans.[6]

For the position of the widows the Puranas say that she should discard her ornaments, fine clothes, and keep unkempt hair.[7] Women, it however appears, were independent of their spouses, so far as independence in religious matters was concerned; they were performing religious rites independent of their husbands. Tara, wife of Bali, was participating alone in the *Svasti Yaga*.

This does not imply that the elevation of the deities signals a progressive rise in the status of women. Yoginis have non-Sanskrit names they can also be labelled as the icon of Mahismardini at Bheraghat and Shahdol. This has been understood as a mask of tribal customs (Gatwood 1985: 232). Even so Yoginis could not remain in orthodox Hinduism permanently. The Yoginis once held so high in the *Skanda* and *Agni Purana* and tantra texts were gradually demarcated and found a place in the Shabara mantras, prevalent in a low-level witchcraft. They are among the list of ghosts and spirits.[8]

In the period when the *lokadharma* of the Puranas was popular, the Yoginis reveal a particular social reality, rather than concealing it. Here we find women as daughters, deities, and devotees, and the ways and extent to which they show deviation from the orthodox framework. If one can borrow Parl Ricoeur's terminology (1970): 'there are those who engage in a "hermeneutic of recovery" and those who engage in a "hermeneutic of suspicion".'

The question here is, whether this entire discussion regarding women's place in Shaktism delinates women's place in general. It appears strange that feminist historiography should treat the Goddess as a metaphor, and seek solace in her symbol.

The problem is that we are trying to see a religious phenomenon from today's social reality. The Goddess has been depicted as saviour, or mother, Jagadamba (mother of the world). Just because she is a feminine power, her presence cannot be translated into the position of women. The Goddess was the need of religion. She was the requirement of a political structure. Her emergence in AD 600 had brought the marginalized goddesses into focus. The attributes of the tribal goddesses were merged into one Great Goddess. Because of the acceptance of tribal rituals and customs, Shaktism was liberal towards women in general and of low origin in particular. It was owing to the political need that the suppressed voices of women were brought to centre.

The question of a Goddess ensconced in a patriarchal framework does not arise here. Male Gods worshipping the Goddess may not present a symbol of the powerful position of woman in the society. The 'feminist' movement is the outcome of a totally different perspective. Goddess worship had always been there in the society. There was no inherent advocacy that a powerful symbol like Goddess be translated into the question of gender.

NOTES

1. Paper presented at Jawaharlal Nehru University, February 2001
2. For a detailed discussion on both these articles please refer to author's paper, *South Asian Goddess: Western Perspective*, being published by IIAS, Shimla.
3. For an interesting discussion on as to how it has influenced Sufi female ascetics see Chapter 2.

4. The *Rajatarangini* perhaps could not make a distinction between female ascetics (Yogini) and the Yoginis with magical powers.

5. In UP at Gorakhpur there is a locality, known as Dominpura and another known as Yoginipura.

6. *Devadasi Brahmadasi Svatantra Sudradasika*
   Dasi Caturvidha Prokta Dve Yadye Ksatriyasam
   　　　　　—Skanda Purana, III, 4.811–12
   There are four types of female slaves—Devadasi, Brhmadasi, Svatantra and Sudradasi. Among them the first two hail from the Ksatriya clan.

7. *Nari Yadbarta akasmattanuste tyaktabhusanam*
   Na Rajate Tatha Sakra Mlanvastrasiroruha
   　　　　　—Matsya Purana, 1893, 154.19
   A widow woman should discard the ornaments, she should keep unkempt hair and the fine clothes don't suit her.

8. The Shabar mantra runs like this:
   Om namo Bismillah Rahimane Ul Rahim
   Bhoot Pret ko chalao chaunsth Yogini ko chalao
   (Hail and Greetings to the Hindus and Muslims and their auspicious signs, then flee the ghosts, imps and sixty-four Yoginis.

Conclusion

THE ARGUMENTS SPREAD across the ten chapters in this volume are dispersed. Yet they may be seen as consciously woven around a single theme, which is to show the specific ways in which the Yoginis may be seen as symbols. I have explored the symbolism of the Yoginis, through these several chapters, as manifesting itself in a special way. As symbols, Yoginis are not speaking for, standing in place of, or substituting a text. Nor are they simply images obscuring social and historical processes. The symbolism is complex, and may be read as the representation of quite a few hidden myths and rituals. Yet, such a reading may open itself to charges of exoticization. Thus every quest towards 'reading' the Yoginis would remain unsatisfactory, leaving a range of 'why' questions unresolved and unaddressed. While each aspect of this reading will remain incomplete in so far as it offers only a partial explanation, every reading may be seen as looking at an 'aspect' of the Yoginis, and thereby complete in itself.

If we turn to the crucial question pertaining to how and why the group of sixty-four Yoginis developed, we find a shroud of mystery surrounding it, in terms of the scarcity of available resources. There are, however, different interpretations that one encounters while exploring this question. One trajectory of development and the corresponding interpretation, sees the emergence of the Yoginis from Yakshinis and their subsequent assimilation in the sixty-four Yoginis. Another level of interpretation sees this development as the acceleration from women of lower origin to priestess and from priestess to divinity.

The popular view is that the sixty-four Yoginis became popular after Matsyendra Nath wrote his *Kaulajnananirnaya*. The legend of Matsyendra Nath and his association with Yoginis is also well known and figures in later texts and folk tales. On the other hand, while the sixty-four Yoginis occur in a number of Puranas, none of these Puranas, mentions Matsyendra Nath. Moreover, it appears that the Yoginis of the Yogini Kaula were different from the Yoginis mentioned in the Puranas. The Puranas had an earlier tradition of the Yoginis. Thus the *Kalika Purana* (about AD 700) mentions eight Yoginis as the attendants of the Goddesss. Furthermore, the temple of Yoginis are different, and may be seen to have been carved according to local needs and prevalent beliefs.

There appears to be a different tradition, which picked up the sixty-four Yoginis according to its myth to suit its religious pursuits. Yogini Kaula, which was started in Kamrupa in Assam by Matsyendra Nath, had been an esoteric cult. Both the *Kularnava Tantra* and *Kaulajnananirnaya*, say that each and every woman at Kamrupa, who was a Yogini knew this text.[1]

As far as the question whether Yogini Kaula a Shaiva or Shakta cult is concerned, one may see it as pointing to a transitory stage, where one sect blends into the other. The legend was taken into folklore too and Matsyendra Nath, Gorakh Nath, and sixty-four Yoginis became popular parts of the folklores of Himachal Pradesh, Kumaon and Garhwal. The episode of Matsyendra Nath and Yoginis became very popular in Bengal and Nepal. Matsyendra Nath along with his disciple Goraksh Nath remain integral to many folk songs. The folklore tradition was, however, entirely different.

One may discern, however, different levels in the development of Yoginis from eight Yoginis of *Kalika Purana* to sixty-four Yoginis of tantricism. Their rise, moreover, was as surprising as their waning out. Tribal and local deities were accepted in their fold but the latter were not the parent source for them. Prevalence of tantrcism could be one of the factors behind it. The Yoginis were initially real women, who were gradually deified. The *Kaulajnananirnaya* and *Kularnava Tantra* emphasize the fact that the Devi may be substituted by women of low origin. The Dash Mahavidyas were also supposed to be mundane women earlier. Some of the Yogini images, especially in Bheraghat, appear to be performing their rituals and concealing their identity with a ferocious exterior.

Some scholars hold that the Yoginis evolved from Yakshinis. Both were originally residing in trees. The Yoginis had their dwellings in Kaula trees. In Himalyan folklore, the Yoginis are equated with the giggling Apsaras. The affinity between the Yakshinis and the Yoginis, however, stops here. Unlike Yoginis, Yakshinis are depicted as benevolent. The *Tantra Sara* says that the Yakshinis bestowed boons, whereas the Yoginis are of malevolent nature. The images of the Yoginis reveal that they are an outcome of the assimilation of the tribal deities into the Brahmanical fold. Tantricism gave them a separate identity other than attendants of the Goddess.

It seems that the fierce exterior of the Yoginis worked as a facilitator, compelling one to delve into the hidden world of the Yoginis, as well as an obstruction, impeding further explorations. In many ways, the fierce exterior of the Yoginis signifies a tussle between the 'authentic self' and the 'other'. In their original forms, tribal deities were priests symbolizing the self. The Sanskritization of these deities may be seen as a process of their 'othering'. The exterior is the 'me' that is hiding the 'other'. In tantricism, there was a tendency to conceal the real identity. The real deity of a *pitha* was not displayed.

It is often asserted that the rituals performed will never be known. But texts like *Kularnava Tantra, Kaulajnananirnaya* (Chapter 8) and *Mahanirnavatantra* narrate the rituals. The most fascinating account, moreover, is presented by the images themselves. The images may reveal answers about rituals, human sacrifice, the depiction of sex organs, worshippers, and priests.

It is not that the images were confined to a depiction of these aspects. An assimilation and 'travelling' of goddesses from one tradition to the other is also revealed. Thus, among the diverse puranic, Buddhist and Jain traditions of Goddesses, there appears to be a stage when the dividing line becomes blurred. Among the 'travelling' Goddesses, the assimilation of the Buddhist deity Aparajita is not surprising. The *Kaulajnananirnaya* shows a stark similarity with the Buddhist tantras. There has been an attempt among scholars to trace shades of sectarian and regional influences on these images. While the images delineate different Shakta and Shavite rituals, the distinction is not blatantly reflected. So far as regionalism is concerned, each and every site has its own individuality and native fingerprints. Although the images show traces of regionalism, the Yogini cult did not emerge anywhere as a regional cult, though the images show a degree of regionalism. Local features and characteristics find strong expression in the images which have been found at diverse sites. This persistence of local characteristics has naturally led to the query whether like the Goddess cult in Bengal, Radha in Vrindavan, and Jagannath in Orissa, the Yogini cult developed as a regional cult. While looked at from the perspective of the art historian, the images may be seen as delineating regional features. But being of an esoteric and mystic nature, they could never become a predominant regional cult.

The mystery of the temples, however, does not cease with a discussion of images. Another pertinent and persistent question is who the builders of these temples were? The question becomes even more befuddling, when one considers that these temples were not confined to specific dynasties or territories, but are found in the territories of different contemporary dynasties. Often the rulers of the said regions have almost 'naturally' been assumed to have been builders of these temples. On the other hand, none of the inscriptions of the concerned rulers proclaim the authorship of these temples. Only two later Andhra inscriptions mention that the Yogini temples were built by the royal people. The general silence on the Yogini temples in the royal inscriptions could perhaps be attributed to gains that rulers expected to garner from secret pursuits pertaining to the Yoginis. Moreover, it was often said that whoever would disclose the secret of Yoginis, would be victim of their wrath. Whatever the reasons for the silence, they have contributed to aggravating the mystery shrouding the Yoginis and their temples.

The ground plans of these temples have been attributed to inspirations ranging from tantric yantra to women's pelvis. The Puranas mention temples of sixty-four and eighty-one rooms. They do mention Yogini images, but are conspicuously silent about the structure of the Yogini temples. In Buddhist mythology, the Dakinis, the counterpart of Yoginis, are supposed to reside in open temples, that generate energy. Such a structure, for Dakinis, has been made in Tibet. While Sonbhadra from Madhya Pradesh reports a circle of stones with a triangle inside, a structure traced back to the Upper Paleolithic period, by and large such structures were limited to Buddhism. Thus it may be said that the peculiar structure of Yogini temples may have had its origins in primitive and contemporary constructions.

Among tribal deities and temples a 'methodological' evolution can be found. First, there is an idea, which later takes the shape of an image, which is subsequently installed in a temple. The Yogini images from Bheraghat, Mitauli, Naresar and Hirapur bear the mark of tribal connection. As mentioned earlier, popularly the idea of Yogini is supposed to have been derived from Yakshinis. The evidence, however, suggests the other way. It seems that the Yoginis became part of folklores when they were equated with Yakshinis.

A different development trajectory may also be traced pointing to an evolution of the idea. At the conceptual level, the Yoginis may be seen as having found expression in the tantras. The Yoginis of the tantric texts are different. As *Mantra* and *Svara* they reside in different organs of the body, and are simultaneously also the residing deities of different regions. They are equated with Vatukas and Bhairavas.

The Yogini of the Puranas, on the other hand, are conceived as the attendants of the Goddess, or different forms of the Goddess. The *Skanda* and *Agni Purana* contain lists of Yogini names, that include some non-Sanskritic names. The texts describe the Yogini tradition differently. The *Kaulajnananirnaya* could become popular only after the fifteenth century in Bengal and Nepal. This may be the reason why the Puranas do not mention the tradition of Matsyendra Nath and his Yogini cult. The Jains while incorporating Shaiva elements, developed their own list of sixty-four Yoginis, with Kshetrapal as their leader. The Buddhists evolved the counter-form of the Yoginis, viz., Dakinis.

Since most Yoginis emerged locally and were later submerged into the great Goddess after their elevation, it is naturally asked whether they signify the Great or Little Tradition. This model, we have seen, is not of relevance to this study. The Yoginis are Great and Little goddesses at the same time. They occur in folk songs and in tantric texts.

Initially, the sixty-four Yoginis are supposed to correspond to 'women' rather than 'icons'. The *Kaulajnananirnaya* clearly says that this text is known to each and every woman of Kamrupa, who were Yoginis. Evidently, the

Kaulajnananirnaya equated Yoginis with real women. Subsequently, however, the women were deified and became goddesses. Even the ten Mahavidyas are supposed to be real women. If one tries to look beyond the images, some of which do appear to be of real women, especially in the temples of Ranipur-Jharial, Bheraghat and Shahdol, they appear to be participating significantly in some ritual.

Questions have been raised as to why no Yogini temple has been found in Assam, Bengal, or Nepal. As mentioned earlier, the Yoginis of temples do not belong to a single tradition. They belong to different traditions and in each case the local goddesses were accepted, assimilated, and elevated. The temples were subsequently constructed to perform rituals. In addition, their representational forms appear to have been distinct as well. Although Assam,[2] Bengal, and Nepal do not report the existence of Yogini temples, the Yoginis were worshipped in geometric form on palm leaf or cloth. The legend of Matsyendra Nath was also prevalent in Assam, Bengal and Nepal. The construction of temples in the regions in which they have been found, may be attributed to political reason as well. It is possible that the kings wanted to fulfil their ambitions through the temples, and second, by accepting the local deities they wanted to please and win over the conquered subjects.

Images of the deities usually address the invisible hands of the artists and the visible devotion of the worshipper. Throughout the depiction of these 'terrifying beauties' the tension between the two is quite obvious. The Yoginis with their beautiful limbs and awesome faces convey the genuine attempt of artists who appear to have been well-versed in local myths and culture. They also reveal that some of them were carved for the worshippers only.

The Yoginis are not only celebrated in the folk songs, there appears to be a connection between Yoginis and Jogati of Andhra Pradesh and Karnataka. The question has been raised whether some of these Yogini sculptures may have been of dancing devadasis. The depiction was not limited to the divinity only. Some of them were not manifestations of the goddess. A stark contrast in the imagery, therefore, emerges, especially if one compares the images of Hirapur and Ranipur-Jharial. If the Hirapur images have been identified with different goddesses, the Ranipur-Jharial images were inspired by the dancing Devadasis.

Despite having become part of the esoteric cult, some Yogini images are still scattered as village deities in the villages of Orissa and Madhya Pradesh. The Yoginis of the Yogini cakra and kaula may not have been known here, but the germination of the cult may be visualized from these native deities.

The sixty-four Yoginis may not be written off merely as a tantric cult of early medieval India. It narrates some more important issues, pertaining to the development of Yoginis from folk deities to the Great Goddess, and simultaneously issues of the plural forms in which the Yogini imagery existed, and extended to include ordinary women, and dancing Devadasis.

There are many layers of enquiry about the sixty-four Yoginis, and several more remain to be opened up, considering that what is largely seen as a secret cult, would not have grown in isolation. Apart from enquiry into the plural traditions of the Yoginis, the Yogini Kaula, the Yogini cakra, the temple, and the Yoginis of folklores of tribes, above all the 'mask' of the Yoginis should be penetrated to reveal the multiple processes that went into the making of the Yogini.

NOTES

1. It was supposed to be transmitted from Shiva to Devi.
2. Assam is one of the few areas where Yogini cakra is still made.

Locations and Narrations

LOCALES OF THE KNOWN YOGINI TEMPLES

Orissa

The Hirapur Yogini temple was built around AD 900. It is situated in the village of Hirapur on the banks of Bhairavi river 15 km. east of Bhubaneshwar. It is the smallest of all the Yogini temples. The temple is still in the practice.

The Ranipur-Jharial Yogini temple was built around late AD 900.It is in the interior of Orissa in Bolangir district near Sambhalpur, a village in Paragana Loha known as Ranipur-Jharial. Its dimension is almost twice the size of Hirapur, but the sculptures are weather-worn.

Central India

The Shahdol temple was probabaly built in AD 1100 or 1200, a short distance from Amarkantaka in Shahdol district. Here there is possibility of two Yogini temples. The sculptures lie in the villages of Antara and Panchagaon, and in the Museums of Dubela and Kolkata. There is a temple of Matsyendra Nath also.

Built around AD 1000–1100, the Bheraghat temple (Jabalpur, MP) though known as Chaunsath Yogini Temple, houses eighty-one Yogini images, most of them are defaced and vandalized. Only one third remain intact. After 200 years another sanctuary in the Nagar style was constructed. An inscription mentions Queen Gosala Devi and her two sons who in 1190 dedicated the temple to 'Bhanagna Khidra', the 'Slayer of Illness'.

Unlike other Yogini temples, the Khajuraho Yogini temple is rectangular. The Yogini temple in Khajuraho is constructed along a vertical north-east-south-west line and a horizontal south-east-north-west line. There is a larger niche, perhaps for the main deity, with sixty-six other niches. The niches are empty. Only three images have survived, which are stored in the local Museum.

The Badoh temple is situated in Vidisha district, MP, 18 km. away from Kulhar village. According to local tradition it was built by a shepherd, that is why it is called the temple of Gadarmal. Badoh temple appears to be built during 1000 and it is rectangular in shape. Instead of sixty-four Yogini images here we have forty-two.

Mitauli is situated near Gwalior two miles away from Padavali. There are sixty-five niches and an altar for Shiva-Bhairava. No Yogini image can be assigned to Mitauli. One sculpture now located in the Fowler Museum in Los Angeles possibly comes from Mitauli temple.[1]

Naresar is 20 km. away from Gwalior in a lovely picturesque surroundings. About twenty Yoginis have been transferred to the Gwalior Museum. Here the Yogini images are inscribed, but the inscriptions postdate the images.

Dudhahi is 20 km. from the town of Lalitpur at Pali. Local people call it 'Badi Dudhahi'. Like Badoh, Dudhahi also contains forty-two niches for Yoginis. The temple is of circular shape and is tenth century in date.

Thirteen kilometres away from Mau in Banda, 80 km. away from Khajuraho, Rikhiyan has a number of temple ruins, but there is no trace of a temple of Yoginis. Currently none of the Yoginis are there at original site.

Lokhari is on the top of the hill in Banda district, UP. There were about twenty Yogini images, but now only a few remained. Lokhari images are remarkable for their beautiful workmanship, sensuous bodies and animal heads.

Hingalajgarh is in Mandsor district of MP at the border of MP and Rajasthan.

SOUTH INDIAN YOGINIS

Kanchipuram

It is a matter of speculation whether the Yogini images published by Jouveu-Debreuil, should be identified as Yoginis. Kanchipuram could be site for Yogini temple. But does it have Yoginis or ferocious looking mothers? They belong to the group of sixteen mothers. The temple may have been built in the second half of tenth century by a local ruler threatened by the increasing power of the Rashtrakutas.

Besides the locations mentioned above, there are places associated with Yoginis: Varanasi and Ujjain.

The Kashi Khanda of the *Skanda Purana* narrates that Shiva sent Yoginis to Kashi. Currently at the river bank there is Chausathi Ghat (sixty-four bank) and in a narrow street there is a temple of Chausathi Devi.[2] Ujjain has been associated with the Yoginis in the myths, legends, and Sanskrit texts.

According to local tradition there was a Yogini temple, now there is a modern construction. On the outskirts of the city there is a shrine of Matsyendra Nath.

YOGINI IMAGE NARRATIONS
(Unless Stated Photographs are taken by the Author)

Bheraghat
(*Photographs Courtesy:* American Institute of Indian Studies)

ILLUS. 7 (Chapter 1). She is boar-headed and three-eyed Goddess. She is seated on lotus in *ardhparyanka asana*. She has four broken arms. Her right leg rests on a lotus and there is a lotus motif at the soul of her right foot. Under her right knee there is a boar running to the right. Beneath her right knee a four-armed goddess is seated on a cushion. She is holding a discus in the upper raised hand. The upper left hand is in *abhaya mudra*. Beneath the left knee there is another female figure holding a sword in her right hand. In the each corner, there are two female garland bearers with a kneeling devotee in front. She is labelled as *Sri Varahi*.

ILLUS. 53 (Chapter 6). She is four-armed and seated on the lotus in *lalitasana*. All her four arms are broken. She is three-eyed and the mouth is wide open. The head is surrounded by skulls. She wears a sari and ornaments. Just under the pedestal of the Goddess an animal is carved. The right foot of the Goddess is seated on a female figure wearing a single stringed garland of skulls. In the lower part is a dancing male figure in *lalitasana*. He has a note book in hand and writing some thing. R.K. Sharma (1978: 58) identifies him with Chitragupta. To the left of the Goddess is a male figure in *tribhanga* posture, holding a mace in his hand. At the backdrop there is a garland bearing female figure. Again a male figure is seen in *tribhanga* posture. He holds a *sankha* (conch) in left hand and right hand is in *abhaya mudra*. In the inscription she is labelled as *Sri Amtakari*.

ILLUS. 42 *Dancing Ganeshini* (Chapter 2). The deity had four arms. All hands are broken. Only the remains of left and right hands are placed on both the thighs respectively. She is wearing uttariya (upper stol), dhoti and ornaments. At the lower right side is a male devotee sitting on a cushion. Another such headless figure can be seen at the left side. At the pedestal some unidentified symbols can be noticed.

ILLUS. 103 (Chapter 9). A four-armed female figure is seated in *lalitasana* on double petal lotus. The left leg is missing. Originally she had four hands. She is wearing a sari and ornaments. Below the lotus seat there is a bull. Behind the Goddess there is a female garland bearer whose head is damaged and she is holding a cup. On the other side there are three figures. In the middle section of the stella, there is *Gajashardula* motif. The inscription reads Sri *Jhangini*.

Illus. 32 (Chapter 2). This is an interesting figure of the female counterpart of Ganesh. It shows three-eyed and four-armed female figure seated in *lalitasana* on a double petal lotus. Her hands, and tusks are broken. Her head is that of an elephant with large ears. She is wearing a crown, a sari, and ornaments. Below the lotus seat is the bent figure of Ganesh squatting and supporting with his left hand the knee of the goddess. Two kneeling figures are seated in front of the garland bearer on the right of the goddess. Of these one is female with folded hands, and the head is damaged. The other figure is also kneeling, but the torso is damaged. The inscription reads *Sri Aingini*.

Illus. 52 (Chapter 6). The goddess is four-armed and three-eyed. She is seated in *lalitasana* on cushion seat over lotus pedestal. The left leg is across the pedestal and the right leg is hanging downwards. Her four arms and left leg are broken. She is wearing a sari, ornaments, and *Kirtimukha*. The seven hooded snake has spread his canopy over the goddess. There is *Sirsacakra* behind the head of the goddess. Below the lotus pedestal there is a bearded male figure lying on the ground with head raised up. There are male figures of devotees at each side of the bearded man. The figure on the right had broken hands and had a sign of dot in his chest. The figure at the left is sitting on a cushion with folded hands. Behind him is a female figure standing with folded hands. Her head is damaged. A garland bearing female is standing at the each side. There is motif of *Gajashardula* in the middle section in both outer and inner sides. The inscription reads *Sri Phanendri*.

Illus. 74 (Chapter 9). It is a three-faced female figure seated in *lalitasana* on double lotus petal. Right leg is hanging and the left is placed across the pedestal. Hands are broken, only few remaining fingers show that they were holding the pearls. Of the three faces the front one is wearing a crown and is weather worn, the face at the right side is missing, and left side has a serious expression. The lotus pedestal is being carried by a goose. A bell is tied around its neck.On both sides of the goddess the mutilated figures of female garland bearers can be seen. In front of the goddess there are two garland bearing attendants. The first figure is that of the kneeling female, holding a tray of fruits in both her hands. The second figure is of the male and he is holding a Veena in his both hands. Both the figures have damaged faces. Two more figures may be seen at the ends of the pedestal. The first figure is of a female holding a fly whisk and the other is male. The heads of both the figures are broken. The inscription reads it *Sri Brahmani*.

ILLUS. 93 (Chapter 9). She is four armed boar headed goddess, seated in *ardhparyanka asana* with her left leg bent across the lotus pedestal and right leg hanging. Her head is adorned with *Jatamukha* and decked with *Kirtimukha*. The right hand is in *Varada Mudra*. The fingers are adorned with rings. There is an antelope under the lotus pedestal with long horns. The neck and back of the animal are decorated with chain. On each side there are female and male devotees. The female attendant at left is holding a garland, at right is holding a fly whisk. The inscription reads *Sri Erudi*.

ILLUS. 167. Four-armed and three-eyed goddess is seated on a lotus pedestal in *lalitasana* with her left leg bent across the pedestal and the right leg hanging down. All her four arms are broken. The lotus pedestal is being supported by the back of an animal. On the right of the central figure is a female in the dancing posture, holding a skull cup in the right hand and a *trishul* in the left hand. In front of her is another mutilated figure sitting in *padmasana*. On the left centre again there is a female dancing figure holding a club in her right hand and her left hand is damaged. In front of her a female figure is sitting, whose head and hands are damaged. The middle section of the stella is adorned with the usual *Gajashardula* motif. At the upper side the two sides of the goddess are the *Sirsacakras* flanked by *gandharvas* and *apsaras*. At the extreme left a female figure is sitting in *lalitasana*. The inscription reads it *Sri Thakini*.

ILLUS. 49 (Chapter 4). The goddess is sitting with both her legs folded. Below her feet the private part is carved, which is being worshipped by one bearded person and one female worshipper. Two females are sitting there with musical instruments. One bearded person is sitting at the left and one female at right. There are two female attendants at both the sides. Two female garland bearers at the top are carved. Some music players are also depicted there. She has four broken arms. She has a human face. She is wearing a crown, ornaments, and *vanamala*. Her name is inscribed as *Sri Kamada*.

ILLUS. 35 (Chapter 2). The figure is four-armed and sitting on double lotus pedestal in *lalitasana*. All four arms are broken, Though damged the *Jatamukuta* over the head is apparent. Under the lotus seat there is a parrot with beak curved standing right and small bell tied to the neck. On each side of the lower part there are female attendants. Though the figures at the sides of the goddess are damaged, one can make out that at right side the figure is holding a dagger and a mirror and at the left side again a dagger. Under the right leg of the goddess there are two male figures and under the left leg there are two female figures. The inscription reads *Sri Pimgala*.

ILLUS. 75 (Chapter 9). She is four-armed and three-eyed goddess and is seated on a lotus pedestal with her left foot bent across and the right one hanging down. All hands are broken, only upper left is intact and she is holding a shield in it. A bearded male figure of three-eyed demon is lying between her right foot and the pedestal. He is staring at the goddess. He is also wearing the ornaments. On the extreme corner of the pedestal there are two naked figures of Ghouls, whose heads are broken. There is a Ghoul at right side of the goddess also. The inscription reads *Sri Vibhatsa*.

ILLUS. 101 (Chapter 9). She is four-armed goddess, sitting in *lalitasana* on double lotus. All four hands are broken. The left leg is bent across, the middle and lower part is mutilated. Her right leg is broken from the thigh. Below the lotus an animal is on its forelegs. The head of the animal is damaged. The animal is decorated with the band. A female garland bearer is standing at each side of the animal. A male devotee is carved in front of these female figures. And a bearded male figure is seated in reverence before the animal. In the middle section of the image is the usual *Gajashardula* motif. In the upper most section are the *makaras, gandharvas* and *apsaras*. In the extreme corner there are two figures standing on the lotus coming out from the mouth of the makaras. The inscription on the pedestal reads *Sri Satanusamvara*.

ILLUS. 40 (Chapter 2). She is twelve armed and three headed. She is seated in *lalitasana* on a lotus pedestal. The right leg is bent across and the left leg is hanging. All arms are broken. Of the three faces the front face has three eyes, open mouth with protruding teeth. The second face is more benign. The third face is again ferocious. The *Vanamala* is noticeable as it has three strings and three skulls. The lotus pedestal is also significant. The outer row consists of sixteen petals and the inner shows the emblem of fetility with the symbol of *Hrim* in the centre. By the side of this lotus there is a female figure seated on a cushion. She is holding a *khadga* in her right hand and a head from the hair. Behind this figure a standing male figure is carved. This figure has two hands, holding a skull cup in his right hand and a *Khatvanga* in his left hand. On the other end of the pedestal again there is a male devotee. Behind that devotee there is a four-armed female figure. In her lower left hand there is a skull cup and in her upper left hand a shield. In her left leg she is wearing the anklet of skulls. She is inscribed as *Sri Sarvatomukhi*.

ILLUS. 94 (Chapter 9). The deity is sitting on the double lotus pedestal with both legs folded. Her arms are broken. She is profusely ornamented. Her *vanamala* is touching the lotus pedestal. She is surrounded by female worshippers. There are two female garland bearers at the top. Then there are two female attendants, standing. The middle section of the sculpture is broken. At the bottom one female attendant is standing at left. The right one is perhaps broken. Two female attendants are sitting at each side. A ghoul is lying with head raised beneath the lotus pedestal. The inscription reads *Sri Padmavati*.

Illus. 36 (Chapter 2). The figure is six-armed and three-eyed. She is seated in *lalitasana*, her right foot is bent across and left foot is hanging down. All her hands are mutilated. She is wearing a sari and ornaments and a crown. Below the lotus seat there is a lion with wide open mouth and a raised tail. On the right side of the lion a female figure is sitting and holding a sword in the right hand and a shield in the raised left hand. At the right recessed corner a female figure with dropping *damaru* is seated. At the both corners of the pedestal the female garland bearer may be seen. Before one of the garland bearer a female figure in reverence may be observed. In front of her a seated female figure with bow and arrow may be seen. In the middle section of the sculpture at the left side of the goddess *gajashardula* motif is carved and in the upper most section the *makar mukuta* is depicted. The inscription reads *Sri Tokari*.

Illus. 99 (Chapter 9). Only lower part of a female remains sitting in *lalitasana* on a lotus pedestal her right foot bent and left foot hanging. She is wearing a sari and ornaments. The throne of the goddess is supported on the back of a *Garuda* on the right. His chest is expanded and wings outstretched. He is wearing a *dhoti* and a necklace. On the right of the deity there is a female garland bearer in *tribhanga* posture. Below this female figure is another female figure kneeling in reverence and another figure is that of a child. The head of both the figures are damaged. To the left again there is a female garland bearer. The inscription reads it *Sri Rangini*.

Illus. 41 (Chapter 2). This is an image of *Mahisasurmardini*. She is eighteen armed, three-eyed and standing in *atibhanga* posture. On the left side the six hands are damaged. In the remaining three, the one holds a conch and the other two hold shields. On the right side, seven hands are broken, and among the remaining, one is holding a trident, while the other is drawing an arrow out of the quiver hanging over the right shoulder. The right leg of the goddess slightly bent is placed at the back of the Mahisasur. And her left foot is placed on the lotus. She is wearing a sari, ornaments and a crown over her head. The Mahisasur is shown in jumping posture, the severed head of the buffalo demon is shown fallen on the ground. The mount of the goddess, lion is attacking on the buffalo from the behind. Under the body of the Mahisasur a bearded man is sitting in *siddhasana*. Two female figures are depicted sitting at the two corners of the pedestal. At the right and at the left there are two armed female figures. The inscription reads *Sri Teramva*.

Illus. 37 (Chapter 2). The goddess is sitting in *lalitasana* with the left foot across and the right leg is hanging. There is an elephant supporting the goddess and holding the string of Vanamala. She is wearing a *sari*, ornaments and crown. Two female worshippers are sitting at both the lower ends in reverence. At their top two female figures are visible. And at their top two female figures are standing, holding weapons. At the back of the head there is a bar and small triangles are carved there. There is a halo behind the crown and two female garland bearers are depicted at both the ends. Two female figures are seated at the two corners at the top. Over their heads two standing female figures are again carved. The inscription reads *Sri Ranjira*.

Illus. 104 (Chapter 9). The goddess is four-armed, seated in *lalitasana* on a lotus pedestal with right foot bent across and left foot hanging down. All four arms and head of the figure is mutilated. She is wearing lot of ornaments and three skulled armlet in broken right arm and three skulls in right leg. Below the lotus pedestal of the goddess is an elephant looking towards right. The elephant is also wearing a three-stringed necklace. On each side female garland bearer is standing. The head of these female figures are broken. In front of each female figure a ghoul is seated. One of the ghouls at right is holding a dagger and a bell. The ghoul at the left is seated and is also holding skull-cup in his hand. In the middle of the sculpture the *Gajashardula* motif is only partially visible. The inscription reads *Sri Indrajali*.

Illus. 76 (Chapter 9). This is a four-armed goddess seated on a lotus pedestal in *lalitasana* with her left foot bent across and right foot hanging down. The right foot is being held by a *Garuda* seated below the pedestal. Godesses' head and hands are damaged. She is wearing a sari and ornaments. The *Garuda*'s right leg is pushed at the back and the left is thrown in the front. He is having moustaches and beard. He is wearing *dhoti* (lower garment) and ornaments. On either side of the *garuda* two headless male figures can be seen holding a veena. On both sides of the goddess the usual female garland bearers can be seen. There is a lotus nimbus at the head and the *gandharvas*. In the middle of the sculpture there is *Gajashardula* motif. The inscription reads *Sri Vaishnavi*.

Illus. 50 (Chapter 4). She is an animal faced Yogini. She is wearing an elongated crown. She is profusely ornamented and is sitting in the *lalitasana*, and is wearing a *vanamala*. The panel is crowded with the female worshippers. At the top there are female worshippers and in the middle there is *Gajashardula* motif. At least four female worshippers could be located at the bottom. The right leg of the Yogini is shown taking support of a jackal, carved at the bottom. She is inscribed as *Sri Nandini*.

Illus. 34 (Chapter 2) *Ganesh*. A very weather-worn image. Both legs are broken. One hand is also broken. Right hand is in *varada* gesture. There is *akshmala* in that hand. He is wearing garland and *yajnopaveet* (sacred thread) of beads (?*rudraksa*). He has fan like ears. At the right top there is a mutilated garland bearer.

Naresar
(*Photographs Courtesy:* American Institute of Indian Studies)

Illus. 57 (Chapter 4). She is a four-armed headless goddess.She is sitting in *lalitasana*. Her left leg is broken. Her arms are also damaged.The image is profusely ornamented. The vulva from her crotch is coming out. A naked male figure is lying down. His left hand is under his head, so his head is slightly raised. A female worshipper is sitting at the right with folded hands. The inscription at the pedestal reads *Kauveri*.

Illus. 59 (Chapter 7). She is four-armed headless image of the goddess. She is sitting in *lalitasana*. Her right leg is bent and left leg is hanging. She is heavily ornamented with *Sri Vatsa* as armlet in both the arms. The hands after the arms are broken. The right leg of the image is placed on an elephant. The elephant is also wearing ornaments. A female devotee is sitting at left. The inscription identifies her as *Indrani*.

Illus. 111 (Chapter 9). It is a headless two-armed image. It is different from other images in the sense that it is wearing very few ornament and it is very thin. Her right hand is on her right knee and the left hand was perhaps holding a head. Her right hand is holding something round. She is sitting on a male figure, who is sitting on his knee. Two female attendants are standing at each corner and a female worshipper is sitting. It is *Vaishnavi*.

Illus. 60 (Chapter 7). The head of this figure is also damaged. Out of four arms only two remains. She is also heavily ornamented. She holds a club in right and conch in left. She is sitting on a pedestal and a hawk is in between her legs. Two female worshippers are sitting at each side. The inscription states *Vaishnavi*.

Illus. 100 (Chapter 9). It is fully intact image. The image is owl-faced. Out of four arms, two are safe. She is not as profusely ornamented as other images. She is sitting on a ram in *lalitasana*. At the left side of her lap she is holding a baby animal, whose identification is slightly vague. The other hand is in *varada* gesture. Below the pedestal a woman is sitting with folded hands. The inscription reads *Uma*.

Illus. 48 (Chapter 4). It is attractive, but headless figure. Out of four arms only one is left. She is in *lalitasana*. On the pedestal perhaps a ghoul is lying. She is holding a severed head in her left hand. At the right side there is female worshipper. The inscription reads *Nivan*.

Illus. 112 (Chapter 9). It is a headless four-armed image. Three arms are damaged. The right remaining hand is holding some object. Behind her left leg, there is a figure in *tribhanga* posture. At the right side is a female worshipper. Her left leg is supported by a boar. The inscription reads *Varahi*.

ILLUS. 65 (Chapter 9). The head is damaged. She has four broken arms and right leg is also damaged. She is profusely ornamented. She is sitting on her mount, mouse. On the right side of the pedestal a female worshipper is sitting. She is goddess *Maghali*.

Hirapur

ILLUS. 12 (Chapter 1). Temple

ILLUS. 13 (Chapter 1). Temple Entrance

ILLUS. 14 (Chapter 1). She is standing on a dead body. Though the face is damaged, it appears to be a human face. She has four arms two of which are totally damaged. She is wearing a sari. Her ornaments and hair style show local influence. She is identified as *Chandika*.

ILLUS. 15 (Chapter 1). She is also standing on a corpse. She has two arms of which one arm is broken. Legs are in dancing posture. She has a human face. She is wearing a sari. The hair style and ornaments show native features. She is identified as *Tara*.

ILLUS. 26 (Chapter 1). She is standing on lotus and elephant. She has two arms and wearing a garland. She is drinking from a skull in left hand. She is also wearing a sari with hair-do and ornaments showing local trend. She is identified as *Narmada*, though some scholars identify her as *Surapriya*.

ILLUS. 27 (Chapter 1). The figure is standing on a tortoise in *Ardhparyanka* posture. She is four-armed. Three arms are broken the remaining one is holding a skull cup. She is also wearing a sari as lower garment. She has a human face, but her hair style is different, it is spread on the head. She is identified as *Yamuna*.

ILLUS. 28 (Chapter 1). She is standing on a full blown lotus. She has a very benign human face. She also has heavy hair-do and ear ornaments, She has two arms, which are broken. Her lower garment is like a skirt which comes up to her knee. She is identified as *Mahananda*.

ILLUS. 29 (Chapter 1). The figure is standing on the waves of the water. Both hands are damaged, but they are raised upwards, it appears that she was holding some object by both hands. Both legs are joined together. She has mutilated face, but it was of human. She is wearing heavy hair-do and ear ornaments. She is identified as *Varuni*.

Illus. 96 (Chapter 9). She has four arms two of which are completely broken. She has a human face. She is standing on an alligator. She is identified as *Gauri*.

Illus. 38 (Chapter 2). She is standing on an elephant. Though her arms and legs are broken, she appears to be in a dancing position. She has a human face, which is mutilated. She is wearing a heavy hair-do. She is identified as *Indrani*.

Illus. 115 (Chapter 9). She is standing on a buffalo. She has four damaged arms, in one of the damaged arms she is holding the cup and bow. She has an animal face and elongated hair-do. She is identified as *Varahi*.

Illus. 46 (Chapter 2). She is standing on a snake. She is wearing a garland of snake around her neck and has two arms. In the right raised arm she is holding a Khadga. She is wearing a headgear of skulls on head. She is identified with the Jaina snake deity *Padmavati*. She is also taken as the *Ranjira* of Bheraghat, but that identification is doubtful.

Illus. 102 (Chapter 9). She is standing on a camel. She has four broken arms and and a monkey face. Her lower garment is different. She is identified with *Ushtragriva*.

Illus. 116 (Chapter 9). She is standing on a boar, has two arms, local hairstyle and human face. She is identified with *Pancavarahi*.

Illus. 117 (Chapter 9). She is standing on a stringed drum, has two broken arms, human face but mouth open with protruding teeth. She is wearing a sari. She is identified as *Bhadra Rupi*.

Illus. 108 (Chapter 9). She is standing on an owl. She has two arms and human face. Her lower garment is not clear. Her hair is spread. She is identified with *Vaishnavi*.

Illus. 165. She is standing on a demon. She has two broken arms and a smiling human face. She is identified with *Carcika*.

Illus. 163. She is standing on fish. She has two broken arms and has a heavy human face. Her physique is stout. She is wearing a knee length lower garment. She is identified with *Vaitali*.

Illus. 86 (Chapter 9). She is standing on a human head. She has four arms, but are broken. She is holding a spear. She may have held the severe head in one of the hands. She is identified as *Chinnamasta*, but her iconographical details do not tally with the traditional image.

ILLUS. 120. She is standing on hills. She has two arms, which are damaged. She has a mutilated human face and hair is scattered. She is identified as *Vindhyavasini*.

ILLUS. 91 (Chapter 9). She is standing on a frog, both arms are broken. She is wearing a very heavy hairdo and a sari as lower robe. She is identified as *Jalagamini*.

ILLUS. 92 (Chapter 9). She is standing in *Ardhparyanka* posture on a lion. Two hands are raised upwards holding a snake skin. She has a damaged human face. She is identified as *Ghata Varahi*.

ILLUS. 121. She is standing on a dog. She has a human face and very heavy hairdo. One of her legs is twisted and she is adjusting her anklets like one finds at Ranipur-Jharial. She is identified as *Karkari*.

ILLUS. 122. She is standing on a lotus and snake. She has four arms. One hand is holding the musical instrument and the other is holding her cheek. She is identified as *Saraswati*. Saraswati, with snake appears to be a tribal influence.

ILLUS. 124. She is standing on water. Her two arms are broken and has a smiling human face. She is identified as *Virupa*.

ILLUS. 125. She is standing on *Sapta Bhandara* (seven wealth) in *Ardhparyanka* posture. She has a human face and heavy hairdo. She is identified with *Kuberi*.

ILLUS. 126. She is standing on flowers. She is bear-faced. She has two arms, left is broken in the right raised hand she is holding a *damaru*. She is known as *Bhalluka*.

ILLUS. 127. She is standing on flowers. Two hands are completely broken, remaining two hands are holding a pot. She is lion-faced and not wearing a lower robe. She is identified as *Narasimhi*.

ILLUS. 97 (Chapter 9). She is standing on lotus, both hands broken. She has a human face. She is identified as *Viraja*. Viraja also happens to be the presiding deity of Jajnagar.

ILLUS. 128. She has a demon-like face. Her mount is broken. Currently, she is wearing a modern crown. She is identified as *Vikata Nayana*.

ILLUS. 129. She is standing on a lotus. She has two arms and a human face. She is wearing a *vanamala*. In the right hand she is holding a *vajra* and in the left she is holding a shield. She is identified as *Maha Lakshmi*.

ILLUS. 114 (Chapter 9). She is standing on a pea cock. Her right hand is broken and in the left she is holding a flywhisk. She is identified as *Kaumari*.

ILLUS. 130. She is standing on a full-blown lotus. She has a human face. She is identified as *Mahamaya*. Currently she is being worshipped as the main deity.

ILLUS. 131. She is standing on a archer-like figure most probably, *Kamadeva*. She has a boar-like face and her hands are broken. She is identified as *Rati*.

ILLUS. 132. She is standing on a crab. She has a human face and her both hands are broken. She is identified as *Karkari*.

ILLUS. 133. Her mount is broken. She has a snake-like face. Her four arms are broken. She is not wearing any lower garment. She is identified as *Sarpasha*.

ILLUS. 134. She is standing on a stool. She has a human face and elongated hairstyle. Both hands are broken. She is identified as *Yasha*.

ILLUS. 135. She is standing on a goat. Both hands are broken and has a very round and heavy human face. She is identified as *Aghora*.

ILLUS. 136. She is standing on a crow. She has a human face. Her both hands are broken. In the broken right hand, she is holding a sword. She is identified as *Rudrakali*.

ILLUS. 137. She is standing on a donkey. She has face of an elephant. She is wearing leaves as headdress. Her lower robe is only up to her knee. She is identified as *Ganeshini* or *Vainayaki*.

ILLUS. 138. She is standing on a rat. She has a human face. She is in the posture of a huntress. One hand is holding a bow and string. Three broken arrows are depicted in the background. She is identified as *Vindhya Vasini*.

ILLUS. 139. She is standing on a scorpion. She has four broke arms. Two arms are raised. She is wearing crown and *Kirtimukh*. She has a demon-like face. She is identified with *Shivani*.

ILLUS. 140. She is standing on a Bull. She has two broken arms. And has a human face. She is wearing a sari and has a very heavy hairdo. She is identified with *Maheswari*.

ILLUS. 141. She is standing on a mongoose. Actually there are two pedestals at the back of the mongoose. She has four arms. One is broken. Two are on the knees. One upper arm is holding a *damaru*. She has a human face and highly ornamental heavy hairdo. She is identified as *Ambika*.

ILLUS. 142. She is standing on a hen. She has a human face and wearing a *kirtimukha*. She is identified as *Kamakhya*.

ILLUS. 68 (Chapter 9). She is standing on a lion. She has a human face. Both her hands are broken. She is not wearing a bun rather a wavy bunch of hair. She is identified as *Chandra Kanti*.

ILLUS. 119. She is standing on the pedestal of a sandal pot. Her four arms are broken. She has a human face. She is wearing a heavy ornamental hairdo. Sandal pot is depicted in the background. She is identified with *Parvati*.

ILLUS. 70 (Chapter 9). She is standing on Shiva. She has a human face and two broken arms. Her right arm was holding a *trishul*. She is identified as *Kali*.

ILLUS. 71 (Chapter 9). She is beating the drum. She has human face and one hand broken. She is identified as *Bhagavati*.

ILLUS. 72 (Chapter 9). She is standing on flower. Her upper arm is holding *Nagapasha*. And lower left is in *abhaya mudra*, rest of the hands are broken. Her hairstyle is in *Kirtimukha*. She is identified as *Narayani*.

ILLUS. 51 (Chapter 4). She is standing on a conch. She has a human face and a very heavy ornamental hairstyle. Her both hands are broken. She is identified as *Samudri*.

ILLUS. 143. She is standing on books. She has three faces. All three faces are human. The front face is wearing *Kirtimukha*. She has six arms and legs are broken. She is identified as *Brahmani*.

ILLUS. 144. She is standing on a cot. Her both hands are broken. She is animal faced and identified as *Jwalamukhi*.

ILLUS. 87 (Chapter 9). She is standing on a cow. Her right hand is holding a sword, left hand is broken. She has a damaged face. There is water in the background. She is identified as *Agnihotri*.

ILLUS. 145. She is standing on a parrot. Her both hands are damaged. In one hand she must have been holding something. She is identified as *Aditi*.

ILLUS. 118 (Chapter 9). She is standing on a sandal pot. Her both hands are damaged. She has a human face and very heavy hairstyle. She is identified as *Stuti*.

ILLUS. 69 (Chapter 9). She is standing on a Yak. Her face is damaged and both hands are damaged. She is identified as *Svaha*.

ILLUS. 80 (Chapter 9). She is standing on a mask deer. She has a physique of a skeleton. She is wearing the garland of skulls. She has four hands and she is holding a tiger. Her face is damaged. She is identified as *Chamunda*.

Illus. 84 (Chapter 9). She is standing on a deer. Her both hands are damaged and face is also damaged. She is identified as *Maruta*.

Illus. 85 (Chapter 9). She is standing on duck. One hand is damaged and is holding a winnowing fan in the left hand. She is identified as *Dhoomavati*.

Illus. 83 (Chapter 9). She is standing on a donkey. Her face is damaged. Flowers and leaves are at headdress. She is identified as *Gandhari*.

Illus. 88 (Chapter 9). She is standing on a boar. Both arms are broken. She has a human face. Two branches of leaves are coming out of headdress. She is identified as *Parna Shabari*.

Illus. 146. The figure has a human face and ten arms. Dead body being pulled by one hand. Two hands hold *Akshmala*, skull cup and *damaru*. He is identified as *Svacchanda Bhairava*.

Illus. 113 (Chapter 9). The figure is one-legged. There are *Khadga*, shield, and the weapons are made of the shell of fish. He is identified as *Purva Bhairava*.

Illus. 147. The figure is sitting on double lotus. He has ten arms. One leg is on a female figure lying beneath the pedestal. The figure is identified as *Astanga Bhairava*.

Illus. 148. The figure is sitting on a double lotus pedestal. He has ten broken arms. He is identified as *Ek Pada Bhairava*.

Illus. 149. The figure is standing on a deer. She has a human face and four broken arms. One hand was perhaps on the cheek. The mouth is open. She is identified as *Sarva Mangala*.

Illus. 150. She is standing on a horse. She has four broken arms. She is holding bow and arrow. She has a human face, but damaged. She is identified as *Surya Putri*.

Illus. 151. She is standing on a deer. There are two plants at both the sides. She is in dancing or flying posture. She is identified as *Vayuvega*.

Ranipur-Jharial

Illus. 1 (Chapter 1). Yogini in dancing posture. Both legs are in dancing posture. Left hand is placed on stomach and the right hand is broken. She has a human face.

Illus. 67 (Chapter 9). Both legs are in dancing posture. Right hand is raised and both hands are holding some objects. She has a human face.

ILLUS. 152. Both legs are in dancing position. Both hands are holding weapons. She has a human face.

ILLUS. 66 (Chapter 9). Both legs are broken. Hands are also broken, but remains appear to be folded on stomach. Face is damaged and appear to be wearing very crude necklace and ear ornaments. Hair is tied in spire.

ILLUS. 153. Both legs are in *ardhparyanka*. Yogini is sitting in squatting position, hands are on knees, face is human but damaged.

ILLUS. 4 (Chapter 1). Both legs are in dancing position. The image is sitting in a squatting position. She has a human face and very high hairdo. One hand is broken and the other hand (finger) is on the cheek.

ILLUS. 154. Only two legs have remained in dancing position.

ILLUS. 155. Both legs are in dancing position. She has six hands. Two are placed on the stomach in a dancing gesture. One hand is raised upwards holding a sword, while two hands are broken. She has an animal face.

ILLUS. 2 (Chapter 1). Both legs are in dancing position. She has four hands. Two are folded at stomach in dancing position and rest two are holding weapons, in the right hand a club like weapon. She has an animal face.

ILLUS. 156. Both legs are in dancing position. She has four hands. Two are broken. Right one is on the knee and the left is holding a cup. She has a human face.

ILLUS. 157. Both legs are in dancing position. Both hands are raised and must have been holding some object. She has benign human face.

ILLUS. 3 (Chapter 1). Both legs are in dancing position. All four hands are damaged. She has a snake face.

ILLUS. 158. Both legs are in dancing position. Both hands are broken. She has a human face.

ILLUS. 57 (Chapter 7). She is sitting in a squatting position. Both hands are damaged. She has a divine human face with eyes closed.

ILLUS. 58 (Chapter 7). Both legs are in dancing position. Both hands are damged But it seems at right side she was holding a quiver with three arrows. She has a human face.

ILLUS. 159. Both legs are in dancing position. The hands are broken. She has a human face. She is wearing heavy and crude ornaments.

ILLUS. 160. Left leg is in dancing position. Right leg is broken. Both hands are broken. She has a human smiling face.

ILLUS. 20 (Chapter 1). Both legs are in dancing position. Right hand is broken. Left hand is on the knee. She has a human face, wearing ornaments and crown like hairdo.

ILLUS. 18 (Chapter 1). She has four hands. Two folded on the stomach and two are stretched over head. She has a human face.

ILLUS. 73 (Chapter 9). Both legs are in dancing position. She has four hands. One is broken and she is holding weapon in rest three. She has an animal face.

ILLUS. 5 (Chapter 1). Her legs are in squatting position. The crotch is also obvious. The left hand is broken and right is on the lips. She has a conical hair do.

ILLUS. 162. Her legs are in dancing position. She has four arms holding the weapons. She has a divine human face and she is wearing a crown.

ILLUS. 6 (Chapter 1). Her legs are in dancing position. Right leg is broken. Left hand is holding a mirror and right hand is applying cosmetic at the fore head. She has a human face and spiral like hairdo.

ILLUS. 17 (Chapter 1). Both legs are in dancing posture. She is holding club in both the hands. She has a human face and spiral like hair do.

ILLUS. 31 (Chapter 1). Image of Shiva Bhairava in the dancing posture. He has three faces.

ILLUS. 30 (Chapter 1). The temple exterior.

ILLUS. 16 (Chapter 1). Sitting Image. Right hand and right leg are broken. Finger of left hand is on the left cheek.

ILLUS. 22 (Chapter 1). Legs are in dancing posture. Right hand is broken. Left hand is on the stomach. Face is weatherworn.

ILLUS. 23 (Chapter 1). Right hand and right leg are broken. Left hand is on the left leg. Face is weatherworn.

ILLUS. 24 (Chapter 1). Right leg is damaged. Left leg is in dancing posture. She has four hands. One hand is broken. Two upper raised hands are holding some object. She has divine human face.

ILLUS. 25 (Chapter 1). She appears like a divine image. Right hand is mutilated. Left is placed on knee. She is sitting with eyes closed.

ILLUS. 30. The temple complex.

Mitauli

Illus. 54 (Chapter 6). The temple mound.

Lokhari
(Photographs after V. Dehejia, *Yogini Cult and Temple*)

Illus. 11 (Chapter 1). She is sitting in *lalitasana*. Her right leg is bent and left leg is hanging on the platform. Both her hands are on the knees and are holding some object. She is animal faced and has several horns over her head. Her name is *Mrigashira*.

Illus. 8 (Chapter 1). She is sitting with legs crossed. Left hand holding a *kamandala* and right hand is in *varada* gesture. She has a face of a rabit. A small rabit is sitting under her right leg. She is known as *Shashanana*.

Illus. 9 (Chapter 1). She is sitting in *lalitasana*. Her right leg is placed on a reclining elephant. Her both hands are holding some objects and they are placed on the knees. She is snake-faced and her name is *Sarpa Mukhi*.

Illus. 10 (Chapter 1). She is *Hayanana*. She is sitting in *lalitasansa* with both her feet placed on horse. She is horse-faced. In her left hand she is holding a musical instrument, most probably a pipe.

Illus. 43 (Chapter 2). She is *Ajanana*. Her legs are in *lalitasana*. Right leg is hanging and left leg is bent across. Both legs are placed on a goat. Her right hand is in *varada* gesture and left hand is holding a vase. She has face of a goat.

Illus. 39 (Chapter 2). She is *Vrishanana*. Her right leg is on the large bird and right is hanging. The bird's peak is in the round object in the deity's right hand. She is holding a club like weapon in the left hand. She has face of a buffalo with very prominent horns.

Illus. 44 (Chapter 2). She is *Gomukhi*. She is sitting on a cow with right leg bent across and left leg hanging down. She is holding a cup in her right hand and a long stick with top of a skull in her left hand. She has the face of a cow.

Illus. 62 (Chapter 7). She is *Hayagriva*. She is sitting on a naked male figure in *lalitasana*. Her left leg folded and right leg hanging down. She is looking up. She is horse-faced. There is a kid in the left side of her lap. That is also horse-faced and looking up in the same way.

Illus. 63 (Chapter 7). She is *Rksanana*. She is sitting on a bear with right leg bent and left leg hanging. She has four hands. One right hand is on the knee and the other right hand is holding a club. Her left hand is on the knee and there is small female figure also on the left knee. In her other left hand she is holding a weapon. She is bear-faced.

ILLUS. 61 (Chapter 7). She is *Chamunda*. She has kept her both legs on a human figure. Her whole body looks like a skeleton. She has four hands. She is holding a skull cup in her right hand. The other right hand is raised upwards. The left hand is folded from the palm and is raised towards mouth. The other left hand is on the knee. She has an awesome face with open mouth and protruding eyes. She is wearing a crown of skull over her head.

Shahdol

ILLUS. 77 (Chapter 9). *Sri Krishna Bhagavati*. She is sitting in *lalitasana*. She had ten hands and out of them four hands are intact. One right hand is in *abhaya* gesture while the other is in *varada* gesture. The left upper hand is holding a bell and the other left hand is placed on the leg. She has a human face. At the pedestal there is a crowd of people holding weapons and animals, who are obviously not worshippers.

ILLUS. 78 (Chapter 9). *Sri Jyoti*. She is sitting in *lalitasana*. Her left leg is bent and is placed on the double lotus pedestal. Her right leg also has a lotus at its sole and is placed on the lion. She had at least six hands and one is intact and is placed on left leg. She is surrounded by nine or ten worshippers perhaps involved in some ritual. She has a human face.

ILLUS. 79 (Chapter 9). Name not known. She is sitting in *lalitasana* on lotus pedestal. She has a halo and human face. She is also surrounded by female worshippers from bottom to top. One worshipper is lying at the bottom of deity's right leg. At the bottom some worshippers appear to be preparing something. At the top some worshippers are lying with folded hands.

ILLUS. 98 (Chapter 9). *Sri Tarala*. She is sitting in *lalitasana* on a lion. Her right and left legs are on different lotuses. Her six hands are broken. She is animal faced and wearing a crown. She is wearing ornaments and a sari like lower garment. There are at least three female worshippers at each side. There is a *damaru* at the top, perhaps held by one of the worshippers.

ILLUS. 105 (Chapter 9). *Yogini Tarini*. She has a divine face. She is wearing a crown. Her right hand is broken, and in her left hand she is holding a weapon. She is sitting in latitasana. There are flying devotees at the top.

ILLUS. 106 (Chapter 9). *Sri Varahi*. Her right leg is on a cow. The broken left hand is holding the horn of the cow. Two boar figures are sitting at the bottom. The left figure is holding a severed head. One standing boar figure is peeping from the left side. Rest at the top is broken.

ILLUS. 164. *Sri Tamaka*. The pedestal is interesting. The right leg of the deity is on a half lying male figure. The male figure is profusely ornamented and looking behind. There is an animal faced female figure holding a club and a cup. Behind this female figure is a jackal and another smaller female figure. After the lying male figure there is another animal faced female figure holding a weapon. The deity is sitting on a double lotus pedestal and a sari like lower garment is obvious.

ILLUS. 81 (Chapter 9). *Sri Vrishbha* (*Vasabha*). She is sitting in *lalitasana* with an animal kid in her lap. There is a halo and she is buffalo-faced. Two female worshippers are at both the sides. Two women are preparing something at right bottom. At the left bottom an elephant-faced female is depicted. A club with skull motif is carved at the top. The Goddess is sitting on the lion. There is a *Ganeshini* at the left bottom.

ILLUS. 89 (Chapter 9). *Sri Narasita*. She is sitting on double lotus pedestal in *lalitasana*, supported by a lion. The lion is looking up. She is lion-faced, wearing a crown and a halo behind the head. There are three female worshippers at each side, one standing and the other two sitting. Just like Sri Vrishbha, one is holding a weapon or performing some ritual. Two lion figures are there in the centre corner. There are again some female figures at the top of the panel.

ILLUS. 64 (Chapter 9). *Sri Naini*. She is sitting in *lalitasana* on double lotus. The lower garment appears like a sari. She has a human face, wearing a crown and covered by a snake canopy. She has ten hands. Only two has remained intact. Out of which the right is in *varada* gesture and left is holding a weapon. The remains of a palm at left can be seen touching the hood of the snake. The lotus pedestal is supported by a lion. Her right leg is placed on the lion. She is surrounded by female worshippers from top to bottom at both sides.

ILLUS. 110 (Chapter 9). *Sri Kapalini*. She is in standing posture, wearing a *vanamala,* and a crown over her head. There is a halo behind her head. She has a human face. She has six hands. The right lower is in *abhaya* gesture and the upper is holding a wheel (? Disc). The left lower hand is holding a fish. She is wearing a lower garment may be a sari. She is surrounded by female worshippers from top to bottom.

ILLUS. 107 (Chapter 9). *Mahismardini*. She is killing the buffalo. Her right leg is on the buffalo. The lion is attacking from the back of the buffalo. Out of the ten hands, only two are intact. The right hand is holding the weapon to kill the buffalo demon. One more intact right hand is raised above. Her face is mutilated. She is surrounded by female worshippers.

ILLUS. 45 (Chapter 2). *Sri Badari*. She is standing and dancing in *tandava* posture. She is wearing a *vanamala*. Her four hands are broken. But they also give the impression of being in the dancing gesture. She is surrounded by female worshippers. At the top of the panel they are sitting with the folded hands while at the bottom of the panel some are dancing and some are playing musical instruments.

ILLUS. 123. *Hayavadana*. She is horse-faced and is wearing a crown and a halo. She is wearing a *vanamala* and standing. Her figure is relatively quite slender. The four arms are broken. There is a bell at the top.

ILLUS. 166. *Sri Thabha*. She is in standing posture. She has a human face and a halo behind the head. She is wearing a *vanamala*. She has six hands, out of which four are broken. She is holding *damaru*, *trishul*, and a club in the remaining two hands. She is surrounded by female worshippers, two among them are standing and are holding the weapons.

ILLUS. 90 (Chapter 9). *Sri Tarala*. She is sitting. She has a human face and is wearing a crown. She has eight hands.

Jeerapur

ILLUS. 172. Current temple with modern additions.

ILLUS. 173. Courtyard with assembled images.

ILLUS. 174. Sitting Yogini, resembling Hingalajgarh Yogini.

ILLUS. 175. Damaged picture of Yogini in sitting posture. She is holding weapons in both hands.

ILLUS. 176. Two panels. In the bottom panel, Yogini is sitting in *lalitasana*, with weapons in both hands.

ILLUS. 177. Yogini is standing. In her left hand she is holding a mirror and from the right she is arranging her hair just like an image from Ranipur-Jharial.

ILLUS. 178. Two Yogini sculptures, one is sitting, while other is standing.

ILLUS. 179. Yogini is sitting. Left hand is holding a *trishul*.

ILLUS. 180. Yogini is standing. Right hand is in *varada* gesture. Left hand is broken. She is wearing a garland. *Trishul* is at right perhaps held by broken hand.

ILLUS. 181. Quite a few images in a slab like we find at Rikhiyan. There is a standing Yogini, holding a sword wearing a garland. Worshipper or some other figure may be found at right. Presumably Mahismardini.

ILLUS. 182. Quite a few Yogini sculptures. Some are sitting and some are standing. The standing figure is holding a weapon in left hand. The sitting image is in *lalitasana*.

ILLUS. 183. Two left upper hands holding *trishul* and some other weapons. Only upper torso is intact, bottom is broken.

ILLUS. 184. Modern Shrine.

ILLUS. 185. The sitting Yogini, holding weapons.

ILLUS. 186. Image is standing. *Trishul* is in the right hand. At the bottom there is a buffalo. The right leg is on the buffalo and the left is broken. Currently known as 'Langari Ma'.

ILLUS. 187. Damaged. Standing on an animal.

Miscellaneous

ILLUS. 168. *Nagi.* Standing. She has a human face. There is a serpent canopy over the head. One hand is in *varda* gesture. She is flanked by two female attendants. Find place—Kota.

ILLUS. 170. *Yogini Parvati.* Standing figure wearing a sari. She has four hands. The two upper hands are holding *akshmala* in right and string of bow in left. Her right lower hand is in *abhaya* gesture and the left is holding a *kamandala*. There are two female attendants at the bottom and two female garland bearers at each side at the top. A lotus like disc is at the left top. She has a human face, beautiful hair do and a halo behind. Find spot—Kota.

ILLUS. 171. It is a headless sitting Yogini. Most probably she had eight arms, currently one at right remains intact. In the intact hand she is holding some broken object, perhaps a skull cup. On lower broken hand at right, she is holding a fish. She is profusely ornamented. She is sitting on inverted double lotus pedestal, which has a string of skulls over it. An ornamented male figure is lying under the pedestal. His one leg is raised up and supporting the pedestal and his head is also raised above. There are two female attendants at both the sides. The image appear to be of Shahdol and Naresar tradition. Find spot—Gwalior.

ILLUS. 188. It is a standing figure. She is holding spear in right hand. She is attacking a buffalo. A lion is depicted at the back. In her left hand she is holding another weapon. The panel is badly mutilated. It is *Mahismardini* panel. Find spot is Hingalajgarh.

Illus. 19 (Chapter 1). She is sitting in *lalitasana* with left leg bent and right hanging. She is carved in a panel. She has four hands. The upper right hand is holding a *trishul* and lower right hand is in *varada* gesture. The lower left hand is holding a *kalash* and upper is holding some weapon. She has a human face and wearing a long crown. She is *Maheswari* from Hingalajgarh.

Illus. 21 (Chapter 1). It is a headless image. She has four hands. Two hands are damged and two are intact. The left hand is holding a spear. The lower robe appear like sari. There are two female worshippers at both ends. At the right she is sitting and offering and the right one is standing and headless. The image is standing on double lotus. She is reported as Yogini from Mandsor.

Illus. 169. The image is standing. She has four hands. She is holding a spear in left hand and the right hand is slightly curved at the top. She has a human face and a halo. There are two garland bearers at the top. She is reported as Parvati Yogini from Kota, currently at Gwalior Museum.

Khajuraho

Illus. 55 (Chapter 7). Temple Architecture.

Illus. 56 (Chapter 7). Temple Exterior.

Yogini Cakra

Illus. 109. Yogini Cakra on paper.

NOTES

1. This is the assumption of Dehejia. The basis of her hypothesis is that a sculpture of the same iconography from Naresar workshop is housed in San Antonio Museum of Art in USA.
2. Fifteen Yoginis have been identified by Dr B.S. Mehata along with their current location and a list of Varanasi Yoginis which is discussed in the appendix.

ILLUS. 119: Parvati
(Hirapur)

ILLUS. 120: Vindhyavasini
(Hirapur)

Illus. 121: Karkari
(Hirapur)

ILLUS. 122: Saraswati
(Hirapur)

ILLUS. 123: Hayavadana
(Shahdol)

ILLUS. 124: Virupa
(Hirapur)

ILLUS. 125: Kuberi
(Hirapur)

ILLUS. 126: Bhalluka
(Hirapur)

ILLUS. 127: Narasimhi
(Hirapur)

ILLUS. 128: Vikata Nayana
(Hirapur)

ILLUS. 129: Maha Lakshmi
(Hirapur)

ILLUS. 130: Mahamaya (currently Main Deity)
(Hirapur)

ILLUS. 131: Rati
(Hirapur)

ILLUS. 132: Karkari
(Hirapur)

ILLUS. 133: Sarpasa
(Hirapur)

ILLUS. 134: Yasha
(Hirapur)

Illus. 135: Aghora
(Hirapur)

ILLUS. 136: Rudrakali
(Hirapur)

ILLUS. 137: Ganeshini
(Hirapur)

ILLUS. 138: Vindhya Vasini
(Hirapur)

ILLUS. 139: Shivani
(Hirapur)

ILLUS. 140: Maheswari
(Hirapur)

ILLUS. 141: Ambika
(Hirapur)

Illus. 142: Kamakhya
(Hirapur)

ILLUS. 143: Brahmi
(Hirapur)

ILLUS. 144: Jwalamukhi
(Hirapur)

ILLUS. 145: Aditi
(Hirapur)

ILLUS. 146: Svacchanda Bhairava
(Hirapur)

ILLUS. 147: Astang Bhairava
(Hirapur)

ILLUS. 148: Ek Pada Bhairava
(Hirapur)

ILLUS. 149: Sarvamangla
(Hirapur)

ILLUS. 150: Suryaputri
(Hirapur)

ILLUS. 151: Vayuvega
(Hirapur)

ILLUS. 152: Yogini in Dancing Pose
(Ranipur-Jharial)

ILLUS. 153: Hands on Thigh
(Ranipur-Jharial)

ILLUS. 154: Details of Legs in Odissi
(Ranipur-Jharial)

ILLUS. 155: Yogini in Dancing Posture
(Ranipur-Jharial)

ILLUS. 156: Two Hands Holding Weapons two in Dancing Position
(Ranipur-Jharial)

ILLUS. 157: Yogini Holding a Cup
(Ranipur-Jharial)

ILLUS. 158: Yogini in Dancing Posture
(Ranipur-Jharial)

ILLUS. 159: Yogini in Dancing Posture
(Ranipur-Jharial)

ILLUS. 160: Yogini in Dancing Posture
(Ranipur-Jharial)

ILLUS. 161: Sri Chapala
(Shahdol)

ILLUS. 162: Dancing Yogini
(Ranipur-Jharial)

ILLUS. 163: Vaitali
(Hirapur)

ILLUS. 164: Sri Tamaka
(Shahdol)

Illus. 165: Carcika
(Hirapur)

Illus. 166: Sri Thabha
(Shahdol)

ILLUS. 167: Sri Thakini
(Bheraghat)

ILLUS. 168: Nagi
(Kota)

ILLUS. 169: Parvati Yogini
(Gwalior Museum)

ILLUS. 170: Yogini (Parvati) Kota, MP

ILLUS. 171: Yogini
(Gwalior Museum)

An Unreported Yogini Temple

THE PRESENT TEMPLE is situated in Jeerapur on the main route from Dhar to Mandava in MP (Illus. 180). It could be reached by the right hand side of the forest chowki of village Lunhera. Village Lunhera is 22 km. away from Dhar and Jeerapur is 15 km. away from Lunhera. The temple is locally known as 'Chaunsatha Yogini Mata Ka Mandir' (temple of Chaunsatha Yogini Goddess). Now there is only a partial ruin of the old temple.[1] A modern temple has been constructed on the ruins. The sculptures (Illus. 173 to 187) of the old temple bear a resemblance with the sculptures of Rikhiyan and Hingalajgarh. An image of Bhairava is also reported, whose identity is based only on speculation. An interesting couplet is popular here:

Mansarovar talab chausatha Yogini bavan Bhairav Daulasa Pir Kotawala
Nau sau genda mal na jaane is par ya us par Daulsa Pir Kotawala.

(At the tank of Mansarovar there are sixty-four Yoginis fifty-two Bhairava and Pir Kotawala. The booty weighing equal to nine hundred rhinos was shifted either this way or that way.)

This establishes that the temple at one stage was associated with the sixty-four Yoginis. Very closer to the temple there is a Muslim shrine also (Illus. 180). The couplet is significant as not only it establishes the identity of the temple, it also echoes the 'Shabara Mantra', which is used for the lowest type of superstition and practices:

Katora chalao chaunsath Yogini bulao bavan Bhairav bulao Ismail bulao

(Move the vessel and invoke sixty-four Yoginis, fifty-two Bhairavas and Ismail.)

Literary evidence associates Dhar with the Yogini tradition. Dhar during the reign of the Paramara had a Yogini Pith (centre).[2] An interesting narration testifies to it. The cause of a battle between Chalukya Jayasimha and Paramara Yashovarman is stated to be a Yogini. According to Hemchandra, it was a Yogini's advice to Jayasimha to go to the holy city to worship Kalika and other Yoginis if he wanted higher religious merit. She also impressed upon him the necessity of establishing friendly relations with Yashovarman in order to obtain permission to enter Malwa. This enraged Siddharaj, and who decided to launch an attack on the Paramar kingdom.[3] The *Vasant Vilasa*[4] informs us that Jayasimha brought from Ujjain the Yogini Pitha and defeated and imprisoned the lord of Dhara like a parrot in a cage. In the Jain tradition also Ujjain is associated with the sixty-four Yoginis. Vikramaditya (57 BC) of Ujjain was associated with the Yoginis: thirty-two Yoginis used to dance under his throne (Simhasan Battisi). Like all other contemporary kings, the Paramaras also do not vouch the construction of this temple.[5]

The temple may have seen the height of Paramar power, but currently it is associated with the religion and festivals of the common people. Every Tuesday there is a fair in these premises and on Ram Navami a festival is held. At Baisakh eight days before the Aksaya Tritiya, a celebration is organized at Daulasa Pir's shrine.

It establishes alliance of Yoginis with the lower rituals. It seems that gradually the Yoginis lost their Goddess form and descended to a lower pedestal. This popular aspect of the temple reminds us of the debate regarding Great and Little Traditions and Srinivas' theory of Sanskritization, which models upward mobility.

How did the two differing traditions develop? Why did one tradition give way to the other? The belief and practices of the masses became such an integral part of the temple that it has totally eclipsed the fact that once it had been a centre of mysterious practices.

NOTES

1. In Varanasi also there is a ruined chaunsathi Devi's temple. Currently, only one single icon of Mahismatrdini remains.
2. Modern city of Ujjain has a Yogini centre and a shrine of Macchandar Nath at the outskirts of the city. The shrine had been under Muslim worship for quite some time.
3. Dvyasraya Kavya Canto XIVVV.
4. Canto III, V 21–23.
5. Only one inscription of the twelfth century AD from Andhra Pradesh mention the sixty-four Yoginis and their boons to Mahasamanta.

ILLUS. 172: Current Temple with Modern Additions
(Jeerapur)

ILLUS. 173: Fragment of the Sculptures and the Remaining Part of the Original Temple
(Jeerapur)

ILLUS. 174: Yogini Sculptures Resembling Hingalajgarh Temple
(Jeerapur)

ILLUS. 175: Yogini Sculpture
(Jeerapur)

ILLUS. 176: Seated Yogini
(Jeerapur)

ILLUS. 177: Yogini Sculpture
(Jeerapur)

Illus. 178: Yogini Sculpture
(Jeerapur)

Illus. 179: Yogini Sculpture
(Jeerapur)

ILLUS. 180: Standing Yogini
(Jeerapur)

ILLUS. 181: Presumably Mahismardini
(Jeerapur)

ILLUS. 182: Yogini Sculpture with Some Other Sculptures
(Jeerapur)

ILLUS. 183: Bust of a Yogini Figure
(Jeerapur)

ILLUS. 184: Modern Shrine
(Jeerapur)

ILLUS. 185: Yogini Sculpture
(Jeerapur)

ILLUS. 186: Mahismardini, Currently Known as
'Langari Ma' (Lame Mother)
(Jeerapur)

ILLUS. 187: Standing Yogini
(Jeerapur)

Illus. 188: Mahismardini, Hingalajgarh

Bibliography

SANSKRIT TEXTS

Agni Puranam, Baladeva Upadhyaya, Varanasi: Chaukhamba Sanskrit Series, 1966.

Brhaddharma Puranam, Haraprasad Sastri, Varanasi, 1974.

Brahma Yamal Tantra, Nepal National Archives MSS no. I-743, Nepal German Manuscript Preservation Project, Reel no. AI66/I.439.

Brahmanda Purana, Acarya Jagdish Shastri, Delhi: Motilal Banarsidass, 1973.

Brhannaradiya Purana, Hrishikesha Shastri, Varanasi, 1975.

Brhat Samhita of Varahmihir, ed. and tr. M. Krishna Bhatt, 2 vols., Delhi: Motilal Banarsidass, 1981–2.

Brahmavaivarta Purana, ed. Vinayak Ganesh Apte, 2 vols., Pune, Anandasrama Sanskrit Series, no. 102, Anandasram Press, Poona, 1935.

Chandi Purana, Sarala Das, Kuttak, 1949.

Dasakumaracarita of Dandin, tr. Isabelle Onians (What ten Young Men Did), New York: New York Press, 2005.

Dvayasraya Kavya, Pune, Bhandarkar Oriental Research Institute, Poona, 1936.

Devi Bhagavatam, Ramteja Pandeya, Varanasi, 1960.

Devi-Mahatmyam, or *Sri Durga Saptasati*, ed. and tr. Swami Jagdishwarananda, Madras: Sri Ramakrishna Math, 1969.

Devi Bhagavat Purana, Varanasi: Kashi Pandit Pustakalaya, 1960.

Gopath Brahman of the Atharvaveda, ed. Rajendralal Mitra and Harachandra Vidyabhushan, Calcutta: Ganesha Press, 1872.

Hevajra Tantra, 2 vols., ed. and tr. D.L. Sheyagrov, London: Oxford University Press, 1959.

Kalika Purana, Bombay: Venkatesvara Press, 1891.

Kathasaritsagara by Somadevabhatta, ed. Jagadishlal Sastri, Delhi: Motilal Banarsidass, 1970.

Karpoor Manjari, ed. S. Konow and tr. C.R. Lanman, '*Raja Sekhar's Karpor Manjari*', repr. Delhi, 1963, Eastern Book Corporation, 2007.

Kaulajnananirnaya of the School of Nath, Matsyendra, P.C. Bagchi, 1934, repr., tr. Michael Magee, Varanasi: Prachya Prakashan, 1986.

Kaulavali Nirnaya of Jnanananda Paramahamsa, Arthur Avalon, Calcutta, 1941.

Kularnava Tantra, V. Taranatha, intro. Arthur Avalon, Calcutta, 1916 repr., Delhi, Motilal Banarsidass, 1975.

Lalita Sahasranama, with Bhaskararaya's commentary, R. Ananthakrishna Sastry, Adyar, 1951.

Linga Purana, ed. J.L. Sastri, Delhi: Motilal Banarsidass, 1973.

Mahabharata, ed. Vishnu S. Sukthankar et al., 19 vols., Bombay: Bhandarkar Oriental Research Institute, 1932–59.

Mahanirvana Tantra, Sir John Woodroffe, 3rd edn., Madras: Ganesh & Co., 1953.

Manasollasa of Bhuloka Malla Someshvara, 2nd edn., 3 vols., ed. G.K. Srigondekar, Gaekwad's Oriental Series, nos. 28, 84, 138. Baroda Oriental Institute 1925, 39 rpts., Baroda, 1961.

Matottatra Tantra, incomplete edition published as Goraksha Samhita, Pt. 1, ed. Janardan Pandeya, Sarasvatibhavan Granthmala, vol.110, Benaras: Sampurnananda Sanskrit Visvavidyalaya, 1976.

Mrcchakatikam of Sudraka, the little clay cart, tr. Arthur William Ryder, Cambridge Massachusetts, Harvard University, 1905.

Nispannayogavali by Abhyankar Gupta, ed. Benoytosh Bhattacharya, 1949.

Nitya-Sodasikarnava, Brajvallabh Dwivedi, Varanasi, 1968.

Padma Purana, ed. Hari Narayan Apte, Pune: Anandasharam Sanskrit Series, 1893.

Phetkarini Tantra in Tantra Sangraha, 4 vols., ed. B Gopinath Kaviraj (vols.1–3) and Ramprasad Tripathi (vol. 4), Benaras: Sampurnananda Sanskrit Vishvavidyalaya 1973–81.

Prabodh Chandrodaya of Krishna Chandra Misra, tr.. Sita Krishna Nambiar, Delhi: Motilal Banarsidass, 1971.

Rajatarangini of Kalhan, 2 parts, text ed. in Bombay Sanskrit Series, 1852–84, repr., tr. R.S. Pandit, Delhi: Sahitya Academy, 1977.

Rudrayamala Tantra, ed. Yogatantra Department, Yogatantra Granthmala, no. 7, Benares: Sampurnananda Sanskrit Vishvavidyalaya Press, 1980.

Sakti Sangama Tantra, B. Bhattacharya, Baroda, 1932.

Satapatha Brahmana, ed. Albecht Weber, Banares: Chaukhamba Sanskrit Series, 1964.

Saundarya Lahari Or Flood of Beauty, ed. and tr. W. Norman Brown. Cambridge Mass: Harvard University Press, 1958.

Skanda Purana, Shree Venkateshvara Steam Press, Bombay, 1867.

Silpa Prakash, Medieval Orissan Sanskrit text on Temple Architecture by Ramachandra Kulachara. tr. Alice Boner and Sadasiva Rath Sarma, Leiden: Brill, 1966.

Silpa Ratna Kosa, A glossary of Orissan Temple Architecture by Sthapak Niranjana Mahapatra, tr. Bettina Baumer, Rajendra Prasad Das, Delhi, 1984.

Tantraraja Tantra, ed. Misra Sada Shiva and, Sir Woodroffe, John, Calcutta, Agamanusandhan Samiti, Sanskrit Press Depository, 1865–1936.

Tara Rahasyam, Saryuprasad Shastri, Varanasi, 1970.

Varahi Tantra, ed. B.S.Sharma, Brihad Suchi Patram, pt. III, 1971.

Yogini-Hridayam, With Commentaries Dipika of Amrtananda and Setubandha of Bhaskararaya, ed. Gopinath Kaviraj, Varanasi: Sampurnananda Sanskrit Vishvavidyalaya, 1979.

Yogini Sadhna, ed. Dhana Shamasher, vol. 4, Kathmandu, 1974.

Yogini Tantra, ed. Pt. K. Mishra, Bombay, 1957.

ARCHAEOLOGICAL EVIDENCE

Corpus Inscriptionun Indicarum, vol. III, ed. B. Chhabra and G.S.Gai, 'Inscriptions of the Early Gupta Kings and their Successors', Delhi, 1981.

Corpus Inscriptionum Indicarum, vol. IV, Inscriptions of Kalachuri Chedi Era, pt. I, ed. V.V. Mirashi, Ootacamund, 1985.

Corpus Inscriptionum Indicarum, vol. VII, 3 pts., 'Inscriptions of the Paramaras, Chandellas, Kachchhapaghatas And Two Minor Dynasties', ed. H.V. Trivedi, Delhi, 1989.

Epigraphia Indica, vol. III, ed. E. Hultzsch, The Director General, ASI, Delhi, 1894–5, 1979.

SECONDARY SOURCES

Agrawala, R.C., 'Some unpublished sculptures from south-western Rajasthan', *Lalit Kala*, vol. 6, 1959, pp. 63–71.

Agrawala, V.S., *Ancient Indian Folk Cults*, Varanasi: Prithvi Prakashan, 1970.

Aryan, K.C., *The Little Goddesses*, New Delhi, 1980.

Arthur Avlon, ed. and tr., *Karpuradi Stotra*, Ganesh & Co., Madras, 1953.

Aufrecht, Theodor, *Catalogus Catalogorum*, Weisbaden, 1962.

Awasthi, A.B.L., *Studies in the Skanda Purana*, 1966.

Banerjea, J.N., *The Development of Hindu Iconography*, New Delhi, 1941 repr., Munshiram Manoharlal, 1974.

Barua, B.K., *A Cultural History of Assam*, Nowgong, 1951.

Behera, K.S., 'Evolution of Shakti Cult at Jajpur, Bhubanesvara and Puri', in *Shakti Cult And Tara*, ed. D.C. Sircar, Calcutta: Calcutta University, 1967, pp. 74–86.

Benard, Elisabeth, Anne, *Chinnamasta The Awful Buddhist and Hindu Tantric Goddess*, Delhi: Motilal Banarsidass, 2000.

Bharati, Swami Agehanand, *Great Tradition Little Tradition: Indological Investigations in Anthropology*, Varanasi: Chaukhamba Sanskrit Series Office, 1978.

Bhattacharya, B., *Saktisangama Tantra*, Baroda, 1932.

———, *Saivism and the Phallic World*. 2 vols., Delhi, 1975.

Bhattacharya, N.N., *The Indian Mother Goddess*, Delhi: Indian Studies Past & Present, 1977.

Briggs, G.W., *Gorakhnath and the Kanphata Yogis*, Calcutta, 1938, repr. Delhi: Motilal Banarsidass, 1982.

Brighenti, F., *Sakti Cult in Orissa*, New Delhi: D.K. Printworld, 2001.

Chakrabarti, Kunal, *Religious Process and the Making of a Regional Tradition in the Puranas*, Delhi: Oxford University Press, 2001.

Chakravarti, Uma, 'Beyond the Altekarian Paradigm: Towards a New Understanding of Gender Relations in Early Indian History', in *Early Indian History*, ed. Kumkum Roy, Delhi: Manohar, 1999.

Chandra, Pramod, 'The Kaula-Kapalika Cults at Khajuraho', *Lalit Kala*, vols. 1–2, ed. Karl Khandelwal, Delhi: Lalit Kala Academy, 1955–6, pp. 98–107.

Chattopadhyaya, B.D., *The Making of Early Medieval India*, Delhi: Oxford University Press, 1994.

———, *Studying Early India,* Delhi: Permanent Black, 2003.

Chattopadhyaya, D.P., *Lokayat: A Study in Ancient Indian Materialism*, 1959 repr. New Delhi: Peoples Publishing House, 1981.

Chattopadhyaya, S., *Evolution of Hindu Sects,* Delhi: Munshiram Manoharlal, 1970.

Chaudhary, Vijai Laxmi, 'The Inscription of Karnataka', ed. Parnabanada Jash, *Religion and Society, S.Chattopadhyay, Commemorative Volume,* Calcutta, 1984.

Coburn, Thomas, S.B., *Devi Mahatmya: The Crystallization of the Goddess Tradition,* Delhi: Motilal Banarsidass, 1984.

———, *Encountering the Goddess: A Translation of the Devi Mahatmya and a Study of Its Intrepretation*, Albany: SUNY Series in Hindu Studies, 1991.

Coomarswamy, A.K., *History of Indian and Indonesian Art*, Dover Publications INC New York, 1927 repr., Delhi: Motilal Banarsidass, 1972.

———, *Yaksas*, 2 vols., Dover Publications INC, New York, 1928–31 repr. Delhi: Munshiram Manoharlal, 1980.

Das, Balram, *Bata Avakash*, Cuttak, 1930.

Das, H.C. and Panda P., *Tantricism: A Study of the Yogini Cult*, Delhi: Sterling Publishers, 1981.

Dasgupta, S.B., *An Introduction to Tantric Buddhism*, Calcutta: Firma KLM Private Ltd., 1950.

———, *Obscure Religious Cults*, A. Mukherji and Co., Calcutta, 1974.

Dasgupta, S.N., *A History of Indian Philosophy*, Cambridge: Cambridge University Press, 1932, repr., vol. I, Delhi: Motilal Banarsidass, 1975.

Dash, M.P., *A Descriptive Catalogue of Sanskrit Manuscripst in Orissa*, vol. V, Bhubaneshwar, 1965.

Davis, N.Z., 'From Popular Religion to Religious Cultures', ed. Steven Ozment, *Reformation Europe: A Guide to Research,* Centre for Reformation Research, St.Louis, 1982.

Dehejia, Vidya, *Yogini Cult and Temples: A Tantric Tradition,* Delhi: National Museum, 1986.

———, ed., 'Kalachuris and the Temple of sixty-four Yoginis', in *Patronage of Great Temple Art, Marg,* Bombay: East India Book Co., 1988.

———, ed., *Devi: The Great Goddess Female Divinity in South Asian Art,* Washington DC, Arthur M. Sackler Gallery, 2000.

Desai, Devangana, *Religious Imagery of Khajuraho,* Mumbai, Project for Cultural Studies Publications IV, 1996.

———, 'The Goddess Hinghalaja at Khajuraho', *Journal of the Asiatic Society of Mumbai,* vol. 80, Mumbai, 2005–6.

Donaldson, Thomas, *Tantra and Sakta Art of Orissa*, 3 vols., Delhi: D.K. Printsworld, 2002.

Douglas, Nick, *Tantra Yoga*, Delhi: Munshiram Manoharlal, 1971.

———, *Yogini Cakra,* Delhi, 1971.

Dube, S.K., *Parampara Itihas Bodh Evam Sansakriti* (Hindi), Delhi: Radhakrishna, 1991.

Dupuis, Stella, *The Yogini Temples of India In the Pursuits of a Mystery*, Varanasi: Pilgrims, 2008.

Dwivedi, H.P., *Nath Sampradaya* (Hindi), Varanasi: Rajkamal Prakashan, 1967.

Dyczkowski, Mark, *The Cannons of Saivagama and Kubjika Tantra of Western Kaula Tradition*, Albany: State University of New York Press, 1988.

Elliot, Walter, 'Notice of a remarkable hypaethral temple in the hill tracts of Orissa', *Indian Antiquary*, vol. VII, 1978, pp. 19–21.

Ewing, A.H., 'The Sharada-Tilaka Tantra', *Journal of the American Oriental Society*, vol. XXIII, 1902, pp. 65–76.

Eschmann, A., 'Hinduization of Tribal deities in Orissa: The Sakta and Siva Typology', in *The Cult of Jagannath*, eds. A. Eschmann et al., Delhi: Manohar, 1984, pp.79–89.

Fabri, Charles, *The History of Art of Orissa*, Delhi: Orient Longman, 1974.

Gatwood, Lynn E., *Devi and the spouse Goddess, Women, Sexuality and Marriage within India*, The Riverdale Company, Riverdale, Md., 1985.

Ghurye, G.S., *Devi: Female Principle Bridges the Gulf Between the Folk & Elite*, Bombay: Popular Book Depot, 1962.

Ghonda, J., *Le religion dell India Veda e antico, Induissmo*, Milano Italian translation of Id. Die Religionen Indiens Stuttgart, 1981.

Goldman Sutherland J. Sally, 'Speaking Gender: Vac and the Vedic Construction of the Feminine', in *Invented Identities: The Inter play of Gender, Religion and Politics in India*, eds. Julia Leslie and Mary McGee, Delhi: Oxford University Press, 2000, pp. 57–83.

Gupta, Sanjukta, Dirk Jan Heens and Teun Goudriaan, *Hindu Tantrism*, Leiden: E.J. Brilll, 1979.

Hardiman David, *The Coming of Devi*, Delhi: Oxford University Press, 1984.

Harper, Anne Katherine, *Seven Hindu Goddesses of Spiritual Transformation: Iconography of Sapta Matrikas*, New York: The Edwin Mellen Press, 1989.

Hiltebeitel, Alf and Kathleen M. Erndl, eds., *Is The Goddess a Feminist: The Politics of South Asian Goddesses*, Delhi: Oxford University Press, 2003.

Hazra, R.C., *Studies in the Upapuranas*, 2 vols., Calcutta: Sanskrit College, Research Series, 1958 and 1963.

Kaimal, Padma, 'Learning to see the Goddess Once Again: Male and Female in Balance at the Kailasanath Temple in Kanchipuram', *Journal of the American Academy of Religion*, 2005, pp. 45–87.

Karambelkar, V.W., 'Matsyendranath and his Yogini Cult', *Indian Historical Quarterly*, vol. XXXI, 1955, pp. 362–74.

Kaviraj, Gopinath, *Tripura Rahasyam XIX*, Benares: Ramanashram edition, 1927–33.

Kenoyer, J.M., Clark, J.D., Pal, J.N. and Sharma, G.R., 'An Upper Palaeolithic Shrine in India?', *Antiquity*, vol. LVII, 1983, pp. 88–9.

Khanna, Madhu, 'Unmasking the Mask of Adharma: The celebration of Guru Padma Sambhava at the Hemis festival, Laddakh', in *Man Mind And Mask*, ed. S.C. Malik, Delhi: Indira Gandhi Internatonal Centre for Art and Aryan Books International, 2001, pp. 304–15.

King, Ursula, ed., *Women in World's Religions: Past and Present (God:The Contemporary Discussion Series)*, New York: Paragon House, 1987.

Kinsley, David, *The Hindu Goddesses: The Vision of the Divine Feminine in India*, Berkeley and Los Angeles: University of California Press, 1986.

Kosambi, D.D., *Myth and Reality*, Bombay: Popular Prakashan, 1962.

Kramrisch, Stella, *The Hindu Temple*, Delhi, 1976 repr., Delhi: Motilal Banarsidass, 2007.

Lohani, Bhaskaranand, *Kumayun Acarya* (Hindi), Lucknow, 1994.

Lalye, P.G., *Studies in Devi Bhagavata*, Bombay: Popular Prakashan, 1973.

Lorenzen, David N., *Kapalika and Kalamukhas: Two lost Saivite Sects*, New Delhi: Thomson Press (India) Ltd., 1972.

Manjusri, *The Position of Women in the Yajnavalkya Smriti*, Delhi, 1990.

Marglin, Frederique Apffel, *Wives of the God King: The Rituals of the Devadasis of Puri*, Delhi: Oxford University Press, 1985.

Marriott, Mckim, 'Little Communities in an Indigenous Civilization', in *Village India: Studies in the Little Community*, ed. Mckim Marriott, Chicago: The University of Chicago Press, 1955.

Miller, Stoller, Barbara, ed., *Powers of Art: Patronage in Indian Culture*, Delhi: Oxford University Press, 1992.

Mirashi, V.V., 'The Saiva Acharyas of the Matta-Mayura Clan', *Indian Historical Quarterly*, vol. XXVI, 1950, pp. 1–16.

Mitchell, W.J.T., *Iconology: Image, Text Indology*, Chicago: Chicago University Press, 1987.

Mookerji, Ajit, *Tantra Art: Its Philosophy and Physics*, New Delhi: Ravi Kumar, 1966.

Narayanan, M.G.S. and Veluthat Kesavan, 'Bhakti Movement in South India', in D.N. Jha, ed., *Feudal Social Formation in Early India,* Delhi, 1987.

Nautiyal, Shivanand, *Gadhval Ka Sanskritik Vaibhava* (Hindi), Allahabad: Uttara Madhya Sanskrtika Kendra, 1994.

Pal Pratapaditya, *The Arts of Nepal*, vol. 2, Leiden: E.J. Brill, 1978.

Panda, L.K., *Saivism in Orissa*, Delhi: Sandeep Prakashan, 1985.

Panigrahi, K.C., *History of Orissa* (Hindu Period), Cuttack, 1961.

Patton, Laurie, 'The Fate of the Female Rsi Lopamudra', in *The Making of Indian Myth,* ed. Julia Leslie, London: Curzon Press, 1996, pp. 21–38.

Payne, E.A., *The Saktas: An Introductory and Comparative Study*, 1933, repr., New York & London: Garland Publishing Inc., 1979.

Pitchman, Tracy, 'The Ambiguous Female: Conceptions of Female Principle in Brahmanical Tradition and the Roles of Women in India', ed. Ninian Smart and Shivesh Thakur, *Ethical and Political Dilemmas of Modern India*, New York: St Martin's Press, 1993, pp. 144–59.

———, *The Rise of the Goddess in Hindu Tradition*, Delhi: Sri Satguru Publications, 1997.

Pocock, D.F., 'The Movement of Castes', *Man*, vol. 55, 1955.

Pradhan, B.C., *Shakti Worship in Orissa*, Ph.D. Dissertation, Sambhalpur University, 1983.

Rajaguru, S.N., *Invocatory Verses from Inscriptions*, vol. II, Delhi, 1971.

Ray, N.R., 'Medieval Factor in Indian History', *Proceedings of Indian History Congress*, Patiala, 1967.

Ray, S.K., *Folk Art of India*, Calcutta, 1967.

Rawson, Philip, *The Art of Tantra*, London: Thames & Hudson, 1973.

Redfield, Robert, *Peasant Society and Culture*, Chicago: The University of Chicago Press, 1956.

Roy, Aparna, *Women in the Purana Traditions*, Allahabad: Raka Prakashan, 2004.

Roy, S.N., *Historical & Cultural Studies in the Puranas*, Allahabad: Pauranic Publications, 1977.

Sarkar, Sabita Ranjan, 'Masks of West Bengal', in *Mind Man and Mask*, ed. S.C. Malik, Delhi: Indira Gandhi Centre for Art and Aryan Books International, 2001, pp. 221–31.

Saundararajan, K.V., *Early Kalinga Art*, Delhi, 1984.

Sen, Aloka Parasher, 'The "Self" and the "Other" in Early Indian Tradition', in *Mind, Man and Mask,* ed. S.C. Malik, Delhi: Indira Gandhi Centre for Art and Aryan Books International, 2001, pp. 28–49.

Sharma, Arvind, *Classical Hindu Thought: An Introduction,* Delhi: Oxford University Press, 2000.

Sharma, G.R., *The Excavations at Kausambi 1957–59*, Allahabad, Published by the Department of Ancient History Culture and Archaeology, Allahabad University, 1960.

Sharma, R.K. *The Temple of Chaunsatha Yogini at Bheraghat*, Delhi: Agam Kala Prakashan, 1978.

Sharma, R.S., *Early Medieval Indian Society: A Study in Feudalization,* Delhi: Orient Longman, 2001.

Sharma, Rita, 'Sa Ham I am She; Women, Goddess', ed. Alf Hiltebeitel and Kathleen M. Erndl, *Is the Goddess a Feminist?,* Delhi: Oxford University Press, 2003.

Singer, Milton, 'The Social Organization of Indian Civilization', *When a Great Tradition Modernizes, An Anthropological Approach,* New Delhi: Vikas Publishing House Private Ltd., 1972.

Singh, Jaideva, *Vijnaanabhairava*, or Divine Conciousness, Delhi, 2003.

Singh, Lalan, P., *Tantras: its Mystic and Scientific Basis*, Delhi, 1976.

Singh, Mohan, *Gorakhnath and Medieval Hindu Mysticism*, Lahore, 1937.

Sircar, D.C., 'Tara of Chandra Dvipa', ed. D.C. Sircar, *The Sakti Cult and Tara,* Calcutta: Calcutta Unversity, 1967.

Sirinivas, M.N., 'A Note on Sanskritization and Westernization', *The Far Eastern Quarterly*, vol. 15, no. 4, 1956.

Spivak Chakravarti Gayatri, 'Moving Devi', ed. Vidya Dehejia, *Devi: The Great Goddess,* Washington DC, Freer and Sackler Gallery, 1999.

Sivaramamurti, C., *The Art of India*, New York, 1977.

Stephanie Jamieson, *Sacrificed Wife: Women Ritual and Hospitality in Ancient India*, New York, 1996.

Thomsen, Margrit, *Kult and ikonographie der, un 64 Yoginis,* unpublished Ph.D. thesis, Berlin, 1976.

Thinley Norbu, *Magic Dance,* New Delhi: Shambhala Publications, 2003.

Tripathi, L.K., 'Chaunsath Yogini Temple, Khajuraho', *Journal of Indian Society of Oriental Art*, 1974–5.

Vergati, Anne, 'Men and Masks in Kathmandu Valley', in *Mind, Man, and Mask,* ed. S.C. Malik, Delhi: Indira Gandhi Centre for Art and Aryan Books International, 2001.

Wadley, Susan, S., 'Women and the Hindu Tradition', Doranne Jacobson and Susan S. Wadley, eds., *Women in India: Two Perspectives,* Columbia, Mo: South Asian Books, 1997.

White, Gordon David, *The Kiss of Yogini,* Chicago: The University of Chicago Press, 2000.

Young Serenity, ed., *An Anthology of Sacred Texts by and about Women'*, New York, NY: Cross Road, 1993.

Index